"History as told by Heller is so comic and heartbreaking that you wonder why anyone would want to live there."
San Francisco Chronicle

"Pure renegade Heller—at best, as sharp (and thoroughly American) as Lizzie Borden's axe."
Vogue

"Thought-provoking entertainment... It is as difficult to write *about* as it probably was to write."
New York Daily News

"Tickles our sensibilities... If Heller had written nothing we would be deprived of his devastating comic gift and literature would be a little stuffier."
Detroit Free Press

"Heller's humor is biting.... He takes shots at everybody, pointing out that even the geniuses of the past were just human. *Picture This* is worth reading. It's funny, well-researched and well-written. And expect the unexpected, as usual, from Heller."
The Grand Rapids Press

"A satiric tour de force that's unlike any other novel you've ever read... *Picture This* is a novel about a painting that's about a philosopher thinking about a poet. This self-reflexive artistry represents state-of-the-art narrative technique, but behind all of his dazzling display Joseph Heller remains an old-fashioned moralist who tells stories in the hope of making people better by reminding them of their common flaws."
Kansas City Star

"It does the kind of thing Socrates, who figures large in these pages, used to do for a non-living. This, then, is Heller-the-gadfly, the noodge, the pain in our pretenses, the mangler of our myths.... This is his best book since the publication of the one that made 'Catch-22' a contemporary cliche."
Newport News Daily Press

"*Picture This* is a book to read twice in its entirety—the first time for amusement and for the odd fact about art, history or philosophy, the second for the challenge of seeing how far these ideas can take us.... A profound message hidden in a unique and imaginative story."
San Antonio Express-News

Also by Joseph Heller:

CATCH-22

SOMETHING HAPPENED*

GOOD AS GOLD

GOD KNOWS

NO LAUGHING MATTER (with Speed Vogel)

*Published by Ballantine Books

PICTURE THIS

Joseph Heller

BALLANTINE BOOKS • NEW YORK

Library of Congress Catalog Card Number: 88-4552

ISBN 0-345-35886-4

This edition published by arrangement with G.P. Putnam's Sons, a
division of the Putnam Publishing Group, Inc.

Printed in Canada

First Ballantine Books Edition: July 1989

ACKNOWLEDGMENTS

I am especially grateful to the Brooklyn-born art historian, writer, and publisher Gary Schwartz of Maarssen, Holland, whose newest book on Rembrandt was of immeasurable value to me, as was the acerbic wit he exercises in it. In letters and conversations, he gave generously of his time and several fields of expertise. For help with matters of fact I am indebted as well to the art historian Stephanie Dickey of Bedford, New York, who did much of the research on Rembrandt's paintings and lawsuits; to the historian Simon Schama of Harvard University, whose letters and recent *The Embarrassment of Riches* set me straight on a number of historical facts; to the two New York classicists Lillian Feder of City University and a second Gary Schwartz of Lehman College, who corrected my mistakes, refined my classical vocabulary, and referred me to Diogenes Laertius; and to Robert Cahn, an art historian at the Fashion Institute of Technology, who came into my picture late but in time to correct a few factual errors and direct my attention to the monumental dimensions of Rembrandt's original *The Conspiracy of Claudius Civilis: The Oath*. For any errors that remain I am myself responsible. I am not known as a patient listener and was not always as attentive to historical details as these tolerant and large-hearted mentors might have wished me to be.

JOSEPH HELLER,
East Hampton, New York, 1988

Tragedy is an imitation of an action. . . .

ARISTOTLE, *Poetics*

An upright soul respects honor before wealth.

REMBRANDT

I think the Devil shits Dutchmen.

SIR WILLIAM BATTEN,
Surveyor of the Navy,
overheard by Samuel Pepys,
19 July 1667, *Diary*

History is bunk, says Henry Ford, the
American industrial genius, who knew almost none.

I

PICTURE
THIS

1

ARISTOTLE CONTEMPLATING THE BUST OF HOMER THOUGHT often of Socrates while Rembrandt dressed him with paint in a white Renaissance surplice and a medieval black robe and encased him in shadows. "Crito, I owe a cock to Asclepius," Plato has Socrates saying after he had swallowed his cup of poison and felt the numbing effects steal up through his groin into his torso and approach his heart. "Will you remember to pay the debt?"

Now Socrates, of course, did not owe a cock to Asclepius, the god of medicine.

And the leather merchant Asclepius, you will find written here, son of the physician Eurymynedes, was as baffled as anyone to learn of the bequest from the slave who appeared on his doorstep in the morning with a live rooster in his arms. The authorities were curious also and took him into custody for questioning. They put him to death when he continued to profess his ignorance and would not reveal the code.

2

REMBRANDT PAINTING ARISTOTLE CONTEMPLATING THE bust of Homer was himself contemplating the bust of Homer where it stood on the red cloth covering the square table in the left foreground and wondering how much money it might fetch at the public auction of his belongings that he was already contemplating was sooner or later going to be more or less inevitable.

Aristotle could have told him it would not fetch much. The bust of Homer was a copy.

It was an authentic Hellenistic imitation of a Hellenic reproduction of a statue for which there had never been an authentic original subject.

There is record that Shakespeare lived but insufficient proof he could have written his plays. We have the *Iliad* and the *Odyssey* but no proof that the composer of these epics was real.

On this point scholars agree: It is out of the question that both works could have been written entirely by one person, unless, of course, it was a person with the genius of Homer.

Aristotle remembered that such busts of Homer were common in Thessaly, Thrace, Macedonia, Attica, and Euboea in his lifetime. Except for the eye sockets and the mouth open in song, the faces differed. All were called Homer. Aristotle could not have said why a blind man would want to sing.

About the money to be paid for the painting there could be no doubt. The terms had been set beforehand in correspondence between the Sicilian nobleman ordering the work and Dutch agents in Amsterdam, one of whom, probably, should be credited with proposing Rembrandt for the commission and bringing together these two figures significant in the art world of the seventeenth century who would never meet, whose association as patron and performer spanned more than eleven years, and between whom there would pass at least one acrimonious exchange of messages in which the purchaser complained he was cheated and the artist responded he was not.

The Sicilian nobleman was Don Antonio Ruffo, and it is possible that this avid and discriminating collector of art had not laid eyes on anything but prints of Rembrandt's before ordering from him the Dutch painting of a philosopher he wanted for the art collection he was amassing in his castle in Messina. Not for years did Ruffo find out that the man in the painting was Aristotle. He never found out that the bust of the man in the painting upon whose head Aristotle rested his hand was Homer. Today we accept that the face on the medallion suspended from the heavy gold chain presented to the philosopher by the impecunious artist was intended to be Alexander's but might, through slipshod intelligence, have been a likeness of the goddess Athena, whose face, of course, had never been drawn by anyone who had seen her.

No one doing a painting or statue of Athena, not even the sculptor Phidias, whose great figure of the goddess was one of the eye-catching astonishments of the Acropolis, had any idea what she looked like.

The price of the painting was five hundred guilders.

Five hundred guilders was a good piece of money in the

Netherlands back in 1653, even in Amsterdam, where the cost of living tended to be higher than elsewhere in the province of Holland and in the six other provinces making up the newly recognized and rather loosely organized federation of the United Netherlands, or the Dutch Republic.

Five hundred guilders was eight times the amount, Don Antonio Ruffo complained angrily in writing nine years later, that he would have had to pay to an Italian artist for a picture the size he had commissioned. He did not know that it was perhaps *ten* times the amount Rembrandt could then have demanded in Amsterdam, where he was past the peak of his fashionability and facing a financial catastrophe whose drastic consequences were to keep him impoverished for the rest of his life.

Amsterdam, with a population just about one-third that of ancient Athens in the age of Pericles, was the dominant commercial power on the European continent and the nerve center of a far-flung overseas empire more extensive than anything dreamed of by the most ambitious Greek merchant or militarist, other than Alexander.

Contained in the vast network of Dutch trading posts and territorial possessions that extended east and west more than halfway around the globe was an immense stretch of fertile land on the eastern shores of the new world that reached from the Chesapeake Bay in the south up to Newfoundland in the north, the whole of this expanse christened the New Netherland and encompassing in its ranging borders those few precious acres on the west side of Fifth Avenue at Eighty-second Street on the island of Manhattan with which Aristotle was to become joined indissolubly.

For on this parcel, in time, would rise the Metropolitan Museum of Art in the City of New York, a building of deplorable look, in which the painting *Aristotle Contemplating the Bust of Homer* would come to rest after a journey of three hundred seven years, an odyssey much longer in time and miles than Homer's original and one richly provided with chapters of danger, adventure, mystery, and treasure, and with comical episodes of mistaken identity.

The details would be fascinating if we knew what they were. For something like sixty-five years the whereabouts of the painting are undocumented.

It vanished from Sicily when the Ruffo line ended. It reappeared in London in 1815—as a portrait of the Dutch poet and historian Pieter Corneliszoon Hooft—the possession of one Sir Abraham Hume of Ashridge Park in Berkhampstead, Hertfordshire.

When the noted art dealer Joseph Duveen bought the painting from the estate of the French art collector Rodolphe Kann in France in 1907 and sold it to Mrs. Arabella Huntington, widow of the American railroad magnate Collis P. Huntington, none of the people involved in these transactions knew it was Rembrandt's painting of Aristotle they were buying and selling, or that Rembrandt had done such a work.

In 1961, the cost of the painting to the Metropolitan Museum of Art was a record $2,300,000.

For five hundred guilders in Amsterdam in 1653, a busy artisan or shopkeeper could support himself and his family rather well for a full year. A house in the city could be bought for that much.

For the widower Rembrandt van Rijn, who had bought his house for thirteen thousand guilders and who had lived *very* well in the ten or eleven years in which his reputation had dimmed and the income he had grown used to had lessened, five hundred guilders was not going to be enough.

After fourteen years, he still owed more than nine thousand guilders on his house, an obligation he was to have satisfied in six. The country was at war with England, her occasional Protestant ally in her long revolution against Spain. And this time it was already clear that the Dutch were not going to win. There was plague in the city. Financial discouragement was epidemic. The economy was poor, capital was growing scarce, and the owners of the debt were insisting they be paid.

Rembrandt's house was a luxurious urban mansion of the Dutch kind in a choice residential area on one of the broadest and most fashionable avenues in the east side of the city, the St. Anthoniesbreestraat. The word *breestraat*, by which the excellent thoroughfare was known in its diminutive, translates literally into "broad street."

It was next to a corner site amid other dwellings of similar restrained elegance in which resided a number of the city's wealthiest burghers and officials, several of whom had been his first patrons and sponsors. When Rembrandt bought it, the initial expenses had been met with money from the dowry of his wife, Saskia, combined with his own considerable earnings in the years he was extolled in Amsterdam and his career as a painter was flourishing.

Between 1632 and 1633, it is reported, young Rembrandt executed fifty paintings in a deluge of commissions he received after moving from Leiden to Amsterdam in 1631, when he was twenty-five. Fifty in two years averages out to just about one painting every two weeks.

If the figure is a lie, it is a very impressive lie, and there is no doubt that Rembrandt and Saskia, who was the orphaned daughter of a former burgomaster of Leeuwarden in Friesland, and the cousin of his esteemed art dealer in Amsterdam, had considerable social legitimacy with the city's middle class. In Holland in the seventeenth century, the middle class was the upper class.

Now, Rembrandt had debts that he could not meet.

Rembrandt contemplated often as he worked on Aristotle contemplating the bust of Homer that he was going to have to either sell the house or borrow from friends to finish paying for it, and he knew already that he was going to borrow.

As he added more and more black to Aristotle's robe and put still more mixtures of black into a background of innumerable dark shadings—he enjoyed watching the way his canvases drank up black—he contemplated also that after he had borrowed from friends to finish paying for the house, he would put the house in the name of his small son, Titus, to protect it from seizure by these friends when he decided not to repay them.

He could not take more money from the legacy of Titus, who was too young to know that his father had taken any money from him at all.

Rembrandt was forty-seven, and facing ruin.

Saskia had died eleven years earlier. Of the four children born to Mr. and Mrs. Rembrandt van Rijn in the eight years of their marriage, Titus, the last of the four, was the only one to live longer than two months.

Aristotle contemplating Rembrandt contemplating Aristotle often imagined, when Rembrandt's face fell into a moody look of downcast introspection, similar in feeling and somber hue to the one Rembrandt was painting on him, that Rembrandt contemplating Aristotle contemplating the bust of Homer might also be contemplating in lamentation his years with Saskia. The death of a happy marriage, Aristotle knew from experience, is no small thing, nor is the death of three children.

Rembrandt lived now with a woman named Hendrickje Stoffels, who had come into his house as a maidservant and soon would be carrying his child.

Aristotle could understand that too.

In his will Aristotle, who had not neglected to be generous to the woman who was his mistress, had asked to be buried beside his wife.

Aristotle emancipated his slaves. His daughter, Pythias, and his sons, Nicanor and Nicomachus, had outlived him. A tear welled in his eye when he remembered with longing the satisfying family life he had once enjoyed. Rembrandt brushed it away.

The year after Rembrandt and Saskia married, each made a will appointing the other sole legatee.

In 1642, nine days before her death, Saskia made a new will naming Titus her heir. In effect she was disinheriting Rembrandt; but she designated him sole guardian and exempted him from accounting for his stewardship to the Chamber of Orphans.

A smarter woman would have known by then that Rembrandt could not manage money. He had a passion for status and for buying paintings, drawings, sculptures, and exotic garments and other curiosities of all description, and the artist was a familiar sight stalking avidly the auction rooms and galleries of the city.

When Saskia was alive, both she and Rembrandt had been dubbed extravagant by a near relation of hers with a residual interest in her inheritance, and they had sued for libel and lost.

A mercantile society, suggested Plato, was inclined to be quarrelsome and litigious, and this was especially true of the mercantile society of which Rembrandt was a member.

Under the common law of Holland, half of everything in a marriage belonged separately to both partners. In leaving her share to Titus, for whose upbringing Rembrandt was responsible, Saskia left him half the total; when Rembrandt's half was gone, everything spent for either came from the share left the child.

Of the twenty thousand guilders estimated retroactively to have been the value of the inheritance of Titus, he was able, as a young adult, to recapture less than seven.

When Titus obtained that money, he committed it with endearing filial devotion to the support of himself and his father, until he married at twenty-seven, less than one year before his death.

There is reason to suspect that Rembrandt, in debt, sold paintings abroad secretly to evade paying his creditors, complicating still further for posterity the task of separating genuine Rembrandts from fakes.

Aristotle, so thorough and correct in drawing his own will, had to wonder occasionally what went on in the mind of the notary who had assisted Saskia van Uylenburgh with hers.

But had she not switched her legacy to Titus, neither father nor son, as it turned out, would have had anything left after Rembrandt filed formally for bankruptcy.

Aristotle could hear, of course, after Rembrandt gave him an ear—and then to his enormous surprise and glee, adorned it with an earring whose worth, were it fabricated of real gold instead of simulated with paint, would have been more than nominal in the jewelry markets of the city. And Aristotle heard enough to understand that the artist creating him had more on his mind than completing this particular canvas for Don Antonio Ruffo and the several other paintings in the studio on which he was also working. Rembrandt would turn away abruptly from one painting to another in spells of fatigue or boredom, or impulsively in bursts of renewed inspiration, or while waiting for paint to dry on some while going ahead with a different one.

Often he would not wait for paint to dry but would intently make up his mind to drag new paint on a brush almost dry through areas still soft, to scumble the texture of the surface with more impasto and enrich with variegation the reflective surfaces of the different pigments.

Rembrandt's best years were behind him and his best paintings were ahead, of which the *Aristotle*, we now know, would be among the first in the flow of startling masterpieces with which the last sad decades of his life were crowned.

He did his most successful work while living like a failure, and his melancholy anxiety over money began to filter regularly into the expressions of the faces he painted, even those of Aristotle and Homer.

"Why do all your people look so sad now?" inquired the tall man modeling for Aristotle.

"They worry."

"What do they worry about?"

"Money," said the artist.

But that kind of tremulous solemnity was absent from his own face in the domineering self-portrait of 1652 on the opposite side of the attic, in which Rembrandt stood upright in his working tunic with his hands on his hips and appears defiant and invincible today to any onlooker who dares meet his eyes in the Kunsthistorisches Museum in Vienna.

Pensive torment he reserved for his paintings of others.

It is mildly ironic that it was not until 1936 that this distinguished painting of Aristotle was given the name by which we know it now.

Not until 1917, one year after the Ruffo archives were opened, could the work be positively identified as the one commissioned from Rembrandt by Don Antonio Ruffo in 1652 and the man in it authenticated as Aristotle.

There is nothing in papers anywhere that we know of to verify that the bust is Homer.

It is ironic too that one of the best of Rembrandt's worst paintings was to become his most famous and the one for which he is praised most widely.

This painting is an outdoor group portrait in daytime showing eighteen armed members of the civic military company of Captain Frans Banning Cocq moving forward into a glaring patch of yellow sunlight.

It is called *The Nightwatch*.

The desire of some men for immortality, as Plato says, finds expression in doing things that will cause them to be remembered with favor by succeeding generations. With Egyptian royalty it could occasionally be a pyramid. With Americans it sometimes takes the form of a museum. With the Dutch it was staid portraits, usually in black, of figures who were dignified, stern, and substantial.

Of the eighteen gentlemen who had paid one hundred guilders each for the privilege of being included in the Rembrandt painting *The Company of Captain Frans Banning Cocq*, we can guess that at least sixteen could have had grounds for dissatisfaction.

They had subscribed to an official group portrait of the kind most familiar throughout the city, one in which the figures are as formal as playing cards and the face of each sitter is large and bright and instantly noticed and recognized.

What they got was a picture of embarrassing theatricality

in which they are costumed like actors and are as busy as workmen. Their faces are small, turned, obstructed, or in shadows. Even the two central officers striding into the foreground, Captain Frans Banning Cocq himself and his lieutenant, William van Ruytenburch, are subordinated too much to the wishes of the artist, according to one contemporary critic, who predicted, nevertheless, that the picture would survive its competitors.

The Nightwatch survives.

It is the work by which Rembrandt's genius as an artist is most generally verified and, even by baroque standards, is absolutely awful in almost every pertinent respect, including the conception of the artist in his dramatic break with tradition. The colors are garish, the poses operatic. The chiaroscuro is diffuse, the accents dissipated. Caravaggio would have turned in his grave had he been alive to see it.

The painting is the most popular single attraction in the Rijksmuseum in Amsterdam.

In 1915 a shoemaker, unable to find work, cut a square out of Lieutenant van Ruytenburch's right boot.

Experts restored the canvas by repairing the boot. The offer by the repentant shoemaker to do the job free was declined by authorities.

And in 1975, a former schoolteacher assaulted the lower section of the canvas with a serrated bread knife taken from the downtown Amsterdam restaurant in which he had just eaten lunch, making vertical cuts in the bodies of Captain Banning Cocq and Lieutenant van Ruytenburch. The painting was slashed in a dozen places. On the right leg of the captain, a strip of canvas twelve by two and a half inches was ripped away. The attacker told bystanders he had been sent by the Lord.

"I was ordered to do it," the schoolteacher is quoted as saying. "I had to do it." Newspapers related a history of mental illness.

A decade later the schoolteacher died by his own hand.

A description of the damage to the painting reads like a

coroner's report. The painting was cut twelve times with a knife and from the nature of the damage it was deduced that the stabs and cuts were inflicted with great force. Probably as a result of the force, the blade of the knife was bent slightly to the left, some of the cuts being pressed obliquely inward and all the cut edges being frayed. In the area of Banning Cocq's breeches a triangular piece was cut out and fell off the painting to the floor.

The breeches were mended by a tailor from Leiden and the rest of the damage was repaired by professional art restorers of highest caliber.

To this day, there are superstitious covens in abandoned small churches in Amsterdam convinced the vandal was the reincarnation of one of the discontented musketeers who paid one hundred guilders to be memorialized with dignity and found himself reduced to a detail in oil paint in a garish illustration that could have served as a poster for a comic operetta.

There are others who say it was Rembrandt.

Saskia died in that year of *The Nightwatch*, 1642, and Rembrandt painted her features on the gamboling little girl who is darting through the crowd from left to right with her face illuminated. She died at thirty.

It probably is no more than coincidence that the year in which Rembrandt lost his wife was the one in which his fortunes took their downward turn, and biographers do not assert there was anything more.

3

ARISTOTLE IN EXILE FROM ATHENS IN THE LAST YEAR OF HIS life dwelled on his mother's estate on the island of Euboea and drew his will. He was nearing sixty-two. Aristotle sensed he was in the last year of his life and thought often about Socrates in prison awaiting death by execution, three-quarters of a century earlier. Aristotle had fled there from Athens to escape prosecution.

Again and again his stomach troubled him. His appetite failed. He, who knew so much, was not sure why. His father, who'd died when Aristotle was young, was the doctor. Aristotle was the pioneering scholar, with less scientific literature to research than he had written.

Among the many things he knew toward the end of his life was that there were many more he did not.

A thing he did not know, of course, was that in the Dutch Republic in the seventeenth century, Rembrandt would paint his picture in Amsterdam, and that for close to two hundred years just about no one in the world would know who he was.

Of Socrates he had a clear impression.

Yet almost everything he knew of Socrates had come from Plato, whom Aristotle often thought of now as more wishful than profound, and as someone not always reliable with facts.

Nearly all of the rest was put down by the historian, biographer, and mercenary warrior Xenophon, who, in exile from democratic Athens for the last forty years of his life, was not always reliable either, not even as a warrior.

Xenophon too wrote of the trial and execution of Socrates. But Xenophon was in Persia when these occurred. Before he could return, he was banished for serving with Spartans in military engagements in which Athenians were on the other side.

We have fragments from papers by Aeschines the Socratic and Antisthenes the Cynic that tell us Socrates really lived, and which may be spurious.

Then there was *The Clouds* by Aristophanes, in which Socrates is lampooned as a sophist, and this is the earliest mention we have of him. Dated a quarter of a century before Socrates was put on trial, the comedy is evidence that he was widely recognized in the Athenian community when Plato and Xenophon were children still too small to appreciate who he was.

Aristophanes, on the other hand, was a contemporary and friend and could write of Socrates from a personal knowledge the others did not enjoy.

But Socrates, on the other hand, was never a sophist.

But the jury remembered the play and ignored the philosophy, and they sentenced him to death believing he was one.

That was not the principal reason. In the bitter aftermath of the surrender to Sparta, there was also the residue of political antipathies resulting from his friendships in the past with Alcibiades, the traitor, and Critias, the tyrant, and there was not much tolerance left for the satirical dissent for which Socrates was notable, and which, for many, was as treasonable as treason itself, and vastly more irritating.

Sophists taught for money. At his trial Socrates offered

novel evidence that he had never taught for money and had worked all his life for the public good: his poverty.

The jury was unmoved.

By then, we know, the glory that was Greece, of which Athens for most of a century was the epitome, had ended. The war with Sparta was lost, the empire gone, Aeschylus, Sophocles, and Euripides were dead.

It was over longer still by the time Plato founded his Academy and young Aristotle came south to learn from him, was over even before Plato was born. And Plato lived his first twenty-four years in a city embroiled in a war it could not win and one which most people of ancestry as illustrious as his did not want to fight.

Socrates was past forty when Plato was born.

He was more than sixty when they met, and Plato could not have known for as many as ten years the man who was to inspire him with a lifelong devotion to thought and whose death was to embitter him with a disillusioned hatred for the political freedom and materialistic orientation of the democratic city with which both names are associated.

That age of Pericles, which we think of now as the golden age of Athens, came to an end, literally, with the death of Pericles in the second of the twenty-seven years of war into which that most sensible and constructive of political leaders guided his city inflexibly toward total defeat, unconditional surrender, and the loss of power and empire. That was the year of the plague, transported by sea from the upper Nile into the walled city besieged on land for the second summer in a row by Spartan soldiers and Spartan allies. Pericles, already wretched from parliamentary setbacks inflicted on him by the conservative nobility on one side and the radical business community on the other, and by a series of personal tragedies too, was himself finally among the tens of thousands who fell victim to the disease and died.

In keeping with a sensible war strategy he guessed would produce victory and peace with honor in one year, all of the population living outside Athens had been herded again from the countryside and confined inside the long walls that girdled the city and ran down four miles to the ports of Piraeus. Masses of people camped in the streets and perished there. From the parapets of the walls shielding them from the Spartans, these summer country refugees could see for miles around their fields and houses put to the torch. No one was happy. Pericles had reason to be wretched.

Pericles, patrician leader of the radical democratic party, was not a figure in Greek history upon whom either Plato, an aristocrat, or Aristotle, from the professional elite, could look back without considerable distaste and disapprobation.

In bed near death in his last hour, Pericles heard relatives and friends, supposing him unconscious, recount his magnificent achievements: his nine trophies for military victories as commander in chief, the buildings and sculptures of a magnitude of beauty the world had never known, the flowering of literary art and intellectual life, the extension of empire, the growth of commerce and the increase in tribute from subject cities and islands under Athenian domination. Pericles opened his eyes.

"Why do you say nothing of my most glorious claim to fame," he interrupted reproachfully, "that no Athenian ever put on mourning because of me?"

They said nothing about it because it wasn't true.

4

ARISTOTLE WAS SEVENTEEN OR EIGHTEEN WHEN HE TRAV-
eled south from the royal court at Pella in Macedonia, where
his father had been physician to the king, to study with Plato
in the city-state of Athens.

Plato's Academy had been established about twenty-one
years earlier. Plato's dialogues of Socrates had already been
published and had been consumed by the youth with fervor
and admiration. He wanted to know more.

Plato was past sixty and had given up trying to find out.

Aristotle was disappointed to perceive as time passed and
his own powers of determination matured that Plato was ar-
bitrary and fanciful in belief: he had a mystical faith in the
divine properties of numbers and a theory of ideas as realities
independent of human existence that led almost nowhere
Aristotle wanted to follow.

The two had not always gotten on as comfortably as Aristotle would have hoped, although he remained at the Academy for twenty years, until Plato's death at eighty. Then he
left Athens. To a relative of Plato's of mediocre mind went

the position of head of the school, an office Aristotle might have coveted. He returned twelve years later and founded his Lyceum. By then the city had been subjected to Macedonian rule, first by Philip, next by Alexander.

Plato was not stinting in appreciation of Aristotle. He nicknamed him "the Mind" and "the Reader." Plato had a weakness for nicknames. "Plato" itself was a nickname; he was broad of brow and chest, it is said, and when young excelled in wrestling. But Plato is not Plato; he is Aristocles the son of Ariston. His father claimed ancestry in King Codrus of Athens, who existed only in legend. Plato's mother was a collateral descendant of the lawgiver Solon.

There was no shortage of wealth in this family that had produced his uncle, or great-uncle, Critias. In just the one year he held power, Plato's uncle Critias attained distinction as the bloodiest and most venal tyrant in the history of the city.

Critias, far back, had been a disciple of Socrates.

Not since the charismatic Alcibiades turned traitor and deserted to Sparta had there been an Athenian so roundly feared and hated by so much of the populace.

Alcibiades too had been a follower of Socrates.

It took Aristotle a while to detect that there was sometimes a crabby deprecation in Plato's use of these nicknames that was significantly different from the genial irony with which he had invested the personality of Socrates in his *Republic* and numerous playlets.

Aristotle and Plato were much different in philosophy too, as well as in age and temperament.

Plato had his head in the clouds and his thoughts in the heavens and seemed to be preaching that the only things capable of being looked into were those about which nothing more could be found out.

Aristotle had his feet on the ground and his eyes everywhere. He wanted to know more about all he observed.

Plato rejected appearances: knowledge was obtainable only of things that were eternal, and nothing on earth was.

He stressed geometry. Above the entranceway of his Academy was the legend "Let no one enter who is ignorant of geometry."

Aristotle craved definition, explanation, systematic investigation, and proof, even in geometry.

Plato, elderly, preferred to conduct his lessons seated.

Aristotle, young, could hardly restrain himself from jumping up and pacing whenever he was excited by a new concept. "There is motion in movement," he blurted out one day, after Plato had requested with a politeness of sarcasm that he please try to sit still. And there was exhilaration as well. Walking quickened the pulse, he announced he'd discovered, and made the heart beat more rapidly also.

Aristotle's interest in biology, physics, and all the natural and social sciences was something that might have stemmed from the scientific predilections of his father.

"I have this beetle here in one hand," he proclaimed one day, "with a single oval shell and eight jointed legs, and I have here in my other hand this second beetle of lighter hue which has twelve legs and a shell that is longer and segmented. Can you explain the differences?"

"Yes," said Plato. "There is no such thing as a beetle, in either of your hands. There is no such thing as your hand. What you think of as a beetle and a hand are merely reflections of your recognition of the idea of a beetle and a hand. There is only the idea, which existed before these specimens came into being. Otherwise, how could they come into being? And the form of the idea, of course, is always eternal and real, and never changes. What you are holding in what you think are your hands are shadows of that idea. Have you forgotten my illustration of the cave in my *Republic*? Read it once more. That the two beetles you have are different is clear enough proof that neither is real. It therefore follows that only the form or the idea of the form is susceptible to study, and it is something about which we will never be able to learn more than we already know. Ideas alone are worth contemplating. You are not real, my vain young Aristotle,

I'm not real. Socrates himself was but an imitation of himself. All of us are merely inferior copies of the form that is us. I know you understand me.''

Aristotle did not inquire then whether the idea of the beetle to which Plato referred was of one with eight legs or twelve, or whether the idea for Socrates of which the man had been a copy was of a Socrates young or older. If both, he could envision the whole Platonic Theory of Ideas collapsing with self-contradiction and dissolving at once into a nothingness of incomprehensibility.

Plato to the end was in all things ascetic—at banquets, to the scorn of Diogenes, he ate only the olives or figs. He was patronizing to Aristotle for his joy in clothes, jewelry, and women.

Aristotle did not wish to dissent while his teacher was alive, and he had to wait twenty years, until he was almost forty, before Plato was dead.

By then he knew that the ideal of a philosopher-king propounded in the *Republic* was a folly, and he was embarrassed that Plato had pursued into his old age as a practical matter the unrealistic goal of transforming a despot into a philosopher through education. Plato made three trips to Sicily on this quixotic endeavor. He barely escaped with his life on two of them.

Plato overestimated grossly the power of education to reform and the need for knowledge and intelligence in public affairs.

Plato should have remembered, thought Aristotle in exile, that the moral teachings of Socrates had no good influence on Alcibiades or Critias and that the belief he had exercised pernicious ones lay near the source of the animosity borne Socrates by his middle-class fellow citizens.

Aristotle had no greater influence upon Alexander, and no philosophical brief that he should.

But Plato would not surrender his dream.

Plato had been to Sicily twice before Aristotle met him. Then, at almost seventy, with Aristotle witnessing in disbelief, the old man voyaged to Syracuse again on that same hopeless endeavor of trying for the second time to enlighten with kingly virtue the dissolute tyrant-ruler Dionysius II.

There, from the moment he arrived, he was an object of suspicion and sneaky ridicule in a revolutionary court intrigue brewing all around him of which only he, the philosopher from Athens, was oblivious.

He was under house arrest for months before he was permitted to leave.

The most he achieved on any of his three trips was to kindle a brief fad for geometry. Sicilian Greeks in Syracuse played geometry before they went to bed drunk and made love.

Plato was more dour and depressed than ever after this last fiasco, and Aristotle understood in silence that he was taking instruction in philosophy now from a man who was disillusioned and rancorous and who had finally given up hope for the betterment of mankind.

When Plato died, he was working on the *Laws*, his bleak, misanthropic proposal for a totalitarian society in which all members were prisoners of a rigid orthodoxy that would not tolerate thinkers like himself and Socrates and in which the penalties for varieties of common transgressions were unmerciful.

For a first offense of impiety, for example, the punishment was five years in prison. For a second, it was death without burial.

Impiety was one of the two allegations made against Socrates.

It was the charge brought against Aristotle that caused him to flee Athens the year before his death.

In Plato's *Laws*, retailers—people who bought at one price and sold at a higher price—were held in stern contempt.

In this new ideal community of Plato's, intellect survived only as the basic architecture of a social order in which all other intellect was proscribed.

Aristotle knew what Plato did not, that politics and good intentions do not mix.

And Plato, Aristotle believed critically, should have remembered as much from the defense he gave Socrates in the *Apology* he wrote of the trial. How long, Plato says Socrates asked his jurors shortly before they condemned him to die, would a man whose true goal was to do good for his country be allowed by them to survive in government?

Politics and knowledge did not mix either.

A ruler inspired with that love of philosophy of which Socrates and Plato spoke was not going to have much time to rule or be allowed to rule long. And an intellectual in politics was no more than another orator.

Aristotle in exile could recall with continual amusement the night Philip, king of Macedonia, and sober for a change, crossed the great hall at Pella to a small group listening to young Alexander perform on the lyre with exquisite skill. Philip said nothing until the music ended.

"Are you not ashamed of yourself?" he inquired in soft reprimand of the son he might—or might not—have been picturing as heir to the centralized government he was already imposing on the disorganized land of independent Greek cities that had never known one. "Are you not ashamed of yourself to be able to play so well?"

It was enough for a king to enjoy listening, he was saying, because a man who was very good at one thing was not likely to be excellent at anything else.

By that time there was reason at court to wonder whom Philip did have in mind for successor. He had set aside Alexander's mother, Olympias, the tempestuous princess from Epirus who handled snakes in the wild rites in which she reveled and who boasted in flashes of barbaric madness that she had even mated with one to conceive Alexander. Philip had recently fathered a second son, with his new wife, Cleopatra, with whom he appeared to be giddily infatuated. To a number of his disgruntled nobles allied in one way or another with the family of his rejected wife, she seemed disgracefully childish to be ratified as their queen.

Alexander was thirteen when he began studying with Aristotle. They were together three years. That was enough, both saw, for Alexander to learn from Aristotle all that he needed to know to become what he became.

If he were not Alexander, he reportedly said when he was already king—after Diogenes had asked him to step aside out of his sunlight—he would want to be Diogenes.

"If I were Alexander," an adviser recommended when peace terms arrived in the field from the king of Persia, "I would accept these proposals."

And so would he, responded Alexander, were he not Alexander.

Alexander loved Homer, and it is said that he took with him into Asia an *Iliad* edited by Aristotle and that he kept it beneath his pillow.

At sixteen he was regent when Philip was away and at eighteen, at the battle of Chaeronea, he faced the Theban line, superior now to the Spartan, and led the cavalry charge that broke the Sacred Band.

Alexander was twenty when Philip was assassinated.

He was twenty-one when he left Greece for that exhilarating and triumphant journey of fabulous conquests on which he did not live long enough to return.

He crossed the Hellespont and never set foot in his homeland again.

He was thirty-three when he died in Babylon—for some time the auguries at the sacrifices had not been favorable—from a fever or poison.

Philip had died early too, at forty-six, murdered by a young bodyguard at the celebration of a marriage that he had arranged solely to consolidate his power and ensure his safety.

He was about to make his entrance as a god.

A Macedonian party, Aristotle knew from the many he had attended, where the wine was unwatered and the tempers primitive, was never a predictable affair.

With the news of Alexander's death in 323 B.C., there arose immediately in Athens a wave of anti-Macedonian feeling and a revolt against Macedonian rule, and Aristotle, after twelve years of his Lyceum, was charged with impiety.

Aristotle fled, saying, in allusion to the execution of Socrates, that he would not allow Athens to sin against philosophy a second time.

What he meant was that he did not want to stand trial.

Aristotle in exile in the last year of his life had little regard left for the city renowned in his lifetime as the birthplace of literature and learning.

Except for the playwrights, none of the great names in poetry that came quickest to mind were Athenian, not one of the mathematicians, and, but for Plato and Socrates, none of the philosophers. Athens had produced only these two philosophers of note. One never wrote, the other almost never wrote in his own voice.

How ironic that Aristotle, who had always stressed a methodology of observation and verification, should find himself the arbiter of where the thinking of Socrates left off and that of Plato began. He could often only guess. And Plato had not made it easier for anyone by declaring in his *Seventh Epistle* that there neither was nor ever would be a treatise by him on the subject of his own ideas!

Aristotle knew enough by then to know this was a lie.

It seemed obvious to Aristotle that Plato had brought abstruse philosophical theories into his *Phaedo*, *Symposium*, and *Timaeus* that could not have been held by the unprepossessing figure of the Socrates he had dramatized in these works and his *Republic* and that they had to have originated with Plato himself.

Aristotle valued truth more than friendship, he always took pains to say at his Lyceum as a preliminary to disputing his revered former mentor. And by then he thought more of the beliefs of Socrates than those of Plato, although he could not be sure he knew what they were.

"Socrates did not believe in the Theory of Ideas or in the

theory of the soul as Plato represents him doing in his *Phaedo* and *Symposium*," Aristotle would insist to his students as they strolled about the grounds, and had noted on paper as well in the copious preparations for lectures that centuries later were compiled and published by others as books written by him.

But Aristotle could not be that positive, for between Socrates' birth and his own lay almost a century. The two had never met. Socrates had been executed fifteen years before Aristotle was born and was dead more than thirty when Aristotle came to Athens. The old man was a memory. The dignity, sweet reasonableness, and beautiful morality of Socrates on the day of his execution have been described at the beginning and the end of Plato's *Phaedo* in a way not likely to be soon forgotten by anyone who reads it.

But Plato wasn't there, Plato makes clear.

Plato is never present in his dialogues.

The only time he is present is to explain his absence: he was home sick on the day of that death, he says.

And Socrates did not leave a written word. If Plato had not written, we would not know much of Socrates. If he had not written of Socrates, we would not know of Plato.

But Plato was a juror at the trial, he has Socrates state, and probably he was speaking truthfully.

Also in that jury was the tanner Asclepius, who honestly admitted when deposed by interrogators at a closed hearing before his indictment that he had cast his pebbles in favor of Socrates, although he sensed that this truthful disclosure would damage him.

Anytus, the strong voice of stability behind both prosecutions and, like Asclepius, an important factor in the Athenian leather trade, asserted that he could not understand how any honest businessman in Athens would not wish to see a person like Socrates dead.

"Therefore, either you are not honest or you are not telling the truth."

They did not believe Asclepius when he said this was too confusing for him to understand.

They suspected him of arousing their suspicions.

Why was he telling the truth, if he indeed was telling the truth, when he said he was telling the truth?

Why would a man who had nothing to hide refuse to lie?

He could not see that Socrates had done anything harmful to anyone.

That was not the point, Anytus answered him testily. Asclepius had voted to spare a man who had been charged with crimes.

Asclepius respected Socrates' military service at the siege of Potidaea and the debacle at Delium, and especially in the attempt to recapture Amphipolis from the Spartan general Brasidas, when he had gone to fight for his city one more time, at forty-six. Asclepius could not see anything to be gained by trying and executing a man Socrates' age.

"Well, gentlemen, if you had waited just a little while," Aristotle remembered Plato saying of Socrates speaking to the jury that had just decreed his execution by hemlock, "you would have had your way in the course of nature. You can see that I am well on in life and near death."

He was seventy.

II

IN DUTCH

5

TITUS WAS NINE MONTHS OLD WHEN SASKIA DIED, AND REM-brandt had need for a woman under his roof to care for the infant and attend to the house.

We do not know how soon after Geertge Dircx, a trum-peter's widow, entered his employ she began sleeping with him or how soon after that she began wearing the pieces of Saskia's jewelry Rembrandt gave her. The jewelry was said to belong to Titus.

Or how long it took for relatives of Saskia to notice and disapprove.

Among these relatives was Rembrandt's art dealer, Hen-drick van Uylenburgh, Saskia's cousin, in whose house in the Breestraat Rembrandt lived.

We do know the year Geertge sued him for breach of promise after the next maid hired, Hendrickje Stoffels, re-placed her in his affections and the year in which Rembrandt, in collusion with her brother, secured her incarceration in a house of correction, probably on grounds of immorality and mental instability, when her suit against him was not unsuc-cessful.

Rembrandt was obliged by the court to pay two hundred guilders annually for her maintenance.

Desperate efforts to arrive at a private settlement before-hand had failed: Rembrandt consented to support her and had redeemed articles of jewelry she had pawned, on con-dition that she not pawn them again and not alter her will leaving all the jewelry to Titus. This might have sufficed to mollify Saskia's relatives.

She pawned them again.

After *The Nightwatch*, sixteen years passed before Rem-brandt was given a commission for another group portrait, which might tell something about its hostile reception, and does tell much about his difficulties in Holland.

We do not know that Rembrandt ever left Holland after his marriage.

Aristotle, in whom the propensity for observing, classi-fying, correlating, and inferring had remained immutable, could spy the parallel in Socrates approaching his execution and Rembrandt approaching bankruptcy.

To Aristotle, called the father of psychology for his *On the Soul, On Sense and the Sensible, On Memory and Recollec-tion, On Sleep and Waking, On Dreams*, and *On Life and Death*, it did not come as a stunning anomaly that some people prefer death to the shame of financial ruin and that many before and since have elected suicide as an alternative to experiencing both.

Aristotle could see similarities also between the Holland of the Dutch Republic in which he discovered himself being resurrected on canvas and the ancient Athens that had existed before his birth and about which he had heard and read and written; for this tiny and ambitious maritime nation with mo-nopolies and spheres of influence everywhere seemed, like Athens, always to be in conflict with everyone all over the world.

By then, of course, Abel Janszoon Tasman had sailed an

easterly course through the Indian Ocean into the south Pacific and discovered New Zealand, circled Australia and determined it was a continent, and mapped out New Holland in the northwest area as another overseas trading post of the Dutch Republic.

Across the Atlantic from Europe, on the eastern coast of North America, was the Dutch colony of New Netherland, and in western Africa, the Dutch had gone into Angola for slaves useful in South America for the sugar they grew and refined on plantations in Brazil they had taken from the Portuguese.

Both Holland and Athens had dealt with Russia for grain: Holland through the Baltic; Athens past the Hellespont, the Bosporus, and the Greek city of Byzantium into the Black Sea to the Crimea for the wheat, rice, and barley the city needed to survive. Athens went to war often to keep these routes open.

Athenian traders sold grain elsewhere when the prices were higher.

There were differences as well between Socrates and Rembrandt that this exacting philosopher who had invented the definition of definitions was powerless to ignore.

Like most men of Athens who did not work, Socrates spent most of each day outdoors.

Like most Hollanders, Rembrandt hardly ever stopped working and toiled indoors nearly all the time.

The weather of the Netherlands was not as conducive to outdoor life and verbal communication as that of Athens, which enjoys, on average, three hundred days of sunshine annually.

Holland has none.

Rembrandt lived in a house and labored in an attic that was overcrowded with students, whom he charged for lessons, and overcluttered with artwork, his own and acquired, and with fanciful articles of dress, armament, and ornamentation, accumulated fanatically in the more than twenty years since he had moved to Amsterdam.

Soon everything Rembrandt possessed would be offered for sale, including the bust of Homer he was using as the model for the bust of Homer he was bringing to life with paint so stunningly, while Aristotle looked on.

The Greek had not dreamed that such wonders were possible as the one taking place on the canvas or that beauty so moving could come from a person who in all other ways was unimaginative and banal.

Socrates and Plato would not have approved.

Painting was another of the mimetic arts they derogated as imitations of imitations. As with poetry and music, painting would be curtailed by censors in the first of the oppressive utopias projected by Plato in the *Republic* and banned just about entirely in the second of his oppressive utopias, which is outlined in the *Laws*.

Socrates would have jeered at this imitation on canvas in color of this copy in plaster or stone of an imitation in marble of the likeness of a man whom nobody we know of had ever seen and of whose existence there is no reliable written or oral verification. Socrates would have rocked with mirth at Aristotle's long face and ludicrous dress.

To Aristotle by now the painting of which he and Homer were part was much more than an imitation. It had a character uniquely its own, with no prior being, not even in Plato's realm of ideas.

While Aristotle watched, the artist added olive brown and green to the white sleeves of his surplice, and the sleeves remained white!

He drew his dry brush with new opaque colors through paint still soft and suddenly there were folds in the fabric and the cloth was reflective and rich. He used thick short strokes on top of slender long ones, leaving tracks from the bristles on surfaces made coarse and heavier. With the hairs of a delicate fine brush he tenderly put bags beneath Aristotle's eyes and wrinkles on his brow.

He put more thin glazes over heavy layers of paint to deepen and enrich the abundant jewelry. Using small spots of white he made the gold glitter on Aristotle's long heavy chain. As an inspired afterthought, he piled books in back at the left like a staircase, putting firmly in place a geometric boundary to the painting where none had been formerly, a vertical parallel to the head and hat of Aristotle and to the bust of Homer in between. He moved the pendant with the face of Alexander from one place to another until it hung on the chain finally exactly where he wanted it, and again and again he changed his mind in respect to the size of the brim of the hat.

What he did to the bust of Homer was an unbelievable revelation to a man who had marveled in antiquity at the paintings of Alexander by Apelles.

Between the lusterless daubs on the Dutchman's palette and the vibrant tones on the statue on the table, Aristotle witnessed a miracle of transformation. Adding charcoal browns to his cream colors, Rembrandt bestowed for Aristotle an illusion of flesh on an inanimate figure of a human who seemed to grow warm with immortal life beneath Aristotle's hand. Rembrandt clothed Homer with simple brushstrokes that were broad and flat and put folds in his garment with darker browns.

It was mystifying to Aristotle that a person so untalented commanded such genius.

Aristotle, contemplating, was not looking at Homer. Homer, eyeless, is staring at Aristotle.

So affected was Aristotle that he wondered why Rembrandt did not someday paint Homer as a person instead of a statue.

Rembrandt thought it was a good idea and about eight years later, with Aristotle already at home in the castle in Sicily, he shipped on speculation to Don Antonio Ruffo a partly completed painting of Homer dictating to scribes, together with a second commission executed for Ruffo of a half-length figure of Alexander.

Ruffo sent back the Homer to be finished and remonstrated indignantly because the canvas for the Alexander was made up of four pieces stitched together: he was sure he was being hoodwinked with an existing portrait of a head enlarged fraudulently to the dimensions stipulated in the contract.

Knowing Rembrandt, we do not know that Ruffo was wrong.

Rembrandt's brusque written reply to his patron's complaint, which exists only in translation, would be worth much today to a collector of manuscripts if the original could be found or forged.

Today the *Alexander* may or may not hang in Glasgow, the *Homer*, damaged by fire and cut down in size so that only the main subject and the hand of one scribe remain, is in the Mauritshuis in The Hague.

In New York the Metropolitan Museum of Art had to outbid the Cleveland Museum of Art and the Carnegie Institute of Art in Pittsburgh to obtain the *Aristotle*.

Socrates and Rembrandt were both poor at the end.

Socrates owned nothing and owed nothing and was not distressed.

Rembrandt was miserably unhappy.

He took illegally from the tiny legacy left his daughter by the second of the two housemaids to become his mistress.

Titus died the year before Rembrandt. What small estate he possessed belonged to his pregnant wife, who accused Rembrandt of stealing from it.

One of Rembrandt's late paintings is a self-portrait of the artist laughing. It can break your heart. It could have been painted with a palette knife. Today it hangs in a museum in Cologne.

You could not buy it for a million dollars.

In earlier days Socrates owned enough to do military service as a hoplite, a rank requiring the member to provide his own armor and weapons. In his last days he had little more than a wife and three children. To a friend he estimated that if he found a good purchaser, he thought he could get for all of his property, including his house, about five minae.

"You are living a life," he once was told, "that would

drive even a slave to desert his master. Your meat and your drink are the poorest. The cloak you wear is not only a poor thing but is never changed, summer or winter. And you never wear shoes or tunic.''

"But you must try to see," explained Socrates, "my belief is that to have no wants is divine."

He said he felt wealthy when he walked through the marketplace and took count of all of the things he saw there that he knew he could live without.

His attitude toward property is more easily admired than shared.

About the wife of Socrates, Xanthippe, you will find it reported, unreliably (in Diogenes Laertius' *Lives of the Eminent Philosophers* and Xenophon's *Memories of Socrates*), that she was ill humored and would search him out in the marketplace where he idled with friends, to pull the robe from his back and harangue him in public because there was nothing at home, not even him. A modest freeborn Athenian woman never set foot outside the house if she could avoid doing so, and it was a signal of the extremity of the want of the wife of Socrates that she did not own a slave to go to the marketplace and do this for her.

When he was found guilty his accusers demanded his death.

Socrates waived his right to plead for the lesser penalties of imprisonment or exile.

A fine was unsuitable also, Socrates said with some astringency. "Unless, of course, you'd like to fix the penalty at what I could pay," he offered. "Well, perhaps I could afford a mina, and therefore I propose that penalty."

Of course they sentenced him to death.

He'd mentioned also that friends of his wished him to recommend a fine of thirty minae, which they would guarantee, and this, therefore, was what he consented in the end to do.

They sentenced him to death anyway.

He was the only one who did not seem to mind.

An accident of the calendar gave him thirty days. When friends arranged his escape, he would not hear of it.

He would not break the laws of his city.

In four plays by Aristophanes, *The Clouds*, *The Wasps*, *The Birds*, and *The Frogs*, allusions make clear that Socrates was familiar enough for jokes about him to be understood by the general population. Eupolis the comic poet wrote of him:

"I hate Socrates, who has thought everything out but how to provide himself with food."

No one would believe the tanner Asclepius when he swore he had never spoken to Socrates and did not know any of the statements of his for which the city had put him to death.

His accusers did not know any either. At the trial they put into evidence against him but this one example: The sun is a fire and the moon a mass of earth.

These were the well-known doctrines by Anaxagoras, Socrates twitted in rebuttal, and even schoolboys would find him laughable if he tried to claim them as his own, to say nothing of the fact, he added, that such theories were silly.

III

THE
INVENTION
OF MONEY

6

THE INVENTION OF MONEY BY THE LYDIANS IN THE SEVENTH century before Christ brought lasting changes in the economic conduct of societies that carried into Holland in the seventeenth century after Christ and enabled the painter Rembrandt to buy his house on the Breestraat with a down payment of just twelve hundred guilders, due on the day he moved in.

He paid twelve hundred more six months later, and another eight hundred fifty guilders six months after that, the three payments in twelve months amounting to twenty-five percent of the total.

The balance could be paid over five years or six, as Rembrandt found convenient, along with accumulated interest at the conventional rate of five percent annually.

The house cost thirteen thousand.

Rembrandt had confidence he could afford it.

Why would he not?

In his first year in Amsterdam, he completed more commissions than he had executed in his lifetime. The seven years since proved no less lucrative.

Arriving in Amsterdam at twenty-five, he had become almost overnight the most fashionable portrait painter in the city. By 1639, when he and Saskia purchased the house, he had done paintings for Prince Frederick Henry of Orange for his palace in The Hague. Two other of his paintings belonged to King Charles I of England, who, in 1649, would have his head chopped off, but not because of the paintings.

Rembrandt was making so much money at thirty-three. Were there reasons for doubting he would always earn more?

In that section of Amsterdam to which he moved with his family after he lost his house, he lived in quarters spacious enough to accommodate his studio, Hendrickje, their daughter, and Titus, for which the rent was just two hundred twenty-five guilders a year.

When they bought the house in 1639, he and Saskia had been married five years. She was already an orphan by the time they met. Although eight children had shared equally in the estate of Saskia's father, her dowry was nevertheless sufficient when coupled with Rembrandt's own early affluence for both to spend conspicuously and to incite the criticism from relatives that she was squandering her inheritance shamelessly.

Together with her dowry, Saskia brought to this promising bourgeois marriage a patrician social cachet that Rembrandt cherished and might not otherwise have attained. Given the litigious nature that we know was Rembrandt's, and the passive disposition we attribute to Saskia, they apparently were well suited and the marriage probably was thoroughly satisfactory except, no doubt, for Saskia's poor health and the deaths shortly after birth of their first three children.

There is no record of objection from any in her family to her marriage to this miller's son from Leiden who was a celebrated artist in Amsterdam with presumed entry to the court of Prince Frederick Henry, to which, as far as we can document, he hardly if ever went, and then only as a painter in the practice of his work.

There was silence from his family, although his mother in Leiden supplied the necessary written consent, making her mark with an X.

No member of his family attended the wedding; none, perhaps, was invited.

Between Rembrandt and his family from the time he moved, there was silence about everything but death, and it is not known that he ever went back. At least two of his brothers lived in abject poverty before he was forced to.

Even before coming to Amsterdam, young Rembrandt had money enough to lend a thousand guilders to his art dealer there.

One thousand guilders was a mighty sum for a young man to possess and lend.

Possibly, the loan was an investment in the dealership. Probably, it was Uylenburgh who induced him to move to Amsterdam, a larger city than Leiden and one from which his more important commissions had started to arrive. In Amsterdam, Rembrandt at least until his marriage lived in Uylenburgh's home on the Breestraat, the street to which Rembrandt doubtless aspired to return in a house of his own when he thought he could afford one. Saskia and Rembrandt almost certainly met in her cousin Uylenburgh's home on one of her visits to Amsterdam from Friesland. Rembrandt was soon the celebrity resident and the principal attraction at cultural gatherings Uylenburgh sponsored, perhaps with an admission fee.

Now, at forty-seven, for just five hundred guilders, Rembrandt would work for more than a year on the painting of Aristotle contemplating the bust of Homer.

Hendrick van Uylenburgh was a respected Mennonite businessman in a broad-minded city and maintained cordial personal and business relations with powerful people in Amsterdam and elsewhere who were instrumental in deciding how the public offices of Holland would be filled and in choosing those painters to benefit from civic and even private commissions. The great seaport city of Amsterdam was then the richest and busiest shipping center in the world.

The great seaport city of Amsterdam was not a seaport but is situated a good seventy miles from the closest deepwater shipping facilities in the North Sea.

It was the custom of Rembrandt's respected art dealer to borrow money from all of his artists who had it to lend and to recommend them in return to the merchants and professionals of Amsterdam who were fertile sources of commissions for paintings.

Such a person was Dr. Nicolaes Tulp.

For Rembrandt, *The Anatomy Lesson of Dr. Nicolaes Tulp*, dated 1632, was a spectacular debut in this new city to which he had come the year before with a reputation he lost no time living up to.

He was now twenty-six.

His dramatic painting of surgeons attending a dissection in which Dr. Tulp is expounding from a textbook about the arm he has laid open is an extraordinary, bold masterpiece, and almost everything in it is false.

Dr. Tulp had not then dissected the arm about whose dissection he is shown lecturing and upon whose words the others hang. Dissections begin in the visceral cavity, which is shown intact.

The men painted by Rembrandt, all wealthy officials of the surgeons' guild, were not medical students and perhaps none was a physician, and all but one of the principals in the painting are displayed doing something other than what they would have been doing had Rembrandt depicted them doing what they in fact were doing when Rembrandt painted them, which was posing for the painting.

The single true figure in *The Anatomy Lesson of Dr. Nicolaes Tulp* is a man known as Adriaen Adriaensz. 't Kint (*'t Kint* means "the Kid"), who is the corpse.

He was hanged publicly for robbery with violence. He had stolen a coat.

Dr. Tulp, distinguished scholar, professor of anatomy to the Amsterdam guild of surgeons, alderman and member of the town council, and, later on, four times a burgomaster, was the son of a cloth merchant.

In Amsterdam in the early half of the seventeenth century there was no shame in being the son of a cloth merchant.

Or of a merchant of salt, herrings, nutmeg and cloves, pepper and cinnamon, grain, timber, tobacco, arms, and even, as inevitably comes to pass when a culture progresses, of money itself.

Toward the end of that century, some social stigma would be attached to the manufacture of cloth or the curing and shipping of herrings or to any other kind of enterprise involving labor and a product.

Toward the end of the seventeenth century, wealthy merchants, manufacturers, and shippers in Amsterdam were complaining that their very much wealthier public officials no longer engaged in trade or manufacture but instead "derived their income from houses, lands, and money at interest."

Aristotle had evaluated the lending of money for interest as the lowest of the several perversions to which that medium of exchange could be put.

A new aristocracy was emerging and more and more of the children of the rich married only into each other's families, blending fortunes. They began buying summer houses and dressing distinctively and attractively.

When shopkeepers and artisans dressed themselves and their wives and children in the same styles, laws were proposed by members of the middle class to make it a criminal offense for anyone but the middle class to do so.

With so many dressing alike, went the complaint, it was often impossible to distinguish people who deserved courtesy from those who did not.

These laws were not passed, but the spirit of social change and new class divisions they signified is unmistakable.

With the invention of money by the Lydians in the seventh

century before Christ the possibility of profit spread, and as soon as there was profit, there were people who wanted to make it, more than they wanted to make anything else. And whenever there is more money to be made from money than from anything else, the energies of the state are likely to be devoted increasingly to the production of money, for which there is no community need, to the exclusion of those commodities that are required for health, physical well-being, and contemplation. Whenever there is more money than products to buy with money, much money will be spent to buy more money. Banking will wax predominant, the number of lawyers and accountants will increase, and the society will become disorganized and weak militarily.

There will be many who flourish in this environment of finance, and a great many more who can go straight to hell.

In Amsterdam, when Hendrick van Uylenburgh borrowed money from patrons for his business or allowed them to invest, it was his habit to put out as security paintings by Rembrandt and others, knowing they could be copied without the authorization of the artists or any payments to them.

On more than one occasion he pledged as collateral the same paintings to more than one creditor.

Uylenburgh would give etching plates as security for loans and did not bar lenders from running off copies for sale.

Rembrandt sold plates for an etching to a Portuguese Jew and surreptitiously pulled extra copies for himself in violation of the terms of sale.

René Descartes—called the father of modern philosophy and the founder of analytical geometry—lived much of his life in Amsterdam at the same time as Rembrandt and remarked of the city that people were so engrossed in furthering their own interests that he could spend the whole of his life there without being noticed by a soul.

Descartes spent much of the rest of his life in Amsterdam and was not noticed by Rembrandt.

When Rembrandt had been married one month he retained a lawyer to collect small debts owed Saskia in Friesland.

From then until the end of his life there was scarcely a period as long as two years in which he was not embroiled in litigation over money.

When his mistress and housekeeper, Hendrickje Stoffels, was summoned before the governors of her church council on charges of practicing whoredom with the painter Rembrandt, Rembrandt was summoned also. He declined to appear.

When *Aristotle Contemplating the Bust of Homer* was nearing completion, Hendrickje was modeling in the nude for Rembrandt's canvas of Bathsheba ruminating over the letter from David. She also posed in a white chemise for Rembrandt's marvelous work of a woman standing with lifted skirt in water up to her shins.

This simple painting is hardly more than a sketch in paint.

Yet it was thrilling to Aristotle to see the work created, to observe the suggested solidity of that flesh appear, to watch the substance and the form of the human being and the white garment grow out of almost nothing more than an idea and a palette knife, complemented by the sprawl of a contour of a red robe on the ground that appears dropped there casually and an insight almost prophetic into the potentials of color, shape, space, and texture.

Aristotle kept his eyes on the bust of Homer while Hendrickje posed naked or with the skirt of her chemise lifted. That Hendrickje was five months pregnant improved neither her allure to Aristotle nor her chances for exoneration with the governors of her church.

In at least four biographies of Rembrandt in English, nothing good can be found about him but his artwork and the sympathetic treatment in some of his pictures of the poorer Ashkenazi Jews in the city, who had flocked to Amsterdam as refugees from wars in Germany and Poland and whom the city's cultivated Sephardic Jews, in concert with large numbers of Dutch Calvinists and Catholics, detested.

He was not a bohemian.

Of the three women in his life with whom we know him

to have been intimate, Saskia, Geertge, and Hendrickje, all were found in the households in which he was living. His domestic and amatory arrangements were practically the same.

There was an economy of motion in these liaisons that Aristotle, whose theory of creation in the *Metaphysics* rests on a prime mover setting the universe rolling and never looking our way again, could recognize without respecting.

Rembrandt was no more attracted to travel than Socrates, who hardly ever left Athens.

We know of only two times he left Amsterdam, once to Friesland for his marriage and once to Rotterdam on some kind of business. We can be sure that he sometimes went out into the countryside, for there are landscapes by him of incredible dullness that some think of as great.

He did an etching of a monk fornicating in a field.

He did still lifes so poor that people who own them are ashamed to come forward and admit they have them. Not one can be found.

It was told about Rembrandt that his students painted coins on the floor to watch him scoot and stoop to fetch them, but this seems the sort of anecdotal prank art students everywhere would practice or say they did.

Like other Dutch artists of his time, he had students make copies of his paintings, which he sold.

The better the student, the more valuable the imitation.

The more valuable the imitation, the more valuable the student.

There were times Rembrandt made more money selling imitations of himself by his students than selling his originals. The inventory of possessions of a contemporary lists one Rembrandt and six copies after Rembrandt, clearly marked as such.

In Paris was the much-acclaimed collection of the banker and art connoisseur Everard Jabach, which consisted entirely of copies of works he had once owned. Among them was the Rembrandt self-portrait of 1660 showing Rembrandt before his easel with his maulstick, brushes, and palette. The original was later a possession of Louis XIV and hangs now in the Louvre.

This remarkable collection of copies of great works once owned by the French banker Jabach could be sold for a fortune today in counterfeit money.

Rembrandt did some fifty-two self-portraits that have come down to us, and several of these Rembrandts are not by him. It is hard to conceive of self-portraits executed by someone other than the subject, but here they are.

It is hard to conceive of the Dutch, or anyone else, being more than halfway around the world, but there they were.

Zeno the Eleatic would have spied the paradox in the thought of anything being more than halfway around the world had Zeno known that the world was round.

At least four of the copies of Rembrandt self-portraits are judged superior to their originals, which are nowhere to be seen. On two of these copies the draftsmanship and brush control are finer than anything Rembrandt himself ever could accomplish. Unless, of course, the copies are by Rembrandt and all of his originals are by someone else.

This is hard to believe, as Schillig says.

When Rembrandt entered insolvency in 1656, his debts totaled seventeen thousand guilders, of which more than half had been borrowed to save the house he was going to lose. One of his creditors was Geertge Dircx, who claimed maintenance following her release after five years from the state institution to which Rembrandt and her brother had succeeded in having her confined. Geertge died before she could collect a stuiver, which is the twentieth part of a guilder.

Probably, she would not have received a stuiver had she lived.

Of all his creditors, only one, a burgomaster, obtained the whole amount owed him.

With the invention of money in the seventh century before Christ, people became free, like Rembrandt, to borrow at interest and go into debt.

In ancient Athens they went into slavery when they could not repay. Their wives and children went with them. Small farms failed. The city split into creditors and debtors, rich and poor.

With profit the motive, people were expendable, the welfare of the society secondary. Who needed a working class when slaves were so plentiful? Why bother producing what could be imported more cheaply? Why ever sell for less than the traffic would bear? A hundred years before Pericles, wealthy landowners in Athens were shipping their own grain outside the city to better markets while people inside the city went hungry.

Revolution loomed.

Solon, a landowner, was called into power to avert civil war.

He abolished slavery as a penalty for default.

To alleviate the grain shortage, he banned the export of all agricultural products but olive oil, of which there was always a surplus.

Landowners planted more olive trees and grew less grain.

He confided to friends he trusted that he was going to cancel debts but leave the large estates intact.

His friends borrowed money and bought large farms quickly. The debts were canceled, the farms were theirs.

We like to think he personally was blameless.

We know Solon today as the wise lawgiver.

The rich were incensed because they did not get their money, the poor were incensed because they got no land.

Solon wrote poems with couplets like this:

> *Virtue's a thing that none can take away;*
> *But money changes owners all the day.*

They are no less nauseating in the original.

People who kept track of such things as the Lydian invention of money back in the seventh century before Christ had no idea they were living in the seventh century B.C. Socrates, who lived in the fifth century before Christ and for one year into the next, spoke at his trial as though he *were* Christ.

"I have been given to you by God, as a sort of gadfly attached to the state," he said to the jurors in his defense on that day of the trial. "And I am not going to argue for my sake, as you may think, but for yours, that you may not sin against God by condemning me. I am his gift to you. And if you kill me, you will not easily find a successor." All his life, he informed them, he had been private audience to a personal supernatural voice whose enjoining instructions it would be sinful for him to ignore. "Men of Athens, I honor and love you, but I shall obey God rather than you."

It was too late to talk him out of this conviction that would have led to his being burned as a heretic in those enlightened Dark Ages to come, in which Plato was embraced and absorbed and Aristotle was rediscovered and acclaimed "the Philosopher" by such as Aquinas.

And it was too soon to tell him of the lunatic schoolteacher in Amsterdam with the serrated bread knife, who believed he had been commanded by God to go to the painting of *The Nightwatch* in the Rijksmuseum directly from the restaurant in which he had eaten his lunch.

7

When Socrates was sixty-five and Plato twenty-four,
Athens was blockaded by ships financed by Persia and
manned by Spartans, who had learned by then from bitter
experience against the Athenians how to make war at sea.
On land the city was surrounded once more. The population
huddled again inside the walls in this last season of a struggle
whose outbreak had occurred twenty-seven years earlier.

Gold and silver had been stripped from the statues and
monuments in the squares and temples and minted into
money necessary to go on with the war that would make the
miserable conditions of the city worse.

Through all of this the theater thrived.

When Rembrandt was forty-seven and painting his *Aristotle*, the coasts of Holland were blockaded by the English,
who had learned from experiences against the Dutch how to
build larger warships carrying heavier armament, and had
found out too that there was more money in trade than in
agriculture and animal husbandry, as the Dutch had learned
earlier from the Portuguese.

England, lagging commercially and very slow to catch on, had begun to realize that the Netherlands derived huge profits each year from the great herring catch taken by Dutch fleets from the fisheries off the coast of Scotland and farther south and had noticed also that the undyed cloth imported from England to be finished in Holland and resold abroad yielded higher returns to the Dutch than to the sheep raisers, spinners, and weavers in Britain.

Before the end of the century, after practical Holland perceived she could no longer contend against England and her natural advantages in geography and population, practical Dutch underwriters would be giving lessons in insurance and finance to their former adversary by masterminding the organization of the Bank of England, Lloyd's of London, and the London Stock Exchange, shipping capital abroad to strengthen the English economy instead of buttressing their own, and demonstrating by eternal example that money follows different laws from the rest of nature, flows swiftly not where it is most needed but where it will increase fastest, and is without loyalty or nationality.

The military actions took place at sea, the critical battles in this first Anglo-Dutch war fought mostly in the waters of the English Channel, through which Dutch overseas vessels normally had to come and go. There were few physical signs of the war in the city of Amsterdam itself.

Rembrandt, engrossed in his painting and his problems, could not seem to absorb with any lasting comprehension the connection between the financial gloom in the city and the ominous reverses already suffered by the Hollanders.

A frequent visitor named Jan Six had constantly to remind him.

Of the debt on the house, which now was seven years in arrears, more than one thousand guilders, Rembrandt disclosed, was for accumulated interest.

Aristotle kept his mouth shut. Lending at interest was unnatural, he'd written, because the profit gained was not gained through the exchange process that money was invented to serve.

"Of course," said Rembrandt, "I can easily sell the house."

There was a serious recession in the country, said Jan Six. If Rembrandt sold his house he might not get for it what he had paid.

"It's worth much more."

"People are cautious about spending," said Six. "That may be why the owners of your mortgage now wish to be paid."

Six would know. His family owned dye works and silk mills. Rembrandt heard him glumly. Aristotle did not know what to advise.

Six was younger than Rembrandt, a learned man with aesthetic leanings who was involved actively in the vigorous intellectual life of the city. He had published a play of his own called *Medea*, for which Rembrandt had provided an etching.

The artwork was satisfactory, but the etching had lost definition rapidly with repeated impressions.

The fault of the printer, Rembrandt said untruthfully. They never took care.

Several years back, he had done an etching of Jan Six reading by a window that had set a standard for etchings no one in the city could match. Rembrandt himself did not match it again either, although we do not know that he took time to try.

That one did not wear well either.

"The printer, the printer," Rembrandt muttered in blame of the man Six had used to pull more copies. "He didn't take care and he spoiled the plate."

Rembrandt knew, and refused stubbornly to believe, that etchings were not suitable for printings in large quantities. Especially this one of Jan Six. In conjunction with the lines etched by acid, Rembrandt had inventively scratched directly on the plate with both a drypoint needle and a burin, combining the different techniques of etching, engraving, and drypoint, and raising burr that enhanced the soft accents in countless nuances of black but wore down even more quickly and soon left new impressions faint.

Six had no complaints. He seemed greatly intrigued by Rembrandt's procedures, and he stopped up periodically for no better reason than to stare enchantedly at the changes in the paintings of Aristotle, Bathsheba, and the other figures and to comment on the differences. Almost without realizing what he was doing, he would attempt to come right up to the canvases to assay by close inspection the minute components of the effects in each, which he was finding progressively more fascinating.

"I see that you've changed him again, haven't you?" he said of Aristotle. As an optical phenomenon alone, he said, he marveled that so convincing an illusion of a human in profound contemplation could be constructed so movingly out of bristles and colored paint.

"And my knife and my finger too," Rembrandt corrected moodily. He sidled with polite determination between Six and the easel, persisting in blocking him from coming too near. He did not want to share his secrets.

"I would like you to do a painting of me," Jan Six said now suddenly, and added with haste when Rembrandt whirled to gaze at him, "in your own manner, of course."

"My manner?" The artist appeared startled.

"In any way that you choose, I mean. I would not mind if you did it like that one."

"A portrait like this one? This is not a portrait."

"I did not say a portrait. I like that harsh texture, all your shadows and blackness, and that very broad brushwork. You certainly make clear that an artist has been here, and that he is a much more eminent presence than the subject, don't you?"

Rembrandt chuckled. "I try," he admitted.

"I recognize the bust of Homer," said Jan Six, nodding. "The robe on the man is modern, I would guess, the gown antique. Am I mistaken?"

Rembrandt didn't know. They were things he had bought.

"You really don't know? I know you don't like to tell. I don't recognize the hat."

"I'm inventing the hat."

"You've changed it, haven't you? You've made the brim larger."

"I'm changing it back. I'm making it smaller."

"I don't recognize the man. Is it someone I should?"

"Aristotle."

"He looks like a Jew."

Aristotle glared.

Rembrandt toned him right down with a small touch of glaze.

"It's the way that I want him," said Rembrandt. "A friend models for me."

"In that costume? Aristotle?"

"Don't you like the effect?"

"He looks so sad."

"It's the way that I see him. He is growing older. He doesn't know what to do. He's an ancient philosopher and he can't find work."

"Do I see something else? Is that a face on the pendant now?"

"I'm putting one in. I don't know whose it is. It's from something I bought."

"Call it Alexander the Great."

"Why?"

"He was taught by Aristotle. You'll get credit for greater symbolic intelligence. The gold in the chain?"

"I'm making it thicker."

"How do you make it look so real?"

"Please don't stand too close. The smell of the paint will make you sick."

"How much thicker will that be?"

"As thick as I want it to be."

"How much thicker will you want it?"

"I'll know when I know."

"The hands fascinate me."

"I would do yours the same. Would you want them as plain? I can put in detail."

"You've done each one with just a few strokes, haven't you? Yet they're perfectly natural and entirely at rest. I find them amazing."

"I'm not good at motion."

"You don't do people eating, or drinking."

"Not often. Would you like me to do a portrait of a herring?"

"Everyone else does."

"I like people who stare. Whenever I finish a painting now of people doing anything else, I'm not sure that I like it."

"How do you begin? How do you decide what you are going to do?"

"The way I decide to. I don't know how. I would do you much differently, in a three-quarter length. Getting dressed to go out on serious business. Wearing a cloak, pulling on gloves."

"I won't go into business. I think I've already decided."

"Then you'll go into the government."

"I'm not sure I want that."

"Then you'll go into government work anyway, although you might not do much. Your family is too important, and so are you. I can use more friends of influence. I can use more commissions again, to help pay for the house. I think you should look older."

"By then I will look older."

"I will make you look older, the way you are going to look when you're an alderman and a burgomaster." Rembrandt smiled, Six frowned. Rembrandt put down his palette, leaned his maulstick against a chair. In silence, staring past his thumb, he pondered his prospective subject for a minute, bobbing his head once, nodding again, while Six did not move, seemed hardly to breathe. "I'll use much brighter reds and a different gold. I may do your hands with only my palette knife. I'll drag the knife through them before they are dry. I might use my finger.''

"And then you might change your mind." Jan Six laughed quietly. He added in jest, "And will you give me your notorious and gigantic impasto?"

"You might not like it."

"I will not mind."

"Then I promise to give you your money's worth in paint."

"And I'll want your chiaroscuro too, for which you have also become so infamous."

"And for which people make jokes about me too."

"How else will anyone know that I have been painted by Rembrandt?"

"It won't be pretty."

"Do you think of me as someone who wants to look pretty?"

Rembrandt sighed with self-approval and spoke with a snarl. "I am glad there is still somebody left in Holland who doesn't care for the classical."

"I am ordering a painting, not a picture."

Rembrandt grunted, pleased. "I'll use more black than here. I'll give much brighter light. I will invent you a hat much better than this one."

"I will want to be painted wearing one of my own," Jan Six told him firmly.

"You will look like a man I would not want to owe money to," said Rembrandt slyly, smiling, and began adding more gold to Aristotle's chain.

Aristotle frowned: a man like Rembrandt would drive him mad.

Rembrandt hummed loudly after Jan Six left. He could put the house in the name of his son, he said directly to Aristotle as he returned from the door, scrutinizing his subject with hearty delight. "But then he would have to make a will, wouldn't he? But then I could be the beneficiary. I know it's exactly what you would tell me to do, isn't it? Eh? You see,

Mr. Philosopher? You're not the only smart fellow in this house, are you?''

Aristotle was livid. Rembrandt drained the color from his face with a mixture of white and raw umber and then elongated the hollow far back in his cheek.

There were rumors of food shortages in Utrecht and Zeeland. Six was another, Rembrandt mused out loud to Aristotle, from whom he was sure he could borrow.

8

To Aristotle contemplating the bust of Homer, the continuing preoccupation of the world with making money remained an enigma he was not even aware he was unable to decipher. He still could not see that money had any value of its own. It was only a medium of exchange. And he could not understand what there was about money that made the pursuit of it more attractive than a good night's sleep.

A complicated mind like Aristotle's finds unanswerable dilemmas where simpler people do not.

"A man cannot expect to make money out of the community and to receive honor as well," he had written in Athens in his *Nicomachean Ethics*.

In Sicily he was no longer positive.

In London and Paris he began to have doubts.

In New York he knew he was wrong, because all the people who had contributed to the acquisition of his painting by the Metropolitan Museum of Art were making much money out of the community and were held in very great honor, especially after the purchase, for on the brass wall label in the museum the names Isaac D. Fletcher, Henry G. Keasbey, Stephen C. Clark, Charles B. Curtis, Harris B. Dick, Maria DeWitt Jesup, Henry G. Marquand, Joseph Pulitzer, Alfred N. Punnett, Jacob S. Rogers, as well as Robert Lehman, Mrs. Charles Payson, and Charles B. Wrightsman appear alongside the masterpiece with the names of Aristotle, Homer, and Rembrandt.

Homer begged and Rembrandt went bankrupt. Aristotle, who had money for books, his school, and his museum, could not have bought this painting of himself.

Rembrandt could not afford a Rembrandt.

IV

"I AM THE
STRANGEST
OF
MORTALS"

9

THE TRIAL OF SOCRATES TOOK PLACE IN A DEMOCRACY. THAT was another one of the things appalling to Plato, who'd been revolted already by the hideous, brief regime of the Thirty Tyrants, which had fallen to the democratic rebellion five years before. His uncles Critias and Charmides were among the most evil of the Thirty. Plato declined entreaties to enter politics under their auspices.

He was twenty-four then.

He was twenty-nine when Socrates was executed on charges brought against him by Anytus the businessman, Meletus the poet, and Lycon the orator.

Socrates had survived the lawless rule of the Thirty, going freely about the city continuing to be Socrates, although he was brought in once and warned.

The Tyrant Charicles took him before Critias, who said nothing of the days the two had been friendlier, when Critias, as a young man, had followed Socrates about the city to learn from him what he could.

What he learned was debate.

What he did not learn was that the object of debate is not debate.

There was a law, said Critias, that made it illegal to teach the art of words.

Socrates had not known of the law.

"I am decreeing it right now," said Critias. He was enacting it expressly with Socrates in mind.

Socrates protested that he did not understand what the art of words had to do with him.

"I am ready to obey the laws," he proceeded earnestly, starting right in, as usual, with the art of words, "and I want to understand them lest I unwittingly transgress them through ignorance. Will you give me clear directions? Are you saying that the art of words from which you bid me abstain is associated with sound or unsound reasoning?" The Tyrant Critias was already rolling his eyes. "If with sound reasoning, then you are ordering me to abstain from good thinking. If with unsound reasoning, clearly I must try harder to reason soundly. Which do you mean me to do?"

Charicles answered brusquely. "Since you seem to be ignorant, Socrates, we will put our orders into such plain language that even you will not be able to say you do not understand. From now on, you may not hold any conversations whatever with the young."

"Well then," said Socrates, "please fix the age at which a man is to be accounted young, so that there will be no question raised about my obedience."

"As long," said Charicles, "as he is still not old enough to sit in the Council because he lacks wisdom. From now on, you will not converse with anyone who is under thirty."

Socrates nodded. "Suppose," said he, "I want to buy something. Am I not even to ask the price if the seller is under thirty?"

"Oh, yes," said Charicles. "You may in such cases. But the fact is, Socrates, you are in the habit of asking questions to which you know the answer. So that is what you are not to do."

Socrates was not in the least offended by this characterization. "If I am asked a question by somebody young, am I to give the answer or not give it, such as where is Critias, or do I know where Charicles lives?"

"Yes," said Charicles, "in such cases you may."

"But you see, Socrates," said Critias, with the air of a man of rank deciding he has put up with all that he wants to, "you will have to avoid those favorite subjects of yours when talking about those who run the state—your cobblers and builders and metalworkers—for these examples of yours have already been worn to shreds in my opinion, and I am sick of hearing about them. As you know, I have helped have our old friend Alcibiades murdered. Do not think that I will stop at you."

Had Socrates been richer, he might have fared more poorly, for these Thirty Tyrants were tyrants not merely in the classical sense but in the modern as well.

They were seizing greedily for themselves the property of those who resisted them, those who argued against their actions, and those whose wealth they simply coveted, arresting people as criminals without telling them why, and giving the familiar order to drink the hemlock without so much as saying what the charge was against them.

They had been appointed by Sparta to create a new constitution for an Athenian city in vassalage to the conqueror, of which they themselves would begin as ruling oligarchs.

But these were enterprising, right-wing Athenians, vigorous and antidemocratic. They saw no need to draft a constitution enabling them to do what they could accomplish without one, and they leaped right into their orgiastic frenzy of persecution, plunder, imprisonment, and liquidation. Foreigners with money were particularly vulnerable. There prevailed that fear of the unexpected arrest, the sudden knock on the door, of the paid informer and the secret police.

A moderate member of the Thirty was put to death for opposing the cruelties of the group he had helped organize and zealously become part of.

In the eight-month rule of the Thirty, fifteen hundred people were executed. Hundreds of democrats fled into exile. Five thousand citizens who were not visibly and vocally supporters of the official party line were deported in bunches to Piraeus: there was not enough space in the city for a decent concentration camp, no land for relocation in a penal colony or gulag, no time or manpower or any of our modern facilities for murdering quickly as many as they wanted to.

The policy of the Thirty was to implicate all others in their crimes, so that none in the city could denounce them for deeds in which everyone had not shared.

Love it or leave it was the challenge of the Tyrants to the people of Athens.

Anytus, the accuser of Socrates, was among the democrats who fled to the community of rebellious exiles organizing in Thebes.

Socrates was among the citizens who remained. It seemed hardly to matter to him what kind of government he lived under, as long as it was Athenian. He found fault with all.

And the day came inevitably when he was summoned before Critias on official business, and he was directed with four others to seize Leon of Salamis for execution.

"And what crime are we to tell him he is charged with when he inquires?" asked Socrates of Critias.

"None."

"No crime? Then where is the authority in law to do what you order us to?"

"There is no law. There was no crime. I am the authority. I want his property. Don't bring him here. Take him directly to the prison and have the leader of the Eleven put him to death."

Socrates went home instead to await whatever fate would result from his disobedience. The four others went dutifully to apprehend Leon of Salamis and convey him to jail, where he was poisoned.

The exiles invaded before Socrates could be punished. He was saved by the uprising of the democrats. Critias and Charmides, the uncles of Plato, both perished in Piraeus in their futile assault against the rebels at the battle of Munychia Hill.

The coming of peace does not usually bring an end to the violence of war, and the conclusion of this war did not bring an end to the feelings of hatred and enmity that had spawned it.

In Eleusis, where the survivors of the Thirty and their partisans fled, there was composed this epitaph for Critias and others of their leaders who had fallen:

> In memory of the brave men who had once lanced
> the swollen pride of the damned democrats in
> Athens.

There are people to this day who say that Critias was the best thing that ever happened to Greece and that his only error was his failure to kill all of the democrats.

Between the greed and the will to dominate of the oligarchs and the swollen pride of the militant, damned democrats, a thinker like Socrates with reverence for neither could be squashed to death easily, and an idealist like Plato would have no place to turn, eventually, but to the inner world of isolated thought and to the fantastic illusion of the dictatorial community of his *Republic*.

The reign of terror of the oligarchs had ended.

The reign of terror by the democrats was delayed.

It took five years for Socrates to be brought to trial by Anytus, Meletus, and Lycon. In those five years he had done nothing different from what he had been doing all his life, except, perhaps, to suggest to Anytus that his son, in whom Socrates had detected a strong nature, might wish to do more with his life than spend it in the family leather business.

The affront to Anytus does not seem enough to account for the general hostility of so much of the community.

Reckless levity and ideological nonconformity would be.

Socrates testified about himself at his trial that he never said anything privately that he did not speak of openly.

That could have been the trouble.

"I have always been the same in all my actions, public as well as private, and never have I yielded any base compliance to those who are slanderously termed my disciples," he said, alluding to his alleged responsibility for indoctrinating Critias and Alcibiades when they were young and for their unspeakable official actions afterward. He did not mention that Alcibiades was forty-six when he was slain and would have been fifty-one at the time of the trial, and that Critias was fifty-seven when he died and would then be sixty-one. "Not that I have ever had any regular disciples," he continued. "I have never set myself up as teacher to anyone. But if anyone, young or old, likes to come and hear me conversing, he is not excluded. I do not charge a fee or refuse to talk without one. I am ready to answer questions of rich and poor alike, and I am equally ready to listen to anyone answer my questions. And whether a person turns out to be a bad man or a good one, neither result can be justly imputed to me, for I never taught or professed to teach him anything. And if anyone says he has ever learned or heard anything from me in private which all the world has not heard, let me tell you he is lying. The truth is that I am convinced that I never intentionally wronged anybody. I believe that if it was your practice, as it is with other nations, to give not one day but several days to the hearing of capital cases, I could convince you of that. But under the law we must conclude today. In so short a time, it will not be easy to rid you of great prejudices."

Plato was deeply moved. Plato when old thanked his good fortune because he had been born a man and not an irrational animal; again, because he had been born a Greek and not a barbarian; and again, because his birth had fallen in the time of Socrates.

Anytus, the freedom-loving military hero, leather merchant, and persistent defender of traditional conservative Athenian democratic values, did not consider it his particular good fortune to live in the time of Socrates. He was disappointed in his son and blamed the philosopher. The youth, ordered by his father into the family tanning business, and banned by his parent from participating in any more street-corner discussions with that disreputable, unkempt, and heretical old iconoclast Socrates, was turning to drink and amounting to nothing.

There was this question of logic in the family of Anytus, of first, necessary, and sufficient causes: Was Anytus, Socrates, both, or neither the cause of the youth's disaffection with business and attraction to philosophy?

There was this answer by Anytus: To plan with two others to lay charges against Socrates of serious crimes that were not serious inherently, confident that Socrates, like others, would sooner flee Athens than trust the judicial process.

Meletus the poet would do most of the speaking; Socrates had belittled poetry.

Lycon the orator would prepare most of the speeches; Socrates had vilified rhetoric.

"Who will pay our fines if we fail to get one-third of the jurors?" inquired Meletus the poet.

"Yes," wondered Lycon the orator.

Anytus would.

Lycon gloated: "Socrates is a poor speaker. Since he is not a hypocrite, he will not allow himself to read a defense prepared by somebody else. Each of us must therefore begin or end by praising his elocution abilities and open and close our statements of prosecution by warning the jurors to be on guard against his clever ability to deceive them with words."

The indictment sworn by them against Socrates the son of Sophroniscus of Alopece consisted of three sentences.

Socrates is guilty of refusing to recognize the gods recognized by the state and of introducing other strange deities.

It did not matter to his three prosecutors that Socrates offered sacrifices constantly in his home and at the altars of the state temples, relied on divination, and never offended against piety and religion in deed or word. He disavowed poets who, like Homer and Hesiod, told undignified stories of the gods. For good measure, they added a second com-

plaint that really stuck in the craw of Anytus as iniquitous
and unpardonable: Teaching.

He is also guilty of corrupting the youth.

Anytus relished Lycon's wording of this charge and resolved never to trust him again.

Had they named the son of Anytus, the complaint would
be cause for a civil action instead of a criminal trial. By slyly
naming no one, they brought into the courtroom the specters
and soundless testimony of the Tyrant Critias and the traitor
Alcibiades.

The penalty demanded is death.

10

HE WAS THE STRANGEST OF MORTALS, HE SAID, AND HE KNEW
that he sometimes drove men to their wits' end.

To Protagoras, the eminent Sophist, he taunted when
young in their famous debate: "I have a wretched memory,
and when anyone makes a long speech to me I never remember what he is talking about."

Thrasymachus of Chalcedon flew into a temper with him
in the *Republic*: "I say if you really want to know what justice is, you should not only ask but answer, and you should
not seek honor from the refutation of an opponent, for there
is many a one who can ask and cannot answer. But no, Socrates will do as he always does, refuse to answer himself, but
take and pull to pieces the answer of someone else."

"I know nothing at all," said Socrates innocently. "For I
know not what justice is, and therefore I am not likely to
know whether it is or is not a virtue, nor can I say whether
the just man is happy or unhappy."

To know you do not know is to know a great deal.

Wisdom consists in knowing there is no such thing.

No one would take seriously the honest ignorance he feigned. Man is a political animal and a social animal, and he normally enjoys hearing fantastic answers in preference to none.

"Can goodness be taught or must it be acquired in practice?" questioned Meno. To which Socrates responded: "What is goodness?" Soon Meno was protesting in awe-stricken admiration: "Before I knew you I was told you did nothing but perplex yourself and make others perplexed. You are, if I may speak jocularly, the very image in looks and otherwise of the flat torpedo-fish which paralyzes anyone who comes near it and touches it. That, I think, is what you have done to me. My mind and my tongue are paralyzed and I don't know what answer to give you. I have made an infinite variety of speeches about goodness in the past—and excellent speeches they were, I thought—but now I cannot even say what goodness is."

"It's impossible to get a straight answer from him," said Xanthippe, the wife of Socrates, to the dauntless Alcibiades, who was devilish enough to ask her directly if the report he had heard about her and Socrates was true. Xanthippe would neither confirm nor deny that she had emptied a chamber pot on his head.

"You don't know what he's really like."

"Tell me."

"If you ask him a question," Xanthippe raced on, "he wants to know what you mean. If you tell him to do something he'll pretend he doesn't understand and ask you to explain. When you've finished explaining he'll make you explain some more. When you think you've explained he will ask you still another question and make you continue explaining." Alcibiades had no trouble believing her. "See what you have to go through to get him to take out the garbage." What was garbage, Socrates would ask. "If I tell him he's getting deaf he pretends he doesn't hear. If I tell him he's dumb he calls me a sophist. Try making him empty a chamber pot. Then *you* show him how!" He was driving her mad with his endless illustrations of cobblers and herdsmen and physicians and builders.

Socrates replied to friends who wondered why he did not put her out that living with a wife who was the hardest to get along with of all the women there were was superb training for the real world. If he could endure Xanthippe, he would have no difficulty with the rest of mankind. A horseman training himself, he added in another one of those homely analogies about which she had groaned, will train himself on the most difficult mounts, knowing he later will have no trouble with those more docile.

Socrates was addicted to examples of horsemen, herdsmen, cobblers, and physicians, and his analogies, Aristotle knew on first reading Plato, were often preposterous.

"Many a time I have wished to see him dead," said his good friend Alcibiades in his inebriated accolade to Socrates in the *Symposium* by Plato.

In his youth and early manhood, the dashing Alcibiades had been the most glamorous figure in Athens and the personality most exasperating, setting a style for the young that was infuriating to the old. His son and other young men imitated his walk, his extravagant dress, and even his lisp. Handsome, wealthy, of noble birth, he was hunted by ladies and spoiled by men. He was made richer still by marriage to a respectable woman, to whom he was habitually unfaithful, mainly with the hetaerae in the city, those Ionian prostitutes gifted with education and with practice in social skills that were denied to the women of Athens. (The celebrated consort of Pericles, Aspasia, was celebrated, among other reasons, for overseeing one of the most celebrated hetaerae houses in Athens.) There was no one in Athens more proud, vain, and arrogant than Alcibiades, no one more careless of decorum or more ostentatious in affectations, no one more self-assured or less inclined to repent.

"Without doing anything," Alcibiades went on about Socrates to the friends at the party, to which he had not been invited but had burst in anyway with a loud racket in a great state of intoxication, "he makes me ashamed of my activities and of my weakness with the temptations of popularity. He makes me confess that I should not live the way I do. But when I leave his presence the love of popularity gets the better of me again. And therefore I want to fly from him like a coward whenever I see him."

Socrates was homely, with bulging eyes, thick lips, and a flat nose, and he walked like a strutting pelican stalking along and gazing all about. He had a face like a satyr, Alcibiades said in playful insult.

Socrates was homely in a society in which good looks in men were prized. Handsome youths were called beautiful, and outstanding masculine young men like Alcibiades, Agathon, and Euthydemus were lauded and wooed for their pretty faces and athletic and poetic skills.

Alcibiades, the most slavishly sought after and flirtatious of beautiful young men in his generation, felt hurt, he confessed, that Socrates did not join the ranks of other older men paying amorous court to him. Addled and impressed, he reversed the conventions, making Socrates the beloved and himself the lover, employing flattering ruses to win the sexual affections of this eccentric focus of his curiosity and desire. He admitted his failures and confessed that there grew in him as a result a respect for the character, self-control, and courage of this man he had underrated and misunderstood.

"The really wonderful thing about him is that he is like no other human being, living or dead. If you are looking for a parallel for Achilles, you can find it in Brasidas and others. If Pericles is your subject you may imagine Nestor and Antenor to have been like him, and the same may be said of other famous men. But our friend here is so extraordinary, in both person and conversation, that you will never be able to find any likeness, however remote, among men who now are or who have ever been."

The two had messed together in the infantry at the siege of Potidaea in Asia Minor when Alcibiades was eighteen.

Alcibiades was wounded and Socrates saved his life—"I was wounded but he would not leave me, but he rescued me and my arms"—a fearless action much lauded at the time that did not redound to the credit of Socrates at a later time after Alcibiades had deserted first to Sparta and next to the Persians and was cursed and dreaded.

The medal of valor went to Alcibiades, because of his noble rank, despite the insistence of Alcibiades that Socrates deserved it. Socrates urged Alcibiades to accept it.

"He was more eager than the generals that I and not he should receive the prize—and this again he will not impeach or deny as he sits here listening to me, with that face like a satyr. Am I not telling the truth about you? See, he is silent and seems to be blushing."

The medal of valor was of course a great honor; it was one of those honors that confer more honor on the donors than the recipient, and there was much more honor in awarding it to someone better born than Socrates, to a handsome youth like Alcibiades, who had been reared as a ward in the household of Pericles after his nobleman father had died heroically in the great battle of Coronea.

Coronea was a great battle that Athens lost.

People back home could glow with pride upon learning that the excellent Alcibiades had won the medal for valor and affirm with a sense of honor that it was indeed an honor.

Had Socrates received it, they would be surprised.

And shrug and ask why.

There is not much importance in giving an award of importance to someone of no importance.

Alcibiades related how Socrates in the winter of that campaign would walk on ice with bare feet and endure the bitter cold without extra clothing. Other soldiers looked daggers at him, convinced he despised them.

Alcibiades confirmed what other friends of Socrates knew: he could fall into a trance when seized by thought and stand for hours without moving.

Once during that campaign, Alcibiades related as a witness, Socrates was caught early by some thought and was in the same spot at noon. Word spread that Socrates had been standing and thinking about something since break of day, and others came to stare. Ionian soldiers brought their bedding outside in the evening to see how long he would remain. They grew sleepy while watching. Socrates stood the whole night in that one place. Only at dawn did he finally stir. Then, with the return of light, he simply said a prayer to the sun and went about his business.

Today this state is called catalepsy.

The supernatural voice of which Socrates spoke we call an auditory hallucination.

Eight years later, there was the battle of Delium during the invasion of Boeotia by the Athenians. Delium was another crushing defeat for Athens, a rout so overwhelming that Pericles abandoned forever his grandiose dream of an Athenian land empire. Alcibiades was in the cavalry this time and, as he related, comparatively safe during the retreat. Astride his horse, he had a good view of Socrates moving back with the rest after the battle was lost. Socrates was withdrawing on foot, but with a demeanor of such forbidding composure that pursuing Boeotians recoiled when they saw him and cautiously left him a wide berth, chasing instead after foes who ran about in defenseless panic in their headlong flight.

"I must warn you about him," said Alcibiades, jovial in his cups. "When Socrates is present, no one else has a chance with anybody who is good-looking. The Socrates whom you see has a tendency to fall in love with good-looking young men and is always in their society. See how readily he has found a plausible excuse for getting Agathon beside him. So I warn you, Agathon, not to be deceived by him. But this is exactly the point. He spends his whole life pretending and playing with people, and it makes no difference to him whether a person is good-looking, nor whether he is rich, nor whether he possesses any of the other advantages that rank high in popular esteem. To him all these things are worthless, and we ourselves are of no account. I may add that I am not the only sufferer this way. He has pretended to be in love with others too, when in fact he is himself the beloved rather than the lover. Learn from my experience and be on your guard.''

Alcibiades, it should be remembered, was sued by his wife for divorce because he spent too much time in bed with other women. He strode into court while she pleaded her case, slung her over his shoulder, and carried her back home, where, he felt, the respectable wife of Alcibiades belonged.

The divorce laws in Athens did not favor women.

When the neutral city of Melos was sacked by democratic Athens, Alcibiades brought home for himself as slave a beautiful Melian woman by whom he fathered a child he brought up as his legitimate own.

In Sparta after he switched sides, Alcibiades seduced the wife of the king, and the woman boasted to female friends that the sire of this son, to whom she cooed the pet name of his father, was really the handsome Alcibiades from Athens, who had deserted the city of his birth to become a Lacedaemonian and a Spartan military adviser.

When Alcibiades fled Sparta and settled in the end in the Persian city in which he spent the last evening of his life, he was in bed with a famous courtesan when assassins set fire to the house in which he lay with her and drove him outside, his sword drawn to defend himself, where he was ambushed and outnumbered and struck down by the javelins and bows of those waiting there to kill him.

Alcibiades, proud and boastful now in proclaiming his unrequited passion for Socrates in the past, was not a man who disliked sexual intercourse with women.

''Anyone who sets out to listen to Socrates will probably find his conversation ridiculous at first,'' said Alcibiades in this tribute to Socrates that was published by Plato, ''for he will talk of pack-asses and blacksmiths, cobblers and tanners, and he seems always to be repeating the same ideas over and over again in the same words, so that any inexperienced or foolish person is bound to feel disposed to laugh at his way of speaking. But if a man discriminates within, he will find that his are the only words which have sense to them, and that his talk is almost the talk of a god. Whenever I listen to him my heart beats faster than if I were in a religious frenzy, and I see that numbers of other people have the same experience. Nothing of this kind ever happened to me when I listened to Pericles and other good speakers. They spoke well, but my soul was not thrown into confusion and dismay by the thought that I can hardly endure the life I am leading. He is the only person in whose presence I experience a sensation I might be thought incapable of experiencing, shame. He, and he alone of all the people in the world, makes me positively ashamed of myself, and of the things I do. I know that I cannot answer him or say that I ought not to do as he bids. I am conscious that if I did not shut my ears against him, I would grow old sitting at his feet. So I behave like a runaway slave when I see him, and want to take to my heels. Many a time I know I would be glad to see him vanish from the face of the earth. Yet I know that I should be much more sorry than glad if he were to die. In fact, I simply do not know what to do about him. I am at my wit's end.''

There was much laughter when he stopped for breath, for he seemed to be still in love with Socrates.

No one had ever seen Socrates drunk, Alcibiades recalled almost enviously, and the others would not see him drunk that evening, no matter how much his powers were tested.

''Give me some ribands,'' he called out joyously in a display of mock chagrin, ''that I may crown the head of this universal despot who, in conversation, is the conqueror of all mankind.''

There was a general uproar of good humor when Alcibiades had finished, all order was abolished, and everyone was compelled to drink great quantities of wine.

But Socrates was not drunk when almost all the others, Alcibiades too, had left or fallen asleep.

Near dawn, said one witness, only Aristophanes and Agathon were still awake with Socrates. They were drinking from a large goblet, which they passed around, and Socrates was busy compelling these two prize-winning playwrights to acknowledge that a man who could write a comedy could also write a tragedy, and that the true artist in tragedy was an artist in comedy too.

Aristophanes fell asleep while listening and Agathon dozed off shortly afterward.

As for Socrates, when he saw he had no audience, he stood up and went to the gymnasium, where he bathed and spent the day as he would any other, and then toward evening he finally went home to bed.

Socrates was about ten when Pericles rose to leadership, nullified the prerogatives of the hereditary Areopagus, and transferred the authority to legislate to the Assembly, to which every adult male citizen was now eligible to belong.

A patrician of noblest lineage, he was called, of course, a traitor to his class.

Socrates was about forty when Pericles died, and he could find no more virtue in Athenian democracy than in other forms of government that had preceded it and very much less than in a theoretical ideal toward which no one wished to strive. From Plato and Socrates we learn that when there are two conflicting political viewpoints, it is possible to reject one without embracing the other, and that, even when there are more than two, it is possible to feel repugnance for them all.

The most he could say for the democracy he knew was that it was not something worse.

He kept out of politics except when chosen by lot. In the democracy of Athens most public officials were chosen by lot. Elections, of course, were undemocratic for reasons that are obvious.

Socrates would wonder out loud that people who would not choose a pilot or a builder or any other craftsman by lot would pick that way judges and government officials whose mistakes in statecraft were far more disastrous. He was amused too that a man would pursue a runaway slave or seek a lost sheep yet search not at all for virtue or good character.

Scoffing observations like these were not ingratiating to people who believed their system sacred and superior and exempt from analysis by anyone other than themselves.

"Do you really believe I would have been allowed to survive long enough in politics to do Athens any good?" he said to his jurors in reply to the criticism that, for a person professing the wish to do good, he had not immersed himself in public affairs. "Consider that for what little I have said as a plain man how many of you may now wish to kill me. I am certain that if I had engaged in politics, I should have perished long ago, and done no good to either you or to myself. And do not be offended, O men of Athens, at my telling you the truth, for the truth is, no man who opposes you or any other crowd and tries to prevent the many unjust and illegal acts which are done in the state, will save his life. He who will fight for the right, if he would live even a brief space, must have a private station and not a public one."

Under the Tyranny, he reminded, he had risked death by disobeying the illegal order to arrest Leon the Salaminian.

Under the democracy earlier, he reminded also, it had fallen to his lot to preside in the Assembly the day members wished to condemn to death by a single vote the eight generals who had been victorious in the sea battle of Arginusae: they had routed the Spartans, destroying many of their ships; but they had failed, in the confusion of battle and the pursuit of the enemy, to effect the rescue of floating survivors from their own wrecked triremes and to ensure that the bodies of their dead would be taken up from the waters. The orders were issued belatedly. A sudden storm made their completion impossible.

Trying people en masse was prohibited by the Athenian constitution.

The people were furious when Socrates refused to put the illegal motion to a vote, and they clamored for his arrest. They thought it outrageous that citizens in a free society, by majority vote, should not be allowed to kill whomever they wanted to.

The next day a different man presided.

The generals were tried as one, found guilty, and executed.

To Callicles in the *Gorgias* Socrates had said: "My position has always been that I myself am ignorant of how things are, and that I have never met anyone who could say otherwise and not appear ridiculous."

He could not believe in the illusions of political freedom, that democracy necessarily brought unity, coherence, contentment, good government, intelligence, equality, fairness, honesty, justice, peace, or even political freedom. In democratic Athens there were always factions enraged with each other; and in all of the factions there were men who were just and evil, selfish and generous, vicious and peaceful.

But he would not violate the law to save his life.

He did not know if the law was good, but he knew what it was, and he would not flee Athens to avoid his trial or escape his execution.

"But how shall we bury you?" his friend Crito asked at the end.

"Any way that you like," answered Socrates. "If you can catch me and I don't slip through your fingers."

He believed in God and in the immortality of the soul, says Plato, before anyone else in the world knew what a soul was, and they accused him of impiety and put him to death.

The soul has its genesis in the writings of Plato.

He was cheerful at the end when he drank his cup of poison. He could not, he had said to his good friend Crito, repudiate the laws of the community in which he had lived his life without repudiating the meaning of that life.

He was a dedicated philosopher who had no philosophy, an educator without curriculum or system of education, a teacher without pupils; a professor who professed to know nothing; a sage with faith that a knowledge of virtue exists unborn inside each of us and might, perhaps, be brought to life through persevering search.

He did not like books, which should have nettled Plato, who wrote so many.

He had low regard for people who read them.

He mistrusted books, he said in the *Phaedrus*, because they could neither ask nor answer questions and were apt to be swallowed whole. He said that readers of books read much and learned nothing, that they appeared full of knowledge, but for the most part were without it, and had the show of wisdom without its reality.

He said this in a book.

The book, though, is by Plato, who denounced dramatic representations as spurious because the writer put into the mouths of characters imitating real people whatever the author wished them to say.

Plato said this in a dramatic representation, in which he put into the mouth of Socrates and other real people exactly those things Plato wanted them to say.

Socrates did not think much either of lectures and lecturers. This should have soured Aristotle, who taught by lecturing.

Said Socrates in Plato's *Protagoras*, of teachers who lectured: "If anyone asks them a question, they are as incapable as a book of answering it or themselves putting a question. They behave like a brass pot which gives out a continuous ringing sound if you strike it, till someone puts his hand on it. So the orators, at the least query, go off into a long-drawn speech."

This sounded to Aristotle like a lecture or a long-drawn speech.

He was not anyone's idea of an intellectual.

Other philosophers founded schools, including more of his followers than Plato alone: because he was more skeptical than dogmatic, the schools of philosophy founded by his followers were always diversely in contradiction to each other.

Socrates had no school.

He had no library, as Euripides and many of his contemporaries did.

He had long lost interest in the natural sciences as useful in providing knowledge that mattered.

He had no fellow scholars, colleagues, or associates with whom he worked or formed a group, no movement, methodology, or ideology of which he was the center or inspiration. He was not ambitious. He did not even write for a magazine.

Rumina had no son.[1]

He kept no horns, as certain herdsmen of his system
privates do.

He had lost the interest in the marital sciences as useful
in promoting knowledge and pleasure.

He still no longer inflicted no pleasure in associating with
whom he wished or himself ... greatly, an abnormal ... under
subtlety, or identity of which he was the center of ... the
fine. He was not handsome. He did not even wish the
magazine.

V

RISE OF
THE
DUTCH
REPUBLIC

11

THE LAND IN WHICH ARISTOTLE IN LAVISH COSTUME WAS re-created by Rembrandt in debt had passed by marriage, as, part of a region containing Flanders and Brabant, from the Burgundian estates of the fifteenth century into the Hapsburg dynasty and the Holy Roman Empire and eventually, through natural and divine rights of inheritance and succession, *he* thought, into the sovereign dominions of the king of Spain, Philip II.

Religion, education, exploration, commerce, and the multifarious effects of what later came to be called capitalism brought confusing impediments into this normal historical routine.

One of the effects of capitalism is communism.

In the second half of the twentieth century, the contending superpowers of capitalism and communism coexisted in a symbiotic equilibrium of necessary evils and got on with each other much better than either wanted to admit.

Russia and the United States had been enemies for seventy

years and the only two times they had both gone to war this century they were allies against Germany.

In both countries, as elsewhere, the quality of government was normally very low.

Leaders in both places never seemed to hate each other as much as they hated members of their own populations who differed with them and, as with ancient Athens, smaller nations attempting to evade their domination.

The government of each was helpless without the threat from the other.

It is impossible to picture either nation functioning so smoothly without the horrifying danger of annihilation by the other.

It is easy, however, to picture the chaos that would result in both from a sudden outbreak of peace.

Peace on earth would mean the end of civilization as we know it.

In the interlude of peace that followed World War I there was an international economic depression that was not alleviated until the sovereign nations of the civilized world began preparing for World War II.

In all of the conflicts between Russia and the U.S. in different areas of the globe, ideology was never a cause or an objective of either power.

Each called the other an evil empire.

There were no more crusades.

Even in communist countries the right wing prevails.

In ancient Athens, too, the dynamics of domestic politics overcame all other incentives.

The motives of Athenians in establishing democratic societies elsewhere were not to establish democratic societies but to remove hostile neighbors and obtain absolute compliance from societies guided by governments in liege to them.

In the eighty years of military strife in Greece after victory in the Persian wars, the sole diplomatic principle asserted by Athenians in debate was the right of the strong to suppress the weak.

This was proclaimed under Pericles in the council in Sparta before the start of the Peloponnesian War, by the demagogue Cleon in the Assembly on his motion to destroy the city of Mytilene, and by the delegation of Athenians to the men of Melos.

To obtain absolute compliance from other free cities, the free city of Athens conquered, massacred, deported, and enslaved.

When an Athenian moderate opposed the motion of Cleon to slaughter the men of Mytilene and sell into slavery the women and children, Cleon labeled him lily-livered, anti-Athenian, un-Athenian, a bleeding heart, and a knee-jerk liberal.

The demagogue Cleon was a radical democrat, the first in the line of businessmen political leaders after Pericles.

In ancient Athens, the radical democrats were businessmen.

Cleon ranted effectively in legislative debate. In contrast to the dignified eloquence of his predecessor, Pericles, he harangued and bellowed in his speeches, paced in rage and sawed the air, and earned for himself the resentful contempt of Thucydides and Aristophanes and others in the educated elite who were repelled by the vulgarity of his appeals and the coarseness of his followers.

Almost all members of this new merchant class spoke with the harsh accents of the town and the animated arm and head movements of the common and the foreign, invoking the scorn and discontent of those in the upper classes of the country that had been in the past the wellspring of Athenian culture and the backbone of Athenian history.

Like many in politics who are self-centered and brazen, Cleon was thin-skinned, immovable, histrionic, boisterous, and self-pitying.

He demanded to be told why the same autocratic practices should not suffice in the management of government that had served him so profitably in the management of his leather business, where his laborers were slaves.

Given his way, the democrat Cleon would have forbidden criticism from the stage and rescinded the rights of everyone to oppose him. He sounded more contemporary than classical when he cried out in the Assembly:

"Not for the first time do I realize how impossible it is for a democracy to govern an empire!"

The European emperor Charles V, it's been said, was among the best in the history of the Holy Roman Empire. He abdicated to enter a monastery. To his son Philip II, he bequeathed the throne of Spain, the Spanish possessions of Sicily and Naples, Spanish America, and all of that territory at the north of Europe known as the Netherlands, or the Low Countries.

Philip II spent much of his long life attempting to restore Catholicism in the Netherlands, where the large majority had remained Catholic, and imposing his rule as king upon a population already accepting him as such.

But at the head of his armies he sent the inflexible Duke of Alva, who was tactless and cruel. The severity and brutality of the Duke of Alva aroused terrified protest and hardened opposition finally into an organized rebellion that lasted eighty years.

Tradition too played a role in the revolt of the Netherlands: generations of noblemen, merchants, farmers, and even of royal officials had grown used to a considerable amount of local autonomy, which they were unwilling to surrender to a distant central authority. The presence of foreign soldiers on their soil kindled resentment and consolidated hostility.

William of Orange, who, as stadtholder of Holland, Zeeland, and Utrecht, was the highest representative of the Spanish throne in the Netherlands, aligned himself finally with the Dutch resistance and eventually became its leader.

A German Catholic with tolerant religious attitudes and known Lutheran leanings, William was heir to estates in the German region of Nassau and had lands and noble ancestry in the principality of Orange in southeastern France.

He converted to the religion of the Calvinists when he found them his most dedicated supporters.

As Spanish armies pushed deeper into Flanders, William moved north from Brussels and Antwerp to headquarters in Delft in Holland. The Dutch provinces of the Netherlands were provincial indeed compared to the baroque entertainments of the Flemish court in Belgium, and a man of weaker character might have yielded to Philip to revel again in these luxuries.

The Dutch War of Independence was curious, for it did not begin as a rebellion and was not thought of as a war of independence until, after the first twenty years, a formal act of deposition put the new vision into words.

The Act of Deposition of the Lord of the Low Countries, Philip II formally renounced allegiance to Philip for breaching an implied social contract between ruler and ruled in which governments derive their powers from the just consent of the governed. This declaration of independence by the Dutch preceded the American Declaration of Independence by two hundred years and the civil war in England by sixty.

The Dutch national anthem, composed around 1570, still contained in 1985 a pledge of allegiance to the king of Spain.

Of the seventeen provinces of which the Netherlands consisted originally, only the seven in the north achieved independence. Of these, just a few are known to us by name, Holland, Zeeland, Utrecht, and perhaps Friesland; outside the Netherlands, perhaps inside too, not many people know of Groningen, Overijssel, and Gelderland. Only the two coastal provinces of Holland and Zeeland took major roles in the maritime growth of the country.

William of Orange, known also as William the Silent, was the father of this new country, which was not his own, and at two o'clock one afternoon in 1584, sixty-four years before the war of independence ended, he was assassinated in his home by three balls discharged into his chest from a pistol for which he had provided the money.

The attacker, Balthazar Gérard, inspired in large part by a

reward advertised by King Philip, was a Catholic fanatic who had insinuated himself into the household of William of Orange by posing as a penniless Calvinist fanatic whose father had been burned as a heretic. William gave him money for food and decent raiment and Gérard bought the pistol and ammunition with which he shot his sympathetic benefactor.

Balthazar Gérard was neither Dutch nor Spanish, but a Burgundian, and he was captured trying to escape.

He was questioned and tortured. He was completely at ease in his respites between torture and interrogation and conversed with his captors comfortably.

The sentence against him was execrable, says Motley in his *Rise of the Dutch Republic.*

He was condemned to die: it was decreed that his right hand be burned off with a red-hot iron, that his flesh be torn from his bones with pincers in six different places, that he be quartered and disemboweled while alive, that his heart be torn from his bosom and flung in his face, and that, finally, his head be taken off.

Spectators were awed by the astonishing fortitude with which he bore each step in the sequence. He smiled with the crowd near the end as one of the executioners experienced a bit of comical difficulty on the scaffold. Only when his heart was torn from his bosom and thrown in his face was he seen to flinch. Not long after, it is said, he gave up the ghost.

The bounty promised by Philip went to the parents of Gérard in the form of three lush seignories belonging to William of Orange, costing Philip nothing. Thus, Motley writes with fine rhetorical balance, the generosity of the prince furnished the weapon by which his life was destroyed, and his estates supplied the fund out of which the assassin's family was rewarded.

Nevertheless, the expenses of war proved too much for Philip. By the turn of the century he was eager for peace, and in 1609 came the Twelve Years' Truce between Spain and the Dutch.

With the assassination of William of Orange, leadership

passed to his son Maurice, Count of Nassau, who stemmed the Spanish advance and restored the Dutch borders. He did not succeed, however, in his larger aim of retaking from Spain the occupied territories of the Netherlands, where he had title to family lands, as did other Flemish refugees, who were eager to extend the offensive. His ambitions were obstructed by the hardheaded reluctance of the burghers of Holland to continue paying for a war that no longer seemed necessary to them and often interfered with trade.

Each time there was peace, it was against the wishes of whoever was Prince of Orange.

There is the anecdote of the outspoken merchant from Amsterdam on a trip to The Hague, who, admonished by Prince Frederick Henry for trading with the enemy at Antwerp, told him without fear:

"Not only will I continue to trade with the enemy Antwerp, but if I could make a profit by passing through hell, I would risk burning the sails of my ships in doing so."

Cromwell said of the Dutch that they preferred gain to godliness. To which an Amsterdam merchant might reply that he did not see the difference.

"By God!" Samuel Pepys overheard the Surveyor of the Navy to exclaim later during the Second Anglo-Dutch War. "I think the Devil shits Dutchmen."

When Maurice died of natural causes in 1625, he was succeeded as stadtholder by his younger brother, Prince Frederick Henry, who, it turned out, became Rembrandt's most important patron, purchasing more paintings from him than did any other person, at least seven religious paintings, five of them in a Passion series, and a portrait of his wife, Amalia van Solms.

Rembrandt probably was commended to Frederick Henry by his secretary, Constantijn Huygens, a man of letters with a wide range of literary abilities and artistic interests.

His son, Christiaan Huygens, would become known internationally as an outstanding physicist: he improved telescopic lenses; interpreted correctly the ring structure surrounding Saturn; discovered its satellite Titan; applied the principles of the pendulum to the operation of clocks for the first time; developed a wave theory of light opposed to Isaac Newton's corpuscular theory; formulated the Huygens principle of light waves, which holds that every point on a wave front is a source of new waves; and discovered the polarization of light in calcite.

Aristotle was impressed each time he heard Jan Six talk about the poems of the father and the precocious mathematical and scientific genius of the son, although he himself did not think much of the ring structure of Saturn or the polarization of light in calcite.

The elder Huygens came upon Rembrandt in Leiden when the artist was just past twenty and extolled him as a burgeoning talent of tremendous significance to the future cultural greatness of Holland.

The focus of Huygens' praise was the Rembrandt painting *Judas Returning the Thirty Pieces of Silver*, a puerile work of precocious dexterity and sentimental imagination. For a number of decades, Rembrandt made money from this painting of Judas by lending it out to be copied.

By the time Rembrandt was twenty-seven and in Amsterdam, Huygens had developed a formidable disenchantment with him that never abated. Huygens lived to be ninety and never spoke well of him again.

Seven letters by Rembrandt to Huygens survive. All relate to the paintings in the Passion series and five are requests to be paid more money or be paid more quickly.

In 1639, the final two of these paintings, *The Entombment of Christ* and *The Resurrection of Christ*, were completed hastily and shipped to The Hague before they were dry. This was the same year Rembrandt bought his house. Biographers infer a need for cash.

VI

THE
HERRING
IN
HISTORY

12

It was a ship's captain from Zeeland who, in 1385, perfected a process for curing herring at sea, thereby creating a fishing and a shipbuilding industry and the vast international trade in herring that was the original base of prosperity in a country that would grow into the largest commercial empire the world had seen and the mightiest naval power. As the importance of pickled herring grew, the Dutch needed greater and greater quantities of salt, which they purchased in Biscay, mostly from Portugal, with money from the sale of Norwegian timber and Russian and Polish grain purchased with profits from the sale in the Baltic of their barrels of herring, which were taken in the millions of tons from the teeming fisheries off the coast of Scotland. By the seventeenth century Dutch herring-fishing was the most closely regulated of all industries in the Netherlands.

Each spring when the fishing fleets set sail for the waters off the north of Scotland, they were protected by Dutch men-of-war. The Dutch ruled the waves. On land, the small Dutch military forces, consisting in the main of Protestant mercenaries from other countries and native volunteers from the lower social orders, were considered among the best drilled and disciplined in Europe. Aboard ship, they were the most ferocious fighting men. At sea and abroad, there was no one more warlike than the peace-loving Dutch.

When Spain sacked Antwerp in 1576 and again in 1585, much of the shipping activity normally in this Flemish commercial center began moving northward to Zeeland and Holland in search of safer ports of call, and most was eventually drawn to Amsterdam by the superior acumen of the businessmen there.

When Spain annexed Portugal in 1580 and closed the port of Lisbon to the Dutch, Dutch vessels went searching overseas for the exotic wares they had been buying at one price and, in Plato's unflattering word, "retailing" at a better one. They followed the Portuguese into the Indian Ocean and the Pacific and found what they were looking for in the spice islands of the East.

Soon they were displacing the Portuguese there.

Today, it is hard to envision enough money in cloves and nutmeg, and in cinnamon and pepper also, to launch the Dutch into their historic Golden Century, but a people who had founded a booming national economy on herring was not to be underrated.

In the Golden Century of the Dutch, a thousand new ships were built annually. This averages out to almost twenty a week, with perhaps forty or fifty times that number always in various stages of construction for that many to be completed each year. Just about all the wood, metal, rope, sailcloth, and other materials needed for the building and outfitting of these vessels had to come from abroad, as did the cannons and their mountings, and the cannonballs and gunpowder too.

Even if this figure of a thousand ships a year is a lie, it is a very impressive lie, and the merchantmen and warships of Holland and Zeeland could be found crowding those of other nations in all of the peaceful ports and barring them entirely from markets abroad in which the chartered Dutch companies had obtained monopolies.

A ship of Dutch design called a "flutie" had a greater carrying capacity than all others of the time, was built at lower cost, and was manned by smaller crews, who were paid lower wages but had better food.

No one in Europe carried freight for less.

English monarchs were informed by their envoys that England must not attempt to compete with the Dutch on equal terms: the Dutch would not be overbid or undersold.

By 1648, the year of the Peace of Westphalia and the conclusion of the Thirty Years' War, the city of Amsterdam was the busiest shipping and trading center in the world, and had become so while engaged for some eighty years in the war of independence against Spain. Almost all the spices, silks, beads, and glassware from the East Indies, China, India, and Japan were carried to Europe in ships of the Dutch East India Company. Holland's merchant class was the wealthiest in the world, her industries the most profitable, her commercial practices the most efficient, her navy the strongest on all the seas in which her cargo ships trafficked.

You may wonder how this came about.

Don't ask me.

De Montchrestien termed Dutch prosperity a miracle of human endeavor in a country not fit to live in. To the English ambassador Temple, the key to their common riches lay in each man's spending less than he had coming in. "They wear plain woollen," he wrote, "and feed upon their own fish and roots. They sell the finest of their own cloth to France, and buy coarse out of England for their own wear." Defoe wrote that they bought to sell again, took in to send out, and that the greatest part of their vast commerce consisted in being supplied by all parts of the world, that they might supply all the world.

There were years of truce when Spain sent her silver fleets directly to Amsterdam from Spanish America to pay for the vast quantities of goods bought to preserve her society at home and her international stance against England, France, and also against the Dutch.

Even while at war with Spain, the Hollanders were breezing into the Mediterranean with fleets of Baltic grain and Scandinavian lumber—crops failed in southern Europe for something like five consecutive years, and famine brought optimism and ideal market conditions. Dutch trading vessels sailed past Sicily and Greece into the harbors of the Levant with spices, silks, and porcelains from Asia at prices Asian overland traders, much nearer to sources and markets, were helpless to match.

Dutch opticians invented the telescope in 1600. Six years later Galileo invented the proportional compass and Rembrandt was born in Leiden to Harmen Gerritsz. van Rijn and his wife, Neeltgen. He weighed seven pounds, four ounces: baptismal records in the Pieterskerk in Leiden describe him as "a bouncing baby boy." Two years after his baptism a Dutch scientist invented a better telescope. When Rembrandt reached three, a handful of Dutch families were on their way to settle in Manhattan and Long Island, the Bank of Amsterdam was founded, and Spain and the Netherlands agreed to a twelve-year truce.

VII

BIOGRAPHY

13

THE DUTCH EAST INDIA COMPANY WAS FOUR YEARS OLD
when Rembrandt was born in Leiden in 1606. It was founded
by a consortium of independent shipowners from Zeeland
and Holland who perceived the virtues of administering mo-
nopolies in those places in the Far East where they were able
to take or receive such concessions. The company was chartered with sole rights to do business in the waters and lands
east of the Cape of Good Hope and empowered to arm its
vessels for the protection of its interests. It was capitalized
at nearly seven million guilders, the equivalent of five hundred thousand British pounds. The money was obtained by
public subscription to inexpensive units of ownership. Not
too long after its beginning, the company was posting annual
earnings of between three hundred and five hundred percent
and declaring annual dividends of forty percent. The value
of these units, which were bought and sold easily, skyrock-
eted. They were called "shares," the owners "sharehold-
ers."

Thus was the first modern public corporation brought into being by the first modern European republic.

The first bank checks appeared in the Netherlands, called "letters of cash."

Shares in the Dutch East India Company were so easily transferable and so widely traded that, like tulips later that century, and Rembrandt paintings in our own, they could occasionally replace money as a medium of exchange. In that epidemic of feverish speculation now known as "tulipomania," people in Holland bought and sold even houses for tulip bulbs.

In 1986, an American from Boston paid one Rembrandt to buy $10.3 million.

To a country whose economic health depended on sea voyages, the telescope, like cartography and all other navigational devices, was of primary importance, and even a man of great mind like the Dutch Jew Spinoza earned a respectable living grinding lenses. The philosopher Spinoza was another seeking coherent intelligibility in a universe that had none, and he was excommunicated from his Sephardic congregation for supplying his own when he could not find any.

The heathen influences of Plato are incalculable.

Spinoza died at forty-four, from lungs ruined, it is conjectured, by particles of glass inhaled in the performance of his honest duties as a lens grinder.

The Mercator projections, those maps most familiar to children and adults throughout the world from early education onward, have remained indispensable in schools, travels, and war since the publication of the complete Mercator *Atlas* in 1595. They were conceived by the Flemish cartographer Gerardus Mercator as a technique for depicting our globe accurately on a flat surface. They do not depict the world accurately. No map of the world on a printed page is a map of the world.

He was the fourth of five sons in a family of eight living children, the ninth child of a total ten, and the terms agreed to in the Twelve Years' Truce with Spain were dictated by the Dutch, who were introducing tea from China into Europe while Henry Hudson, an Englishman employed by the Dutch, was exploring the eastern coast of North America and found the river that bears his name.

Dutch prostitutes working the docks preferred tea leaves to money as payment.

So struck was Hudson by the breadth of the entrance to the Hudson River that he assumed he had made that momentous discovery of a northwest sea-passage to the Pacific and Indian oceans.

Whereas, in truth, he had not even discovered a river.

The Hudson River is not a river, although some may wish to argue.

The East River on the opposite side of the island of Manhattan is not a river either. Four of the five boroughs of the City of New York, the country's finest, are not on the continental mainland.

The explorer Henry Hudson was set adrift in a small boat with his son by a mutinous crew and was never seen again.

Rembrandt's father was a miller, his mother the daughter of a baker. By Dutch standards, this would appear to be a marriage made in heaven. When he entered a city grade school at six, the Dutch made a pact with the King of Kandy in Ceylon and skirmished with English settlers in India while trading furs in Manhattan. The Portuguese had already hanged the entire crews of more than a dozen Dutch vessels seized in the Caribbean, outdoing the Athenians who, one year before their inglorious final capitulation, directed through legislation that every Spartan captured at sea have his right hand cut off.

Rembrandt spent three years in grade school, and Dutch settlers established Fort Orange up the Hudson Valley in the vicinity of what is now Albany, and Fort Amsterdam at the lower tip of what is now Manhattan, and the Dutch seaman Adriaen Block, exploring Long Island Sound, came upon Block Island.

Block was astounded by the coincidence of names.

When the Dutch displaced the Portuguese in the Moluccas in the Indian Ocean and established their world monopoly of cloves and nutmeg, Rembrandt, who was nine, was enrolled in Latin school.

Shakespeare died. Rembrandt was ten and still wrestling with Latin while the Dutch mathematician Willebrord Snellius was finding out in his investigations into refraction that the ratio of the sine of the angle i of incidence to the sine of the angle r of refraction is equal to the ratio of the refracting medium's index of refraction n to the original medium's index of refraction n.

I don't know what this means and don't want to have to find out.

In 1617, Rembrandt celebrated his eleventh birthday and Snellius evolved the technique of trigonometrical triangulation for cartography by utilizing the Pole Star to measure the latitudes of the Dutch towns of Alkmaar and Bergen-op-Zoom.

In the eighth year of the Twelve Years' Truce, the Dutch joined with England to send warships to Venice to assist against the Hapsburgs of Austria. Spain was active on the other side. At sea, Dutch and Spanish vessels harried each other whenever one side came upon the other and spied an advantage, and that was how the Dutch Republic and the Spanish monarchy spent the years of their truce.

In Greece, in the cessation of hostilities produced by the Peace of Nicias in 421 B.C., Athens instigated plots against Sparta by other cities and embarked upon the invasion of Syracuse. Sparta participated on the side of Syracuse.

Thus were Athens and Sparta able to observe the terms of the Peace of Nicias while continuing to make war against each other in the cities of the third world.

Rembrandt graduated from Latin school two years before the resumption of the war with Spain two years after William Harvey at St. Bartholomew's Hospital in London first announced his discovery of the circulation of blood while the first Negro slaves were arriving in the English colony of Virginia just twelve years after the city of Jamestown had been settled. And when Jan Pieterszoon Coen, governor general of the overseas territories of the Dutch East India Company, was razing the town of Jakarta and erecting on its ruins the city of Batavia on the site of what is at present Djakarta in what is at present the sovereign state of Indonesia, Rembrandt was admitted to the University of Leiden.

To the directors of the company, who constantly urged moderation in treating with the native populations in his pursuit of immoderate profits for the Dutch East India Company, Coen wrote the following:

"There is nothing in the world that gives one a better right than power and force added to right. The teaching of nature and what has been done by all peoples from age to age has always been sufficient to me."

Coen made his own policies and drove off the Javanese and Asian merchants who for centuries had been trading with the Moluccans, and he imposed by force his monopoly of the cloves and nutmeg cultivated there, dictating prices so low that native workers had to leave off growing spices for him to grow the produce necessary for themselves to continue living in order to continue growing cloves and nutmeg for him.

He had ships circle the islands on search-and-destroy missions, spying through their spyglasses unregistered plots of cloves and nutmeg, which he destroyed with fire, defoliated with chemicals, made barren with salt.

The Dutch knew how to extract salt to make soil fertile again, but no one else did.

By the time the Twelve Years' Truce ended in 1621, the Dutch were in Sumatra and Pulicat in Asia and at the Amazon in South America, and Rembrandt was in the tutelage of Jacob van Swanenburgh in Leiden, mixing pigments in linseed oil and milling ink for etchings with a man not especially esteemed as a painter or teacher, from whom, it is agreed, he could not have learned much more than the rudiments of drawing, painting, and etching.

He was fifteen. In the three years he worked with Swanen-burgh, the Dutch West India Company, modeled upon the Dutch East India Company, was chartered and obtained a government monopoly on all trade between the east coast of the Americas and the west coast of Africa, and the potato was brought from South America to Germany and success-fully cultivated in Europe.

There were people in Europe to whom the potato was more important than the training of Rembrandt or the dis-covery of the circulation of the blood by William Harvey. Measured by the assumption that human life has a value, few foods have been as beneficial to mankind as the potato.

Nowhere in history is this assumption that human life has a value borne out by human events.

All our religions but the Judaic and the Greek think more of us dead than alive.

In time, the potato was transported back across the Atlan-tic for cultivation in North America and Rembrandt was shipped to Amsterdam to train with an artist of better stand-ing, Pieter Lastman.

For a while, gifted young Rembrandt emulated too well Lastman's overwrought inanities. Fortunately, he gradually was drawn more strongly to the sense of inner feelings in himself and his subjects than to the garish tricks of exagger-ated physical exertion and was affected as well with a lifelong fascination with the contrasts of light and dark assimilated from the followers of Caravaggio in the School of Utrecht.

That there was already a school of art in Utrecht in Rem-brandt's time, and another in Leiden, and another in Am-sterdam, in this small, wet land without anything much of an artistic tradition, is one of those cultural mysteries in his-tory that can no better be explained by genetics, geography, or national character than the remarkable emergence of the Jews, the Greeks, and the Romans, or the surge to commer-cial world leadership of the Dutch in their Golden Century.

Though enrolled by his parents in the University of Leiden when he was fourteen, he did not attend.

We can guess that his innate talent and enthusiasm for drawing and coloring outweighed any hunger for a traditional education in science and the humanities. We also guess, from their indulgence of this precocious and speculative aptitude in the child, that his parents were open-minded and doing fairly well.

People who were poor in the Netherlands, as in most other places before and since, were very poor, and there were great numbers of them even in Amsterdam, and a great many more in the inland cities and provinces.

Textile workers in Leiden dwelt in tiny huts with only a straw mat on a floor for furniture. Fortunately, their workday was so long they had little time to spend there.

Happily for the national economy, refugees from Flanders and other war-torn lands nearby streamed into the Dutch Republic to escape the sieges and battles of eighty years of war and helped keep wages low enough to preserve the competitive advantages that Dutch industry and commerce enjoyed.

The poverty of the people made prosperity possible.

Thriving labor recruiters filled contracts for children over six to work in textile mills and other factories.

They filled their contracts for children with supplies from orphanages and with others found begging along the roads. Leiden alone imported four thousand children over six from a single supplier.

Children under six sometimes wanted care and were not worth their hire.

Rich is the country that has plenty of poor.

In periods when prosperity is general, the value of the impoverished to that country increases, and nations not rich in poor must import indigents from inferior countries for the labor now considered degrading for citizens of repute to perform.

The bidding sometimes goes high.

It is fortunate for the progress of civilization that there are always plenty of poor.

Nobody else does the dirty work.

The Dutch, to their credit, were the most enlightened people in the world in matters of social welfare.

In 1646, when the rest of the money on Rembrandt's house was due, children in Holland could no longer be forced to work more than fourteen hours a day.

And Amsterdam bakers of fancy cakes were prohibited from displaying overdecorated wares in their windows "lest they bring sadness to people too poor to buy them and stimulate covetous instincts to arise in their hearts."

In 1632, the year of Rembrandt's *Anatomy Lesson of Dr. Nicolaes Tulp*, the Amsterdam municipality voted to ban further religious disputes between Calvinist groups as inimical to the efficient practice of business.

Slavery was prohibited inside the Dutch Republic. But slave trading was not, and the shipment of blacks from Africa to the Americas was one of the few successful enterprises of the Dutch West India Company, whose performance, over the long run, disappointed expectations.

The cargo was perishable, but the markup on slaves was high, and the company, transporting up to fifteen thousand blacks annually, did an estimated $7,000,000 worth of business in slavery in the twenty-five years of its existence.

Bible-reading Dutch Calvinists captaining the slave ships read their Bibles aloud to crews and captives and were in general known to be kinder to their cargoes than Christians in that era normally were to each other.

In New England, Pilgrims fleeing religious intolerance who landed on Plymouth Rock lost little time instituting religious persecutions of their own.

Another profitable, one-time capital achievement of the Dutch West India Company was the capture in 1628 by Piet Hein of the entire Spanish silver fleet on its way from Cuba to the mother country.

This singular exploit yielded a net gain of *sixty-six pounds* of gold and *one hundred seventy-seven thousand pounds* of silver, along with thirty-one ships carrying six hundred eighty-nine guns, four thousand men, and various other goods and supplies with an estimated worth of more than $1,200,000.

The company declared a fifty-percent dividend, paid off its debt, and gave ten percent of the prize to the stadtholder at The Hague.

Rembrandt had completed his painting *The Money Changer* the year before.

There is no doubt he fared well when he returned to Leiden from Amsterdam at seventeen and set up shop in a studio shared with another artist, Jan Lievens, the same year a trade treaty with Persia was announced and the territory called New Netherland was annexed as a Dutch province formally, if not in political fact. That New World territory was countless times larger than its owner and of no discernible value to a nation desirous more of raw money and resalable products than of lands to colonize. In just one place did the Dutch move inland to settle permanently. That was South Africa and we can see what happened. Lievens was a year younger than Rembrandt but already better known as an artist.

Rembrandt's *The Money Changer* is also known as *The Rich Fool*.

With Rembrandt back in Leiden, the Anglo-Dutch alliance agreed to send ships against Spain in the Atlantic at just about the same time the Dutch executed ten Englishmen who had settled on Amboina in the Moluccas with rash fantasies of going into the spice trade there.

Prince Maurice died when Rembrandt was nineteen and was succeeded by Frederick Henry, who built a small palace at The Hague, established a small court, and bought at least fifteen paintings from Rembrandt before his own death in 1647.

It was not long after Frederick Henry's accession as stadtholder that his cultured secretary, Constantijn Huygens, came upon the two youthful artists in Leiden who excited his admiration and encouraged his hope for a national art that would rival the Italian and surpass the Spanish and Flemish one year before Peter Minuit, governor general of the territories of the Dutch West India Company in North America, purchased the island of Manhattan for twenty-four dollars' worth of trinkets and fishhooks from the Wappinger Indians, who did not own it.

Peter Minuit was replaced, and neither the company nor the country got back the twenty-four dollars' worth of trinkets and fishhooks when the island was ceded to England in 1667 after the Second Anglo-Dutch War.

The Dutch got much the better of the British in that second Anglo-Dutch war, in which they relinquished all their possessions in North America. They sailed intrepidly into the rivers near London to destroy or capture English vessels there that were the pride of His Majesty's fleet and landed raiding parties at will along the English coast.

But England was a monarchy and could create an empire. The Dutch were a republic and created only dealerships.

So by the Treaty of Breda of 1667, the Dutch took the open slave market of Suriname on an unexplored coast of South America in exchange for New Netherland, which English colonists were encroaching upon anyway. Rembrandt was sixty-one and had two more years to live.

Milton published *Paradise Lost*.

The Dutch captured Sumatra the year before Titus married and died.

With the ten percent of the booty he received from the Dutch West India Company, Prince Frederick Henry set out on a land offensive into the southern Netherlands and his erudite secretary, Constantijn Huygens, wrote in Latin the remarkable book of memoirs in which he foresaw for the two young artists of plebeian blood he had found in Leiden an immensity of talent that would exceed all predecessors. Of Rembrandt he wrote that he excelled in penetrating to the heart of his subject matter and was obsessed with translating into paint what he saw in his mind's eye.

Huygens' Latin is difficult and his pronouncements were fallible. The painting *Judas* upon which he lavishes praise is comical enough by contemporary standards to tempt a worldly American in a frivolous mood to burst into laughter.

Huygens advised Lievens to continue with portraits and leave history paintings to Rembrandt.

Whereupon Lievens began doing history paintings. And Rembrandt did more of the portraits and stationary figures that mainly constitute our present-day appreciation of his genius.

Any painting by Rembrandt showing anyone in motion is not much good or not by Rembrandt. Rembrandt's striking *Polish Rider* in the Frick Collection in New York is not much good and not by Rembrandt. (The etching by Rembrandt of a monk fornicating in a field, however, is a work of different kidney.)

Both young artists rejected Huygens' advice to go to Italy to study Raphael and Michelangelo to learn to surpass them.

They insisted presumptuously that the best Italian paintings were already in the north and that they could absorb all the Italian influence they needed from the work of Dutch artists who had been there.

Lievens moved to England instead to make his fortune and went bankrupt. He moved to Antwerp and went bankrupt again.

And Rembrandt moved to Amsterdam one year after fishermen of the Netherlands recorded a total catch of thirteen million gallons of herring, of which eighty percent was exported. He settled into new quarters in his art dealer's house on the Breestraat the same year the Dutch were establishing a settlement on the Delaware River.

After his *Dr. Tulp* in 1632, he began making more money than he ever had dreamed of, more than he imagined, erroneously, he would ever be able to spend. Among the fifty paintings dated by Rembrandt by the end of 1633 was the sensitive portrait of his mother owned by King Charles I of England that is not by Rembrandt.

He did a silverpoint drawing of Saskia in 1633 to celebrate their betrothal, and when the island of Curaçao was occupied in 1634, they married. She seems pleasant and plain, with a tendency toward pudginess commonplace among Dutch women of that period, who, we are told, ate and drank as heartily as the men. They celebrated their honeymoon by retaining a lawyer to collect the debts owed Saskia.

The next year, the Dutch invaded Brazil to enter the lucrative sugar business and landed in Formosa, the Virgin Islands, and Martinique. The Dutch were processing whales in Spitsbergen, but the English were settling in Connecticut, and their first child, Rombartus, was born and died circa the same year Rembrandt did his *Self-Portrait with Saskia* that shows him dissipating exultantly in an ostentatious vulgarity of success that is uncomplimentary to both.

Saskia sits on his lap like a tavern prostitute. Rembrandt has a hand on her waist with possessive unconcern, holds a glass aloft in a toast to himself, and is as proud as the peacock gracing the repast on the table.

In the last years of his life, wrote a Dutch biographer who had never met him, Rembrandt was content to make a meal for the day of some bread and some cheese or herring.

This is one of the two self-portraits by Rembrandt in which he is smiling broadly; the other is the one at sixty in which he looks past eighty and appears pathetically demented with his time-ruined laugh. That painting is flawless.

They had moved from Uylenburgh's house into rented quarters by then, and Rembrandt was spending recklessly in the auction halls and art galleries when Harvard University was founded in Cambridge, Massachusetts, as an institution for the education of Puritan ministers and blossomed into the distinguished school of finance and business for which it is best known today.

In that year of Harvard's founding, Rembrandt completed the first of the three remaining paintings in the Passion series for Frederick Henry while the Dutch settled in Ceylon one year before they expelled the Portuguese from the African Gold Coast and the tulip trade collapsed at home with a tremendous national crash. Those bulbous, easily mutated

Eurasian herbs of the lily family were no longer worth more than their weight in gold. There was ruin and suicide.

The Dutch occupied Mauritius in the Indian Ocean and shortly began clubbing to death the dodo bird.

In 1639 they replaced the Portuguese in Japan, which was closed now to all other Europeans, although in late July a daughter baptized Cornelia was born to the pair and died two weeks later, and Rembrandt and Saskia that year filed suit for libel against those relatives of hers noising it about that she was living extravagantly.

They bought the house on the Breestraat.

And the year after that, in 1640, another daughter was born in July and buried in August.

The year 1641 was especially providential, for the Dutch captured Luanda in Angola and secured the dependable supply of slaves needed to grow sugar in Brazil, began their conquest of Ceylon, took Malacca from the Portuguese on the west coast of Malaya between the Indian Ocean and the China Sea, and Titus was born and lived!

By the time Aristotle was in Amsterdam, more than fifty sugar refineries were operating in the city, and Holland was growing its own tobacco.

But Dutch teeth decayed and Saskia died. Geertge Dircx entered the house to help care for the infant, and civil war broke out in England when Charles I attempted to arrest five members of the House of Commons and sent his queen to her daughter and son-in-law at The Hague and his army of Cavaliers against the Puritan Parliament at York. In New Amsterdam the Dutch governor ordered the massacre of Wappinger Indians who had sought protection by the Dutch from attacks by the Mohawks.

More than fifteen hundred Wappinger Indians were as dead as the dodo.

By 1645 Hendrickje possibly was in the house too, and Rembrandt painted *The Rabbi*, and also did his *Holy Family with Angels*, in which the infant Jesus is an infant, Mary is a mother, and Joseph is a carpenter.

Unfriendly critics chastised him for painting his Bathshe-bas and Danaës with the figures of Dutch "charwomen," as though these human women from the legends of our past had been only ordinary human women from the legends of our past.

His Bathsheba *is* on the heavy side. But so, probably, was David's. So is Joseph's Mary.

The balance on the house was due in 1646. He was not pressed to pay it.

The national economy was booming. There came to him commissions for two more religious paintings for Prince Frederick Henry, a *Nativity* and a *Circumcision*, at prices double the earlier ones, and Frederick Henry died.

If Frederick Henry had lived long enough to look closely at these paintings, he would have noted in Rembrandt a dra-matic change to an individualistic style in which the imagi-nation of the artist was absorbed almost entirely in light, color, paint, and form, and in the glorification of his subjects hardly at all.

Rembrandt now was working as he liked and began to wane in popularity in competition against former students of his like Ferdinand Bol and Govert Flinck, with whom he was not friendly.

Flinck in particular was a facile pragmatist. Choosing Rembrandt to work with for one year in 1635, when that artist was the rage of Amsterdam, he learned quickly to imitate the master so well that many of his oils were thought to be Rembrandt's and were probably sold as such, possibly in complicity with Rembrandt.

Govert Flinck changed styles with the times and was im-itating the transparent finish and precise details of someone else when the new taste for classicism took hold among the conservative upper classes of the Amsterdam business world, and Flinck was one of those artists lording it at the top after the work of Rembrandt, like the person himself, had, to many, turned faintly disreputable.

Uylenburgh was Flinck's dealer too.

If Rembrandt used any of the money from these last paintings for Frederick Henry to pay any of his debt on the house or the interest on the loan, we do not know about it. We do not know that Rembrandt ever paid money he owed unless forced to.

In one misguided business decision he bought back all his own etchings he could, plotting to create a scarcity that would increase the resale value of those he had repurchased.

This venture by Rembrandt into marketing would have paid off handsomely had he lived to be three hundred.

In 1648 peace came to the Netherlands while raging quarrels between Geertge and Rembrandt were building to a head and Spain recognized Dutch independence in the separate peace of the Treaty of Münster while Greek Orthodox peasants went rampaging on a pogrom against European Jews to exterminate all who would not embrace Christianity.

Later in 1648 came the Peace of Westphalia. The Thirty Years' War at last was over, and Poland was at liberty to embark upon an epic pogrom that lasted ten years and brought death to more than one hundred thousand Jews.

Today in Poland they would have a hard time finding that many.

No paintings by Rembrandt are dated 1649, the year Geertge Dircx filed her breach-of-promise suit.

Hendrickje gave testimony of the hysterical outbursts by the plaintiff and Charles was beheaded in England by the revolutionary government led by Oliver Cromwell.

An inventory of the late king's royal possessions tabulated a stud of one hundred thirty-nine horses, with thirty-seven brood mares, and two paintings by Rembrandt.

One of these early Rembrandt masterpieces, his portrait of his mother, was recently judged by the Rembrandt Research Project to be by someone other than Rembrandt, and the net worth of the royal treasury, of Queen Elizabeth II, has been depreciated proportionately.

"I wish she had sold it when I advised her to," regretted

the former minister of finance when the government fell. "The market for that one will never be as good again."

Sir Ian admitted to a "fishy feeling" the one time he saw the picture.

Instead of the many millions of dollars that a genuine Rembrandt commands today, the painting is now worth several hundred thousand as an authenticated Rembrandt fake.

Logically, the painting should be worth more, say some art dealers, inasmuch as there are more genuine Rembrandts than there are authenticated Rembrandt fakes.

We know that Cromwell kept the Rembrandts and disposed of the studs and brood mares, subjugated Ireland, and readmitted the Jews to England, from which they had been expelled by King Edward I three hundred sixty-five years back. Cromwell was persuaded to readmit the Jews by the Sephardic Dutch scholar, writer, and printer Menasseh ben Israel, whose *Hope of Israel*, written and published by him originally in Hebrew, impressed Cromwell so deeply that he invited Menasseh ben Israel to England to talk with him. One impression of Rembrandt's 1636 etching of Samuel Menasseh ben Israel, who died of illness as he traveled back home, can be seen today in the British Museum.

In 1650, two years after the end of the Thirty Years' War, the Dutch had the largest merchant fleet in the world and a powerful navy more than twice the size of those of England and France combined. Two years later they were under blockade.

14

THEY FOUGHT OVER MONEY.

Aristotle was bored.

The specific provocation for this first Anglo-Dutch war was Cromwell's English Navigation Act of 1651, whose intention and effect was to ban Dutch vessels from British ports.

Legislation of that nature often leads to war.

In 432 B.C., Pericles enacted legislation barring Megaran ships from ports in the Athenian empire. It helped lead to war.

And it led as well to that prolonged sequence of events in which Athens suffered defeat; the empire was destroyed; the democracy was outlawed and restored; Socrates and Asclepius were tried, found guilty, and executed; Plato wrote his philosophies and started his school; Aristotle came to Athens as a student and departed as a fugitive and was later, during a different war, painted by Rembrandt in Amsterdam contemplating a bust of Homer that was a copy, and, as a consequence of this, as a conclusion to centuries of hazardous travels, and as a matter of verifiable fact, made in 1961 his triumphant passage from the Parke-Bernet Galleries on Madison Avenue and Seventy-seventh Street in the city now called New York to the Metropolitan Museum of Art on Fifth Avenue and Eighty-second Street before John F. Kennedy was shot between the Korean War and the Vietnam War and was succeeded as president of the United States by Lyndon B. Johnson, who, counseled by an inner circle of educated dumbbells associated mainly with Harvard and other prestigious universities, lied to the American people and the American Congress and secretly and deceitfully took the nation openly into a war in Southeast Asia it could not win and did not, persevering obstinately on that destructive course as resolutely as did Pericles when he moved Athens ahead onto her self-destructive course of war with Sparta.

"We make war that we may live in peace," said Lyndon Johnson, quoting Aristotle, who was embarrassed, and paraphrasing Adolf Hitler.

The desire of some men for peace is a frequent cause of war.

In 1652 the Dutch were defeated in the battle of The Downs, off Folkestone in the Strait of Dover, and Rembrandt received his commission from Don Antonio Ruffo in Sicily for the Dutch painting of a philosopher. In 1653, when Rembrandt's *Aristotle* was just about finished and his *Portrait of Jan Six* was beginning, the Dutch lost naval battles off Portland and North Foreland in the English Channel and were defeated again in home territory off the island of Texel at the entrance to Holland's Zuider Zee. After that, English ships lay at anchor along the Dutch coast and patrolled the North Sea to intercept vessels attempting to run the blockade.

Overseas in New Amsterdam, frightened Dutch colonists built a wall across lower Manhattan to defend against expected attacks by English settlers, thereby creating Wall Street.

Fitting indeed that the people who had devised the first postal system and the first newsletter as accessories to business should supply the eponym for the financial district that exists there now.

"Do you think there'll be riots?" asked the man named Jan Six.

Rembrandt asked why.

Six seemed surprised.

Corn prices were rocketing and herrings had all but disappeared. Banks failed.

"Even when you've finished with him," Jan Six said, jerking his thumb toward Aristotle, "you will not be able to ship it. There are no boats from here to Texel. There are no ships from Texel to Italy."

Aristotle was stuck. He prayed for peace.

"I am finished with him," said Rembrandt. "I'm waiting for it to dry."

Aristotle felt chilly and wet. Cooped up all day in a studio in a country whose cloudy, damp climate he detested, he could not wait for the war to end. His eyes were rheumy. His look was dejected, his complexion jaundiced. The smell of the paint was making *him* sick. He had nothing to do.

"It would be a tragedy," said Rembrandt almost casually, "if I stopped to move now when I am working so well." He had already looked at another house. "But I would rather sell my art collection and continue living here."

"It would be a greater tragedy," said Jan Six, "if you tried to sell anything when people don't want to buy."

Tragedy? Aristotle almost sneered. This wasn't tragedy. Didn't they know that tragedy was an imitation of an action that was serious, complete, and of a proper magnitude, in language that was poetically embellished, that was dramatic rather than narrative in form, and that, by evoking pity and fear, brought about a purging of those emotions? This was pathos, nothing more than one of the ordinary miseries of life, without the salutary compensations of catharsis that tragedy was said by him to confer.

It was tragedy without the happy endings.

Rembrandt said nothing to Jan Six about earnings from

new paintings. Or that, on top of his debts on the house, he owed about eight thousand guilders more, and another twenty thousand guilders, technically, to Titus for the total left him by his mother eleven years earlier. As far as a puzzled Aristotle could ascertain, of the innumerable paintings standing and stacked about the loft, the *Aristotle* and the *Jan Six* were the only two for which the overburdened homeowner, artist, and father could be sure he would be paid. None seemed ever to be finished, although Aristotle and Jan Six both frequently could not see what there was to be done. Rembrandt altered colors and brushwork endlessly, bringing back canvases he had set aside as completed.

His inattention to time was exasperating.

Aristotle contemplating the bust of Homer came close several times to scratching his head, X-ray studies of the painting disclose, but Rembrandt would not allow it and finally determined to extend Aristotle's arm with the hand resting on the head of Homer like a cap, in a pose betokening eternal inquiry.

"I must tell you frankly that I like my painting," said Jan Six, who came frequently now to stand for his portrait, and to watch and to chat.

"I do too," said Rembrandt, pleased.

So did Aristotle.

While Aristotle stood resting on his own easel waiting to go to Sicily, there slowly was emerging on the fresh canvas facing him the fantastic portrait of the younger, widely read man of wealthy family, Jan Six. In life Six was slender and mild-looking, innocuous, delicate; in art he gained strength and acquired domineering presence with every touch of the bristles or palette knife.

Aristotle's heart stopped each time Rembrandt moved near one or the other of them with the palette knife, or approached any of the other paintings with the knife in his fist. Six, resting, stepped from his spot and came to the *Aristotle* to peer inquisitively. Rembrandt tried keeping him back with a hand on his chest.

"The smell of the paint—"

"Will make me sick," Jan Six concluded for him. Six smiled, Rembrandt did not. "Are you really finished with him?"

Rembrandt turned aside with a shrug, not wanting to say. Suddenly, his gaze was arrested by the sight of something unexpected. His head jerked up, he gasped. Without a word he was off like a shot. He lurched to his left and went lumbering across the loft to a corner near the door, casting a hurried look over his shoulder. When he stopped, he bent to reach down to the floor. Then he halted halfway. He plodded back slowly with an abstracted look of disappointment, puffing, growling curses underneath his breath.

Someone had painted another coin on the floor.

"And it was only a stuiver," Aristotle could almost swear he heard him mutter.

Rembrandt stood facing Aristotle with a scowl, glowering balefully. Then he struck with the palette knife.

"Did you know when you did that," inquired Jan Six, beaming, "that the green would come through so vividly?" Six put on the spectacles with which he did not want to be portrayed. "Did you know," he continued, charmed, "when you moved your blade through the wet paint just now that the gold would reflect more brightly, and the silk would look so much deeper with folds?"

"I was trying to find out."

"I think that you knew."

"I knew I could change it again if I did not like what I saw," Rembrandt answered, sulking.

"When I see things like that," said Six, "I begin to think it so natural that the Dutch lead the world in the science of optics. I think you do know precisely what will appear each time you make a change."

"I'm going to change him some more," Rembrandt said, on the spur of the moment.

Jan Six looked amused, Aristotle choked back a sob.

"When do you know that a painting is finished?"

"A painting is finished," Rembrandt replied without turning, "when I say that it is."

"With my portrait too?" Six laughed. "I might wait forever."

"With your portrait," said Rembrandt, drifting toward the work table to take up his palette knife again, his squinting eyes, Aristotle perceived with a slight tremor, fixed back upon him menacingly, "I think you will decide that you will never again want anyone but me painting you and your family."

As it turned out, Six never commissioned another painting from Rembrandt, although Six was so pleased he wrote a verse exalting the finished work, and the portrait may well be the most valuable painting in the world today still in private hands. It is owned by the present heirs of Jan Six and may be seen only when they choose to let you.

Possibly Rembrandt's *Portrait of Jan Six* would go for a hundred million dollars today if sold at auction to a private collector, and probably there are a hundred people in the world who could pay that much.

Hendrickje entered with tea, which was an expensive commodity, and with biscuits sticky with sugar when the afternoon's work was over. Titus trailed her shyly, his sketchbook in one arm; he looked anemic and sleepy. He was a pale, thin child with curly auburn hair, with lovely, dark eyes and a lonely manner, and he usually came with Hendrickje at least once every day into the workshop with his sketchbook, from which Rembrandt gave him short, impassive lessons in drawing. Hendrickje would stay to watch, smiling to herself in silence, with her tilted head resting on her hand, her cheeks plump and ruddy. Titus tried hard and spoke softly. Hanging back near the doorway now, he waved slyly at Aristotle with a playful grin, made a face, winked conspiratorially, and thumbed his nose. He was not quick enough to escape the notice of his father.

"What are you doing?" Rembrandt demanded gruffly.

"He winked at me," said Titus, flustered.

"He did not."

"I swear to God."

Rembrandt smirked. "You mean like this?" With no warning, Rembrandt flipped a smear of paint into Aristotle's eye, closing the lid. Just as swiftly, he rubbed it away with his thumb, and the eye was open.

Titus giggled.

Aristotle took pity on him.

Aristotle remembered his own son Nicomachus and grieved soundlessly for this timid and harmless child of eleven whose father recently had borrowed more than nine thousand guilders, which the philosopher and the artist both knew he would never have the cash to repay.

Jan Six drank his tea standing and put down his cup as he prepared himself to go.

"You draw too?" he asked Titus.

"My father does."

"We'll show him how," Rembrandt said.

Titus opened the pad. Rembrandt guided his hand.

"This way, see? Now it looks full. Now put in some light."

"How?" asked Titus.

"By putting in shadows."

"I think that is funny."

Hendrickje smiled too. Aristotle had pity for both.

"Will we work more tomorrow?" Jan Six asked at the door. "I have time."

"Please bring your red cloak. I want to start putting in color."

"I'm still not used to it," Jan Six said, with an uneasy laugh and a light flush of embarrassment. "Although I continue to like it. It's really so bright. I almost never have nerve enough to wear it."

"You will wear it forever," Rembrandt told him with gloom.

"If ever you finish," Jan Six said with a sigh.

"I've only just started. Bring gloves too."

"What color?"

"That will not matter. Whatever you like. I'll paint my own color. I could do you much better with things from my collection, but you demand to be painted in clothing of your own. I could make you look like him."

"The last thing I would want," said Jan Six pleasantly, "is to look like him."

Aristotle could have killed him.

Aristotle finally got out, although it took almost another year. He had to wait until the Treaty of Westminster, which was signed in the spring of 1654, but his luck was extremely good and he made it back to the Mediterranean before that summer was over. The Dutch purchased peace with a heavy indemnity while the Portuguese were driving them out of Brazil.

Aristotle was glad to be gone from that sinister, dark land of northern Europe. With the Treaty of Westminster his dreams of liberation had come true. He felt free when wrapped from head to toe for his sea voyage and packed inside a wooden crate. He looked ahead bravely in keen anticipation to the new world that awaited him.

He left Amsterdam by tender on June 13, 1654, with a shipping order consigning him to the captain of the freighter *Bartolomeus*, which lay at anchor off the island of Texel, and the ship set sail on June 19 of that year, bound for the city of Naples as the first port of call. In August the *Bartolomeus* docked at last at the port of Messina in northeastern Sicily.

Aristotle rejoiced unnoticed when he heard he was there. He remembered Messina from his reading of Thucydides about the Athenian expedition to Syracuse that had been championed by Alcibiades.

The crate containing Rembrandt's *Aristotle Contemplating the Bust of Homer* was unloaded, claimed, and then carried by cart up a bumpy road to the castle of Don Antonio Ruffo, where its arrival was awaited with rambunctious and tremulous suspense.

Aristotle held his breath while the crate was hammered

open and his painting was unwrapped and lifted out. His reception could not have been better. There were cries of amazement and delight when the people there saw him. Aristotle, who was known to have been showy, was exhilarated beyond measure by his warm welcome and the exclamations of excitement and cheer with which his appearance was greeted. These people were expressive! There was no doubt from the first that they liked his looks. The painting was lifted high and rushed eagerly to the archway of the balcony to be admired in sunlight. There was effusive Italian praise for his attire and his jewelry, for the gold chain first, for the brooch on his shoulder, the medallion, his earring and his pinky ring, for the excellent detail in the fine brushwork of the eyes and the reflections of light in the hat and dark beard. Aristotle glowed with pride, with immodest self-satisfaction, basked without shame in their unrestrained adulation. At last he was with friends who could truly appreciate him.

"I wonder who it is," he heard one gentleman say.

"Albertus Magnus?" another guessed.

"He looks like a phrenologist."

Aristotle was speechless.

VIII

THE AGE
OF
PERICLES

15

THE AGE OF PERICLES BEGAN WITH FIFTEEN YEARS OF WAR and ended with the beginning of the one lasting twenty-seven.

The party of liberal democrats of which Pericles was the head rose to power in 461 B.C. A casualty list for 459 B.C. contains the names of Athenians who died that year in wars in places like Cyprus, Egypt, Halieis, Aegina, and the Megarid. The year officially was a year of peace. The wars they died in were not wars.

They were police actions.

In that year of 459, when Socrates was a boy of ten, Pericles dispatched a large armada to the Nile to aid the Egyptians in an uprising against the Persians.

The venture, so simple in beginning, lasted five years.

In 454, when Socrates was fifteen, Athens dispatched a reinforcing armada of fifty more triremes. They arrived without knowing the first expedition had been wiped out. The fresh fleet rowed boldly into the estuary of the Nile—and went aground when Persians drained the tributaries.

All these men and ships were destroyed or captured.

The Athenian historian Thucydides puts the total loss in Egypt at two hundred fifty ships and fifty thousand men, of whom about six thousand were Athenian citizens. The rest were mercenaries from cities in the Greek empire who found better work in war than in peace. No Greek army had ever suffered so large a defeat. The disaster was the costliest in Athenian history, until Athens set sail forty years later to conquer Syracuse with the greatest armada ever assembled in the Greek world—and lost everything again.

You would think that after this debacle in Egypt Athens would be weaker, poorer, wiser, chastened, and you would be mistaken, for the Athenians, it was said, "knew no holiday except to do their work and deemed the quiet of inaction to be as tedious as the most tiresome business."

Even while engaged in Egypt, Pericles launched wars of aggression on the mainland. Defeated by the Spartan alliance in the battle at Tanagra, and by neighboring Boeotia ten years later, he at last made a truce with Sparta, to which many in Athens objected, and peace with Persia, which displeased many in the Athenian empire.

He made enemies in high places by giving benefits to those in low. He extended the vote to the poor. In the ancient Athens of the past, only the rich had the right to hold public office. Now every male citizen had that right, but the poor, of course, could not afford to, and power remained where it had always been, with the noble and the wealthy, who were often the same. Now the free citizens of Athens were free to choose the oligarchs who would rule them.

He allotted each citizen two obols a day for attendance at public councils so that the poor could afford to be present to vote the way he wanted them to. (Cleon, who rose to power after Pericles died, increased the fee to three obols so the poor could not afford to stay away.) Pericles doled out to the indigent the price of admission to such public festivals as the dramatic competitions, which now were famous throughout the Hellenic world.

Plato, who detested democracy and the idea of pay for

public service, wrote in the *Gorgias* some seventy-five years later that Pericles had made the citizens of Athens indolent, cowardly, greedy, and loquacious.

Pericles built walls four miles long from Athens to the coast, enclosing the city in a walled triangle with the seaports on which its trade and naval empire depended. Athens was invulnerable on land and invincible at sea, and never again in his lifetime did Pericles allow Athens to engage in a land battle with a force stronger than his own.

He began building the Parthenon, which would take much time, require much labor, cost huge amounts, and ease the chronic problem of peacetime unemployment, as would other projects in the public works program he envisioned. He instituted a peacetime military force and kept ships afloat to police the seas. With subsidies, military recruiting, building programs, and government employment, he created a welfare state for the many while broadening his political base.

Pericles boosted national pride with his Alien Exclusion and Immigration Act of 451, a jingoistic measure conferring Athenian citizenship only upon those with Athenian parents on both sides.

There is poetic justice in what struck him later in consequence. Excluded from citizenship was his only surviving son, borne him by his Miletian mistress, Aspasia, with whom he would fall in love when he was fifty, and to whom he would remain attached for the rest of his life.

His truce with Sparta in 446 ended the fighting between these enemy cities and freed Athens to make war now against allies and friends. He dismissed protests from members of the Athenian alliance and suppressed defections ruthlessly. Cities that had thought themselves equals now saw they were subjects.

There were rebellions in Byzantium and Samos.

Byzantium, it appears, needed always to be recaptured, from Greek oligarchs or Persians.

With the island of Samos, her most powerful ally, Athens intervened in an insignificant regional conflict that was none of her business. Pericles sent an ultimatum; the ultimatum was defied.

Pericles himself set sail with the first forty triremes. The campaign was costlier than anyone in Athens had supposed it would be. The siege lasted nine months. When it was over, Athens pulled down the walls of the Samians, seized their shipping, and set a large fine upon them. In this victory by Pericles, Athens exchanged a powerful ally for a ruined city, and lost many men.

Returning to Athens, Pericles made the first of the funeral orations of which we know.

"Athens has lost its youth," he said, "and the spring has gone out of the year."

Those who had died were like the gods. "One cannot see these fallen heroes now," he said memorably. "Neither can one see the gods. But from the honors which they receive, and the blessings which they bestow, we know that they are immortal."

The speech was recalled and repeated for hundreds of years.

The men were all but forgotten by the time he concluded.

16

He was called the Olympian: for the majestic works constructed under his direction, and for his manifest preeminence in dignity, intelligence, honesty, and eloquence.

He was also called "Squill-head" by the comic playwright Cratinus, who called Aspasia a harlot.

Like all great leaders in democracies proudest of freedom of expression, Pericles was intolerant of written criticism. Had there been a press, he would have excoriated it.

He enacted a law prohibiting reference to living Athenians in plays.

His law was revoked by popular demand.

His head was long and likenesses invariably portray him wearing a helmet to cover this distortion in facial scale, the workmen being willing, Plutarch tells, not to expose him.

He was also called "Onion-head."

He was belittled for kissing Aspasia in the doorway of his home each time he left and returned.

He went seldom to sessions of the Council and the Assembly, sending deputies instead, adding weight by his presence to those meetings he did attend.

He kept public appearances to a minimum, would not make a spectacle of himself, and did not speak publicly until he had something to say.

His recorded statements are few, his speeches of state as elevated as the Gettysburg Address of Abraham Lincoln, and, unhappily, motivated by the identical circumstances of war and the commemoration of the war dead.

He did not go to meals or other entertainments in the homes of others. In his own home, the contentments were quiet; he associated most with the teachers and talents with whom he had become close friends: the philosophers Protagoras and Anaxagoras, Damon the musician, Phidias the sculptor and architect. Solitary and grave, distinguished in bearing, Pericles would go about the city alone, from his home to his office in the Council or to the stalls in the market, often to shop for his needs for the day.

Scrupulously avoiding any appearance of impropriety, he had his steward sell all produce from his estates wholesale at the market price as soon as it was gathered, and he bought back retail what was needed. In the first year of the war with Sparta, Pericles announced promptly that if his own estates were spared by the invading Spartans, he would donate them to the city. Such rectitude and frugality were exasperating to others in his household, who felt unjustly deprived of the luxury they coveted and the opportunities for prodigality commensurate with their station.

His eldest son tried living lavishly anyway and wed an expensive young wife. Without authorization, he borrowed money on his father's name and could not repay.

Pericles was unyielding to the borrower and the lender, as disapproving of both as though they had been strangers.

That son feuded with him thereafter. He maliciously reported to snickering audiences the private conversations he overheard at home, salaciously accused the father, the Athenian leader elected chief general for fifteen consecutive years, of seducing his young wife and lying with her at his pleasure.

Pericles would not respond to personal attacks.

Plutarch tells of the day he was berated in the marketplace by a displeased citizen. Pericles went about his business without replying. The man dogged his footsteps, and the barrage of invective and denunciation continued all that afternoon, with no reply from Pericles. As the sun sank and the day darkened, Pericles turned for home. The man followed, with no letup in his abuse. It was night by the time Pericles reached his door. Immediately he was inside, he directed a servant to go out with a torch to light the way for the man back to his own house.

This is a story almost too good to be true, and probably it is not.

But it was for poise of such worth that he was known as the Olympian.

He was never without political enemies. On one side of him were radical democrats clamoring for more wars. On the other were aristocratic conservatives partial to Sparta who did not want any.

Neither radicals nor conservatives thought much of democracy as a viable form of government.

They still don't.

Reactionary warmongers calling themselves neoconservatives deserted the democrats of Pericles to join the aristocrats, and were despised by both parties.

He was never accused of homosexuality.

He was accused of heterosexuality.

Along with the spiteful gossip by the son, there were sniggering rumors that his friend Phidias, employing works in progress as the lure, would attract freeborn Athenian women to his studio and deliver them to the bed of Pericles for that Olympian's lustful fulfillment. There were rumors that his beloved Aspasia would beguile other freeborn Athenian women into engaging friendships to entice them home to the bed of her patron, protector, and lover, and the sire of her one son.

His opponents in Athens, knowing him personally unassailable, attacked associates.

His friend Damon, with whom he enjoyed discussing music and political theory, was ostracized early.

Anaxagoras was charged with atheism for theorizing that the moon and sun were heavenly bodies, not gods, and Pericles was helpless to aid him in all but his escape.

In enlightened democratic Athens the study and teaching of astronomy was forbidden for more than fifty years.

Phidias was tried for embezzlement and then for impiety and died either in exile or in prison, depending on whether you believe Plutarch or someone else.

And then Aspasia too was brought to trial, accused of impiety and pro-Persian activities. And here the Olympian came into public and begged. His opponents relented. Politics was only politics; and now they saw they had gone too far.

And then, in 433 B.C., Pericles, this leader of the democrats, builder of the Parthenon, sponsor of Aeschylus and Phidias, pupil of Zeno and Anaxagoras, and friend of Damon, in the belief that war with Sparta was probable, deliberately took steps to make it inevitable.

The security of Athens was never an issue.

Spartans went to war, says the Athenian Thucydides, because they feared the growth of Athenian power and saw that so much of Greece was already subject to Athens.

Alarmed by the ambitions of Athens, Sparta and other Greek cities forged defensive alliances wherever they could.

Alarmed by these defensive alliances, Athens began to forge defensive alliances of her own against these defensive alliances that had been forged to defend against Athens.

The entire Greek world was a tinderbox of defense.

Each side said the other was the aggressor.

Both sides were right.

Diplomacy failed.

Diplomacy always fails.

Men who know most about diplomacy do not know very much, and an expert in international relations generally is as useful to his country as an expert in palmistry or phrenology.

There comes a time in the life cycle of a nation when no decision that can be made is the right one and no action that can be taken is intelligent.

Pericles began by barring the ships of Megara from the ports in the Athenian empire.

Next, he doubled the tribute demanded from Potidaea, a subject city in Asia Minor founded by Corinthians. When Potidaea would not assent, he dispatched a sizable army, in which Socrates and young Alcibiades served, for a lengthy siege that took two years.

He was no longer living when the city fell.

And he intervened against Corinth in a conflict with the island of Corcyra, far to the north off the western shore of Greece. Corcyra asked help. Athens saw a chance to make hay, while technically observing the terms of the truce. Pericles sent ships to Corcyra on a peacekeeping mission to protect Athenian interests there: Athens had no interests there until he sent in those ships.

"You can now see for yourselves," complained the Corinthians to a council meeting of Spartans, "that Athens is plotting against you and your allies. To us it seems that you have never fully considered how different the Athenians are from you." The spokesmen from Corinth emphasized the contrast. "The Athenians are innovators and are quick to form plans and carry them out. Whereas you never devise anything new and are disposed merely to keep what you have."

A delegation of Athenians was not conciliatory in reply. "Considerations of right and wrong have never yet turned people aside from the opportunities to take what they could get by superior strength."

It had always been a rule that the weak should be subject to the strong.

"The longer a war lasts," warned the Athenians, "the more things tend to depend on accidents, over whose occurrence both sides equally have no control, and whose outcome we cannot foresee."

The Spartans were inclined to oppose them. But their king spoke for negotiation.

Once a war was begun, he echoed the Athenians, it was impossible to predict the course it would take.

"Do not take up arms yet, I advise. Send envoys to them and make complaints. If they heed our envoys, there could be nothing better." Once a country undertakes a war, he said, it was not simple to end it, and an honorable settlement was not easy to come by. He feared a long war that they might bequeath to their children. "And let us not be ashamed of the slowness for which others censure us most. This trait may well be in the truest sense intelligent self-control."

Sparta mobilized and sent emissaries to Athens.

Pericles would not relent; he labeled compromise appeasement. "Let no one of you think that we shall be going to war for a trifling matter. If you yield this one point to them, you will immediately be ordered to yield another, since they will think of you as conceding only through fear."

And he would give the Athenians the same advice as he had given in the past: "You must support the common decisions, hard as that might prove. If they invade our country by land, we will invade theirs by sea. And we must not give way to resentment and risk a decisive battle with them, for they are far superior in numbers. If we win one battle on land, we shall have to fight them again. However, if we lose one battle, our allies will be lost to us too." Athens had the better chance if she would but bide her time on land and take care of the navy, and do nothing to endanger the city herself. "I am more afraid of our own mistakes than of the enemy's plans. We must realize that war is inevitable."

Such were the words of Pericles.

In the first year of the war, Sparta went into Attica unopposed and laid waste the countryside outside the walls, while

Athens sent fighting ships to the shores of the Peloponnese to lay waste the outposts and the countryside there.

Pericles gathered inside the city all the country people and their property; their sheep and cattle they sent to islands. Unused to city life and mistrustful of city people, these summer war refugees did not like being where they were or the dismal conditions in which they abided. They found living space where they could, many in the streets of the city and in the clearings between the long walls. Otherwise, life in the packed city went on as before and traffic in the harbors was as prosperous as ever.

There was now, of course, no peace party that mattered. There were two war parties: there was the war party of Pericles that favored limited war, and the war party of his critics that wanted total war.

Sparta was indomitable on land, Athens unbeatable at sea, and the fighting could continue forever so long as the two did not meet.

But Pericles believed the war would be short: Sparta would see in one year that victory was impossible and accede to a peace without the concessions demanded earlier.

The strategy of Pericles was flawless.

The strategy failed.

In autumn of that year, after the first season of war, the Peloponnesians went home to the west, their Boeotian allies to their cities just north, Euripides presented his *Medea*, and Pericles that winter gave the elegant funeral oration written for him by Thucydides about thirty years after he delivered it.

The remains of those who had fallen in battle were laid away in the public sepulcher, which was situated in the most beautiful suburb of the city. When his time came to speak, Pericles took his stand upon a platform built high in order that his voice might reach as far as possible in the throng.

His oration was a tribute to the greatness of Athens. What he said of the dead had been said before in similar ceremonies. What he said of the city could be said of no other.

Athens, said Pericles, was the school of Hellas, an education for all Greece, a city with a form of government that did not emulate the institutions of its neighbors but was the model for others.

It was indeed the city to which all Greeks with anything remarkable to say or demonstrate came to display their abilities where they would be best appreciated.

"It is true that our government is called a democracy," said Pericles, "because its administration is in the hands not of the few but of the many."

He made no apology for the war or the empire.

Their ancestors by their valor had transmitted to those times a free state. And their own fathers had added to the inheritance they had received, had acquired the empire Athens now possessed, and had bequeathed it to those in Athens who were alive that day.

All the tongues of the world could be heard in the streets and shops.

"When our work is over," he said, "we have provided for all kinds of relaxations for our spirits, and the delight we each day find in these things drives away sadness. All the products of all the earth flow in upon us into our harbors, so that it seems our happy lot to enjoy the goods of foreign lands just as naturally as the goods of our own."

He doubted, he said, if in any other place in the world could be found a man graced by so happy a versatility as the Athenian. Athens alone, when put to the test, was found to be greater than her reputation, and future ages would wonder at them, as the present age wondered then.

"We shall need no Homer to sing our praises."

They had forced every sea and land to grant access to their daring spirit and had everywhere planted everlasting memorials of evil to foes and of good to friends.

Their love of the beautiful did not lead to extravagance and their love of the things of the mind did not make them weak.

With them, it was not a shame, he said, for a man to

acknowledge poverty, but the greater shame was for him not to do his best to repair it.

"We alone regard the man who takes no part in public affairs not as one who minds his own business but as good for nothing."

There were no official secrets.

"We throw our city open to all the world and we never debar anyone from learning or seeing anything from which an enemy might profit by observing."

The Athenian public did not have to rely upon the leaders of antagonistic states to learn whether the leaders of their own had been lying to them again or telling the truth.

They were free and tolerant in their private lives.

"Not only in our government life are we liberal but also as regards our freedom from suspicion of one another in the pursuits of everyday life. We do not resent our neighbor if he does different things than we do, nor do we put on sour looks which, though harmless, are painful to receive. Yet we render obedience to those in authority and to the laws, to those laws that are written and to those which, though unwritten, bring upon the transgressor a disgrace which all men recognize."

He could rouse them with words, he said, to withstand the siege by the enemy the coming spring and summer when the battle around Athens resumed.

"Instead, what I would prefer is that you should daily fix your eyes upon the power and greatness of Athens, and that you should fall in love with her. And then when the vision of her greatness has inspired you, reflect that all this has been acquired by men of courage who knew their duty and in the hour of conflict were moved by a high sense of honor, who, if ever they failed in any enterprise, were resolved that at least their country should not find herself deserted by their valor, but freely sacrificed to her the fairest offering it was in their power to give."

He urged those living to make these fallen their examples,

and, "judging freedom to be happiness and courage to be freedom, be not too anxious about the dangers of war."

He exaggerated the generosity of Athens to her allies, and the everlasting remembrance that would honor those buried that day.

But otherwise, for as far as he went, he was speaking the truth.

17

In the second year of the war, congestion in the city was alleviated by the plague. About one-third of the population died.

Thucydides was stricken but lived to tell about it. The disease appeared first in Ethiopia and spread into Egypt. It entered Athens through Piraeus, where people first thought the cisterns had been poisoned by Spartan collaborators. It came into the upper city with more virulence than elsewhere. The population more than doubled each time the people from the country moved inside the walls again.

Men in good health were seized suddenly with feelings of intense heat of the head and were next afflicted with a redness and inflammation of the eyes and the parts inside the mouth. The throat and the tongue became blood-red. Breathing was unnatural and the mouth exhaled a fetid odor. In a short while there was sneezing and hoarseness and before long the disease descended to the chest and brought severe coughing. When it settled in the stomach, vomits of bile of every kind a physician could name occurred. Externally, the body was not very hot to the touch. But internally there was a feeling of such burning that the people could not bear to have on them the weight of the lightest linen sheets but wanted to be quite uncovered and would have liked best to throw themselves into cold water. They were consumed by a thirst they could not quench. Most patients died on the seventh or ninth day. With many who got over the worst, the malady attacked the extremities—the genitals, the fingers, and the toes—and many lost the use of these, and some went blind. And there were some also who, immediately after recovery, were attacked by a total loss of memory, so that they could not recognize themselves or their friends.

The disease resembles typhus.

Though there were many unburied bodies lying about, the birds and four-footed animals used to feeding on carrion would not come near them or died when they did.

Mortality among the doctors was the highest of all because they came more frequently in contact with the sick. No one remedy was found, for what helped one man hurt another.

Nor did any other human art avail.

Appeals to the oracles and supplications in the temples proved futile, and in the end people were so overcome by the calamity that they desisted from such methods.

And the most dreadful thing of all was the despondency into which people fell when they realized they had caught the disease, for they straightaway yielded to an attitude of despair and gave themselves up for lost.

Terrible too was that people became infected nursing one another and died like sheep.

And this was the cause of more deaths than anything else; for when people were restrained by fear from visiting the sick, the sick perished with no one to look after them; when people did visit the sick, they lost their own lives.

Generally, it was those who had been infected and recovered who had most pity for the dying and the sick, because they had learned what it meant and were themselves by this time confident of their own immunity. And they were not only congratulated by everyone else but themselves cherished the fond fantasy that they would never die of any other disease in the future.

What made matters worse was the removal of people from the country into the city, for there were no real houses for them. Living as they did, in the temples, in the towers on the walls, in the open, or in badly ventilated huts that were stifling in the hot season, they perished in wild disorder.

The bodies of the dying were heaped one on top of another, and half-dead creatures rolled about in the streets or, in their longing for water, flocked around the fountains.

The calamity was so overpowering that men, not knowing what was to become of them next, grew indifferent to all law, sacred and secular.

The religious funeral ceremonies which used to be observed were now thrown into confusion, and people buried their dead as best they could. Arriving first at a funeral pyre that had been raised by others, they would put their own dead upon it and set it afire or, finding another pyre burning, they would throw the body they were carrying upon the one that was already burning and go away.

In other respects also the plague introduced a state of greater lawlessness than had ever been known. People now began to venture openly on acts of self-indulgence which before then they had practiced with concealment. They spent money quickly on pleasures that could be had speedily, regarding their bodies and their wealth alike as equally ephemeral.

And no one was eager to achieve what was esteemed as honor, so doubtful was it whether he would live to enjoy the name for it.

Why behave well when no good could come of it?

The pleasure of the moment came to be regarded as both honorable and valuable.

No fear of god or law of men restrained.

Concerning the gods, it seemed to be the same thing

whether one worshipped them or not, seeing that the good and the irreligious were perishing alike.

As for the violation of human laws, no one expected to live long enough to be called to account for his misdeeds.

This, then, was the calamity which had befallen them and by which the Athenians were sorely oppressed, with men dying within the walls, and their land being ravaged without.

Women died also.

The sister of Pericles.

Pericles too fell ill and perished.

But first he witnessed the death of that son with whom he had quarreled over money. The rift had not been healed.

And then he witnessed the death of the younger of his two legitimate sons. When the moment came to lay the burial wreath on the body of this younger boy, he broke down in public with a passion of tears and sobs, a thing he had never done before.

He was blamed by the people for all the sufferings of Athens. The poor, having less to start with, had been deprived of that little, while the upper classes had lost their estates in the country, the buildings and costly furniture. And worst of all they lived in war.

Eager for peace, they sent envoys to Sparta without his consent.

But Sparta by now had learned a rule from Athens: Never negotiate from a position of strength.

Knowing of the bitterness with which they held him to blame, and of the need in the city for reassurance, Pericles called a meeting of the Assembly. With blunt words, he addressed those present in the last of his splendid orations, reconstructed by Thucydides with his own considerable genius.

"I have been expecting these outbreaks of your wrath against me," he said at the start. "You are dismayed by the hardships you suffer at home. And you are attacking me for having spoken for war and yourselves for having voted for it."

In this speech he told the people a truth he had omitted from the other: They were hated.

"Do not think that what you are fighting for is the simple issue of our freedom. On the contrary, the loss of our empire is also involved and the dangers from the hatred we have incurred in the course of administering it."

And he told them what they were: They were tyrants.

"By this time, the empire we hold is like a tyranny, which it may seem wrong to have assumed, but which certainly it is dangerous to let go."

To be hated and obnoxious for a time, he stressed, had always been the lot of those who had aspired to rule over others.

That a democracy owned an empire was not thought peculiar.

In the end the people voted to keep him in power and abide with his patient strategy for winning the war.

Pericles set sail himself with a fleet of one hundred vessels, with transports of his own devising that carried four thousand citizen hoplites and three hundred cavalry, to capture a walled city in the southern Peloponnese and to lay waste the land and towns on the shoreline. He laid waste the land but failed with the city.

He sent these same ships north with siege machinery to end the resistance at Potidaea. They brought plague with them too. The ships turned for home. Before they arrived, one thousand fifty of the original four thousand hoplites had died from the plague in forty days.

He was voted out of office and accused of embezzlement over a shortage of funds used fifteen years before to bribe a Spartan king.

He was found guilty and fined.

And then he was voted back into office, for it was clear to the people that he was the best man of all for the public necessities, second to no man in Athens either in knowledge of the proper policy or in the ability to expound it, who was moreover not only a patriot but an honest one.

And so in what was nominally a democracy, says Thucydides, power was really in the hands of its first citizen.

It was only with the death of Pericles that true democracy came at last to Athens; the powers of government passed into the hands of her businessmen, and the city was doomed.

Democracy and free enterprise go hand in hand and are unfriendly to each other. They go hand in hand and are deadly enemies, for the only freedom business cares about is the freedom to do business. The desire for justice does not count.

Socialism has not been better, and even Plato had revised his views on public ownership by the time he wrote his *Laws*.

Just government cannot exist in the civilized world. About the rest of the world we do not know.

Voted back into office with his powers restored, Pericles made a humble request. And, by special legislation, Athens granted citizenship to his son by Aspasia. His line was continued, his son could hold office.

There is Sophoclean irony in the final scene.

His son progressed to the office of general and was among those generals executed twenty-five years later after the victory in the sea battle of Arginusae.

The father of Pericles had beaten the Persians at Mycale and the Hellespont for the benefit of all Greeks.

The trophies of Pericles had been earned fighting Greeks for the benefit of Athens.

Ten years back, after quelling the rebellion at Samos, Pericles, when he returned to Athens, took care that those who had died in the war should be honorably buried, and he made the first of his funeral orations, which was quoted by Greeks like Plutarch five hundred years afterward. It was that noble speech in which the Olympian observed that Athens had lost its youth, and the spring had gone out of the year. When he came down from the stage, the women drew near to compliment him and crown him with garlands and adorn him with fillets, like a victorious athlete in the games.

All but one, the sister of his predecessor Cimon, whom Pericles had banished and replaced.

With sarcasm, she said: ''These are brave deeds, Pericles, that you have done, and such as deserve our chaplets, who have lost us many a worthy citizen, not in a war with Phoenicians or Persians, like my brother and your father, but for the overthrow of an allied and kindred city.''

Smiling quietly the Olympian replied:

''Old women should not seek to be perfumed.''

I'm not the only one with no idea what he meant.

IX

WHOSE SIDE WERE THEY ON?

18

NO ONE IN EITHER ATHENS OR SPARTA COULD EXPLAIN SAT-
isfactorily why the long war between these two great powers
had to take place at all. They were not commercial or territorial rivals. Conquest was not something either had in mind.
Sparta did not want a seaport in Attica, Athens did not need
farmland in the Peloponnese. Neither side wished to live in
the land of the other. When the war ended, Sparta went back
home.

Yet once started, it seemed natural that it begin and, having begun, that it continue. Athens allocated money for its
wars and legislated the death penalty for anyone suggesting
it be used for anything else. The generation of Plato knew
nothing but war and no kind of government but a wartime
command.

War seemed as natural as nature itself.

In the summer of the fourth year, the Peloponnesians and
their allies marched into Attica again. They stayed longer
than before and made their ships more active, because the
oligarchs in Mytilene, the largest city on the island of Les-

bos, in collaboration with Sparta, revolted to break free from the Athenian alliance.

Athens responded with a shipment of a thousand hoplites. They landed on the beach and encircled the city with a single wall. Mytilene was blockaded by sea and land.

Inside the city the oligarchs, guided by a Spartan military adviser, issued heavy armor to the common citizens. And these men, once equipped, defied their leadership and threatened to force the surrender of the city unless they were given an equal voice in the decisions of government. Fearing they would, the oligarchs themselves surrendered to the Athenians, on condition they might send an embassy to Athens to plead their cause and that none of the Mytilenes would be imprisoned, enslaved, or put to death until the verdict came back from the citizens of Athens.

The verdict of Athens was to kill them all—to execute all men of military age in the city, including those democrats who had forced the surrender, and to make slaves of the women and children. A ship with those orders was sent that day.

Infuriating to Athenians was that Mytilene had revolted even though she was not a subject state but had been allowed to remain autonomous and free.

The Athenians saw no striking contradiction.

But when people awoke the next day, a feeling of repentance came over many, and they began to reflect that the design they had formed, to destroy the entire population of a city, instead of just those who were guilty, was cruel and monstrous. When these doubts became open, the authorities convened a meeting of the Assembly to debate the question again.

Cleon was enraged, for it was on his motion that the Athenians had voted to put the men of Mytilene to death.

"Whose side are you on?" he roared at the man whose proposal it was to reconsider.

"Not for the first time," Cleon declaimed with scorn in the Assembly, "do I see how impossible it is for a democracy to govern an empire! By being soft on Mytilene now, you are guilty of a weakness which is dangerous and which does not win the gratitude of your allies and subject cities or make them love you any more.''

With jeering impatience, he reiterated the statements of Pericles, whose restrained war strategies he had discarded.

"What you cannot bring yourself to look at is that the democratic empire you hold is now a tyranny, a despotism, that is exercised by you over subjects who do not like it and who submit to your rule only because they have to. Our leadership depends on superior strength and not on goodwill.''

It was a general rule of human nature, he insisted, that people despise those who treat them well and look up to those who are ruthless.

"Today, I see again that simpler people make better citizens than the more intelligent, and that states are better governed by the average man than by those who are intellectual and affect to be wise.'' These latter always wanted to prove that they were wiser than the laws and the leaders. They used matters of great importance to show off their vocabulary, as if there could be no weightier question than their own speeches and opinions. "As a consequence of such conduct, they generally bring their states to ruin.''

The best vengeance was the vengeance administered swiftly. "Whereas, when vengeance is delayed by debate as is happening now, the edge of wrath is duller.''

He wondered, sneering, who among them would dare to disagree and speak in opposition to truths that were self-evident. It would have to be a person so intoxicated with his powers of oratory as to imagine he could charm them into believing as true what was universally known to be false. Or one who had taken a bribe and was secretly on the side of the enemy and would therefore put on an elaborate display to deceive them.

As for himself: "I have not altered my opinion, and I am amazed at those who have proposed a reconsideration of the question of Mytilene. Do not put the blame on the aristocrats and exonerate the common people, for they all alike acted together and rebelled. If these people have a right to secede, it would follow that you are wrong in exercising your dominion over them. But if you wish to maintain your empire, you must forget right and wrong and punish these people promptly as your interests require. Or else you must give up your empire and in discreet safety practice the fine virtues you preach.''

He warned them against any who might speak in disagreement with him: the debate was not an entertainment and they were not spectators at a contest of sophists but men taking counsel for the welfare of the state.

Diodotus was the name of the man who rose to oppose him. ''Most dangerous of all among us,'' he said, ''are those like Cleon who charge beforehand that speakers he knows will dispute him do so only because they have been bribed or because they are betrayers of the best interests of Athens. The good citizen ought to show himself the better speaker by fair argument, not by trying to browbeat those who will oppose him. Those men realize that while they cannot speak well in a bad cause, they can at least slander well and can thus intimidate their opponents and their hearers. And all of this is always to the detriment of the democratic state, which is thus robbed of its councillors through fear.''

Diodotus argued that it was to the advantage of Athens that only those guilty of revolt should be punished, that all who were guilty should be punished, and that those who had not taken part in the revolt should be let dwell in peace.

''Whenever you go to war, you have the populace of the rebellious cities on your side at the beginning. If you destroy the populace of Mytilene, you will have published it abroad that the same punishment is ordained for the innocent and the guilty. And so that each time there are some who rise up against us, all will have to support them, and this is what our enemies would like. Why, even if some of the populace are guilty, you should pretend not to know it, to the end that the only class that is still friendly to us may not become hostile.''

On this occasion, and by the most narrow of margins, Cleon was outvoted.

Athens then immediately dispatched a second trireme with all haste on a dramatic mission of mercy.

The trireme carrying the orders revoking the first decree rowed all night, and the men took turns with their food and at sleeping and rowing, so that they did not stop. And since the earlier ship was sailing in no hurry on so horrible a mission, while the second pressed on with hope, although the first to depart did in fact arrive sooner, the second put in close after it, before the orders could be carried out.

By just so much did Mytilene escape destruction.

The walls of the city were pulled down and the Athenians took possession of the Mytilenean fleet. The land was divided and distributed by lot to Athenian colonists sent out to Lesbos, who leased it back to the Mytilenes to cultivate.

The women and the children were not enslaved. The men of Mytilene held most responsible were put to death in Athens on the motion of Cleon. They numbered more than a thousand.

19

At about that same time, defenders of the democratic city of Plataea, powerless to continue resisting without
the military assistance that Cleon's Athens was not able to
provide, surrendered to the Spartans on condition that the
men would be tried singly and none punished except those
found guilty of a crime.

A Spartan promise then was as good as the word of a
Dutch burgher in a business dealing later.

The Spartan judges did try each man individually and
asked the identical question of every one: "What good service have you rendered to us and our allies in the present
war?"

They were led away singly and slain to a man.

More than two hundred Plataeans were killed this way,
together with twenty-five Athenians who had taken part with
them in the siege. The women were sold as slaves. The small
city, which for ninety-three years had been a democratic ally
of Athens, was razed entirely to the ground and obliterated
from the face of the earth the year after Plato was born.

20

ALSO AT THAT TIME, CIVIL WAR BROKE OUT ON CORCYRA, which we know today as the island of Corfu, and after that throughout practically the whole Greek world. Because Corcyra was the first, what occurred was most memorable. There an underground body of eight hundred oligarchs secretly supported by Corinth made plans for the overthrow of the democratic government by force. In a sudden attack on the Senate they used daggers to murder the democratic leader and some sixty others present, both senators and private persons.

But the people rose against them and drove them back, and there was civil war.

And while in time of peace neither group in a civil dispute would have a pretext for asking the intervention of Athens or Sparta, or any inclination to do so, now that these two states were at war, either faction in any of the various cities, if it desired a revolution, found it easy to bring in allies also, for the discomfiture at one stroke of its opponents and the strengthening of its own cause.

When there is war, there are warmongers, and the demagogue Cleon rejected peace offers from Sparta on terms Pericles would have accepted.

That a democracy should be warlike is not so strange.

That a democracy should wish to deny to others the natural rights claimed for itself is not unusual.

"Whose side are you on?" was the challenging taunt flung out frequently at the opposition by Cleon and his radical circle of businessmen and militarists.

People antagonistic to his war policies and the powers he arrogated to his administration were castigated by him viciously for cowardliness and treason and condemned as pro-Spartan and anti-Athenian.

Each side claimed its rebel factions were fighting for freedom.

Both sides were right.

The democrats were fighting against a tyranny of a minority.

The oligarchs were fighting against a tyranny of the majority.

In general, the rich looked toward Sparta, the poor and not-so-poor toward Athens.

Both Sparta and Athens called the members of the factions they supported "freedom fighters."

Each was equally correct.

They were fighting for freedom from rule by the other.

Cleon thundered of "a conspiracy so immense" as to chill the heart of every red-blooded and patriotic Athenian. He claimed he could produce a list of three hundred fifty Athenians who were treasonably pro-Lacedaemonian.

Everyone who was not pro-war was pro-Lacedaemonian.

"Whose side are you on?" he snarled and growled, as he stamped about on the stage in the Assembly, and he had his cabinet and speechwriters repeat and publish too.

Cleon campaigned for a free hand in everything by denouncing every assemblyman and every statesman and general who opposed him as either an unwitting stooge of

Spartanism or a willing sympathizer of the Spartan government—or worse.

"What you have here," he bellowed from the podium, "is a subversive influence allied with the Spartan government undertaking a very well organized effort to affect the vote in the Assembly. Now this is not an Athenian crime under our system of free government," he granted, "but that does not mean it should be permitted."

When facts failed he spoke of a moral obligation to provide military assistance to all of the separate small factions in other cities requesting it.

"The shame of defeat of our allies anywhere now," he swore, "will bring our own troops in there later."

He did not mention that one or another of the Athenian allies was constantly in opposition to Athenian policies and that many of the bloodiest wars waged by democratic Athens were against allies seeking independence and the right of self-determination.

That in Mytilene and Corcyra and in other cities oligarchical movements did indeed foster coups aimed at overthrowing by force the democratic governments there gave some substance to his arguments and some credibility to his allegations.

He was a cynic who probably did not believe fully all of the sensational tales he told. But he knew they would help him politically, and he enjoyed holding sway over the emotions of his listeners. Everybody knew he employed informers; nobody knew how many or who they were. Even people who were not informers bragged they were agents of the government, and no one could ascertain if they were telling the truth.

Patriots like Aristophanes who favored peace were defamed as seditious. Aristophanes was taken to court by Cleon for a play in which he blamed Pericles for starting the war and Athens and Cleon for continuing it.

There was free speech in Athens, and he was exonerated.

In his play *The Acharnians* the following year, he struck

back from the public stage, stating that he hated Cleon, who ought to be flayed to make shoes for knights, that Cleon had dragged him before the Senate to indict him and had uttered endless slanders, a tempest of abuse, and a deluge of lies, and he accused Cleon of tricks and plotting, and of being a prostitute to the highest bidder.

In *The Knights* the year after that, he called Cleon a "Paphlagonian tanner," "an arrogant rogue," "the incarnation of calumny," a domineering and dishonest slave who had rendered life intolerable for others and had to be gotten rid of, "a brutal master," "a perfect glutton for beans" who "farts and snores loudly," "bad-tempered," "a fawning cur," "a robber," "a brawler," "detested," "a yawning gulf of plunder," "a villain a thousand times a day," "an impostor," "a dull varlet," "a thief," "a cheat who flutters from one extortion to another," and "helps himself with both hands from the public funds," an "Inspector of Arses," with "a pig's education," and a man whose death would be a happy day for the rest of the Athenians and their children.

Aristophanes was writing about an autocratic wartime leader who was at the height of his popularity.

Athens voted first prize to both these plays.

And voted with Cleon to continue the war.

"Whose side are you on?" Cleon ranted and raved. "With this vote on the military aid and actions I want, the democratic party will reveal whether it stands with me and the interests of a free Athens or with the oligarchs of Sparta and Corinth, who make no secret of their goal to destroy Athens and all that we stand for."

Once they were at war, it grew normal for Athens and Sparta each to sow dissension in cities partial to the other. In places where there was no discord, they did their best to create it. Each side engaged in conspiracies to conquer or overthrow by force or other means the governments of even those cities that desired to remain neutral. Unrest grew widespread in this third world, with oligarchs, abetted by Sparta, plotting revolts in the democracies, and democrats, abetted by Athens, plotting rebellions in the oligarchies.

And so there fell upon the Greek world many grievous calamities, such as happen and will always happen as long as human nature is the same.

In peace and prosperity, states and individuals have gentler feelings, but war, which robs men of the easy supply of their daily wants, is a rough schoolmaster, says Thucydides, and creates in most people a temper that matches their condition.

Language was debased.

The ordinary acceptance of words in their relation to things was changed as men saw fit.

Reckless audacity came to be regarded as courageous loyalty to party.

Prudent hesitation as specious cowardice.

Moderation as a cloak for unmanly weakness.

And the ability to see a question from all sides meant that one was pronounced totally unfit to take action in anything.

Fanatical impulsiveness was the mark of a true man, while cautious deliberation was a specious pretext for shirking.

The hot-headed was trusted, and those objecting to him were suspect.

He who succeeded in any kind of plot against an enemy behind his back was a person of clever intelligence, and he who detected a plot before it hatched was shrewder still.

On the other hand, if one was averse to plotting, he was branded a disrupter of party unity and a coward who was scared of the opposition.

In short, it was as praiseworthy to get one's blow in first against someone who might do wrong as to denounce someone who had no intention of doing wrong.

To get revenge upon someone was more important than never to have suffered an injury that might call for revenge.

A victory won by treachery gave one title to superior intelligence.

Indeed, most rogues were more ready to get themselves called clever villains than honest simpletons. They gloried in the first quality and were ashamed of the second. The cause of all these evils was the desire to rule which greed and ambition inspire.

For those who emerged as party leaders, by assuming on either side a fair-sounding name, the one using as its catchword "political equality for the masses under the law," the other offering a "temperate aristocracy" or "the safe and sound government of the conservative aristocracy," were in reality seeking to win control of the machinery of government as the prize for themselves.

In their struggles for ascendance nothing was barred, and they were ready, either by passing an unjust sentence of condemnation or by winning the upper hand through acts of violence, to glut the animosity of the moment.

As for citizens with moderate views who belonged to neither party, they were continually destroyed by both, either because they would not make common cause with them, or through mere jealousy that they should survive.

And so it was that as a result of these revolutions, every form of depravity began to show itself throughout the Greek world, and the simpler way of looking at things, which is so much the mark of a noble nature, was laughed to scorn and disappeared, while mutual antagonism between two ideologically different worlds, combined with mistrust, prevailed far and wide.

And it was generally those of meaner intelligence who showed the greater powers of survival and won the day.

Such people boldly launched upon deeds. Their opponents, on the other hand, assuming there was no need to receive by action what they might obtain by reason and knowledge, were taken off their guard to be destroyed more easily, and perished in greater numbers.

Human nature, now triumphant over the laws and accustomed, even in spite of the laws, to do wrong, took delight in showing that its passions were ungovernable, and that it was the enemy of everything superior to itself.

It was in Corcyra then, with a fleet of sixty Athenian ships looking on, that most of these atrocities were first committed and where people were the first to display the passions of revolution and civil war.

It was worse than the plague.

They seized upon all their enemies whom they could find and put them to death.

Next they went into the temple of Hera, where the rest of the oligarchical party, at least four hundred of them, had taken up positions of suppliants. They persuaded about fifty of the suppliants there to submit to trial and condemned all to death.

Most of the others, when they saw what was happening, set about destroying one another in the sacred precinct itself. Some hanged themselves on the trees, and still others made away with themselves as best they could.

During the seven days that the Athenian admiral stayed there with all his sixty ships, the Corcyreans continued slaughtering such of their fellow citizens as they considered to be their personal enemies.

Death in every shape and form ensued, and whatever horrors are wont to be perpetrated at such times all happened then—and even worse.

It is hard to believe it, but fathers slew sons.

It is easier to find credible that men were dragged from the temples and slain near them, or were butchered on the altars. And some were walled up in the temple of Dionysus and perished there.

For the final massacre, much of the responsibility, says Thucydides, must rest with the Athenian generals: first, they allowed themselves to be tricked into delivering to the populace prisoners who had surrendered under promises of safekeeping and trial in Athens; and next, they were satisfied to look the other way.

The Corcyreans shut the prisoners up in a large building. Afterward they led them out in groups of twenty, and they marched them down between two lines of hoplites, the prisoners being bound to one another and receiving blows and stabs from the men who stood in the lines and between whom they passed, especially if any of these saw among them a personal enemy. Men with scourges went along to hurry on their way with lashings of their whips such of them as proceeded too slowly.

In this manner about sixty men were led out and killed without the knowledge of the men remaining in the house, who supposed that their companions were being transferred to some other place of concentration.

But when they perceived what was going on, they appealed to the Athenians for help, and urged the Athenians, if they wished to see them dead, to kill them with their own hands.

And the rest of them refused to come out or to allow anyone to enter if they could prevent it.

The Corcyreans did not force the doors. But climbing onto the top of the building and breaking through the roof, they hurled tiles and shot arrows upon them from above.

The men inside tried to defend themselves as best they could, and at the same time many of them set to work to kill themselves by thrusting into their throats the arrows the enemy had shot or by strangling themselves with the cords from some beds that happened to be there or with strips made from their own garments.

Thus for the greater part of the night—for night fell upon their misery—dispatching themselves in every fashion, and struck by the arrows and missiles of the men on the roof, they perished.

When day came, the Corcyreans loaded the bodies on wagons, laying them lengthwise and crosswise, and hauled them out of the city to a mass grave.

The women who'd been captured were sold into captivity.

In this way the revolution, which had lasted long, was ended by the popular party, so far at least as this war was concerned; for there were no longer enough of the oligarchs left to be of any account.

When the Athenians from their ships saw that order was

restored, they sailed for Sicily to carry on the war in conjunction with allies there.

War is a rough schoolmaster, as Thucydides said.

There was no atrocity by one side that was not repeated by the other.

Throats were cut.

In Athens life went on. There were the *Oedipus Rex* and *Electra* of Sophocles and the *Hippolytus* of Euripides, despite the summer invasions and sieges by the Spartans, which rarely lasted as long as forty days. The Olympic Games continued in the Greek world without interruption. Ambassadors, spies, and terrorist leaders attended for the sport and to forge new coalitions. In one grandiose display later on, Alcibiades squandered a small fortune entering seven four-horse teams in the chariot race and won three of the first four prizes. He gave private banquets celebrating his victory, and to impress upon others the eminence he enjoyed at home, he used silverware belonging to Athens as though it were his own.

X

MONEY TALKS

21

ARISTOTLE COULD SEE, ONCE REMBRANDT HAD GIVEN HIM eyes, that the man modeling for him did not look in the least like the person he remembered himself to be: short, bandy-legged, bald, with a bit of the self-approving air of a dandy.

This man was tall, olive-skinned, with a long black beard, black melancholy eyes, and Slavic, Eastern, perhaps Semitic features.

He had posed for Rembrandt before. They talked easily.

They talked of real estate.

The neighborhood was changing. More Sephardic Jews were moving to the Breestraat from the quarter around the corner. The avenue was already called informally, and without prejudice, the Jodenbreestraat and would be so named officially by the close of the century.

Rembrandt wondered if real estate values would go down because of them. The man had no idea. Aristotle guessed that the blockade and depressed economy would affect prices more.

Aristotle contemplating the bust of Homer took stock of

the world in which he found himself and concluded that not much had improved since his exile and death. No wonder he was downcast. Bustling countries like Holland and England, with their small boundaries and proliferating fleets, reminded him of grasping Athens and her scores of prowling triremes. He predicted for both a very bad end.

The evolution of city-states into nation-states had merely escalated the wars between them to a larger scale, and the same earthly and dreary cataclysms as were occurring in Plato's Athens were occurring in Rembrandt's Netherlands two thousand years later when Aristotle discovered himself taking shape on Rembrandt's easel and learned with a momentary look of startled surprise, which Rembrandt coolly soothed and allayed, that it was *he*, Aristotle, of all people, whom the artist believed he was bringing back to life.

For a while in the beginning, when Rembrandt took up a brush and used black paint directly on the canvas to outline the forms, he had not been able to tell. Once he knew, he could hardly wait to see what he looked like. He could not say he was pleased.

Protestant England was at war with the Protestant government of the Netherlands. Catholic Spain was at war with Catholic France, while Catholics took Jewish lives in Poland and the Balkans and English and Scottish Protestants took Catholic lives in Catholic Ireland.

There were no more crusades.

If they were fighting over money, Aristotle could have taught them it was not worth the struggle. True Aristotelians would know they were fighting over something that he could prove with logic had no intrinsic value. And he knew now that no true Aristotelian would believe him.

His *Politics* was ignored, his *Ethics* also. His scientific speculations—accepted for centuries as gospel truth—were one by one being proven false. He had to wonder that anyone in Holland still thought much of him.

Aristotle contemplating Rembrandt painting *Aristotle Contemplating the Bust of Homer* had to wonder also why

Rembrandt, who had never studied Greek, was painting him at all and why, of all things, painting him contemplating a bust of Homer, of whose works he had grown weary by the time he completed his edition of the *Iliad* for Alexander. He thanked God that Rembrandt had not painted Homer singing or dictating, as he did a decade later in another commission for Don Antonio. Aristotle as an adult had not liked being sung to or read to.

Furthermore, in his *Poetics* he had downgraded Homer inferentially by rating epics below tragedy, as he had downgraded Plato for the first time in his *On Philosophy*.

His *Poetics* embarrassed him now, and not just because he had failed to complete it. Why in heaven's name was he perambulating about his Lyceum lecturing on Aeschylus, Sophocles, and Euripides when Aeschylus had been dead a hundred twenty-five years and Sophocles and Euripides about seventy-five?

Had he turned without knowing it, he asked himself in exile in the last year of his life, into one of those pompous and detestable people with whom Athens was infested who had an opinion of equal fervor and authority on every subject and a compulsion of equal fervor to express it?

Aristotle had written on poetry for the same reason he had written on bugs and stars, as a phenomenon for analysis that lay in the proper jurisdiction of philosophical study, and for no better reason than he had written on rhetoric. He hoped fervently that others would not remember, while he tried grimly to forget, that the august creator of his *Ethics* and *Metaphysics* was not in his *Rhetoric* above teaching others to employ tricks to win arguments fallaciously through the artful use of words, or, as Aristophanes had gibed about Socrates in *The Clouds*, to make the poorer argument seem the better, and the better argument seem the worse.

Was that ethical?

Aristotle grew darker and darker in aspect as the painting of him by Rembrandt progressed. The misty gray European weather complemented his mood. When the fog was low, the sodden atmosphere of the city was rank with the smell of herring, beer, and tobacco. There were times now in Holland when he was as pessimistic as Plato.

The amount of "retailing" that went on would have made Plato vomit.

Strange man, that Plato, revealing nothing of himself while writing fluently of others. What humor he possessed he gave to Socrates. Aristotle tried to guess what Socrates would really have thought of Plato and his philosophies. Probably no more than did the cynical Diogenes. And very much less, Aristotle would bet—bet money, of course—than did credulous St. Augustine, who, Aristotle believed, swallowed more Plato on pure faith than Socrates would have done.

The Socrates dramatized by Plato in most of his written imitations of the living imitation of the man was, by and large, a pragmatic and skeptical personality.

One had to know Plato personally to appreciate the love he suppressed puritanically for the music, poetry, and drama he censured in his philosophy and censored in his model communities. They moved him too deeply.

There were no slaves in Holland, Aristotle perceived in a state of stupefied shock, until he finally comprehended that the Dutch did not need any: they had always enough poor to work like niggers and, for a living wage, to go to sea and to war for whoever paid most. English sailors taken prisoner enlisted with the Dutch for better and more dependable pay than they could count on receiving from the depleted treasury of King Charles II.

The niggers from Africa were shipped instead to where they were needed, to the underpopulated rich new world of the Americas. Aristotle envied the slave-owning classes in Brazil, Virginia, and the Carolinas. He dreamily pictured the cane growers of Spanish America and the tobacco and cotton growers of North America, in possession of all the goods he had catalogued as essential for happiness, spending day after day of their idyllic, serene, enriched, and soul-satisfying lives in the uninterrupted contemplation of science and philosophy.

All men, Aristotle had written, desire by nature to know.

In Rembrandt he found an exception.

All Rembrandt wished to know one afternoon in late 1653 as he laid out on his work table in two rows the busts he owned of Roman emperors and famous Greeks was how much all of them might bring if sold as a collection.

Would they be worth more individually?

The man posing for Aristotle had no idea.

The tall, dark-bearded, sad-eyed man posing for Rembrandt as Aristotle had been as surprised as Aristotle to find out it was Aristotle for whom he was going to be the model. He was puzzled now by an inconsistency in logic and what he saw as an incongruity in reasoning and in art. Aristotle looked on unobtrusively while the man scratched his head and, puffing his pipe, gazed quizzically at the two ranks of busts Rembrandt had lined up to contemplate and appraise. In a bass voice that was always slightly hoarse and mildly apologetic, he asked:

"Rembrandt, let me try to understand you. You say you have a bust of Aristotle there?"

"And I may want to sell it." Rembrandt smiled complacently, like a salesman certain of his wares. "And there is Homer and here is Socrates too. I have more than a dozen emperors. You can read their names. Here we have Augustus, Tiberius, Caligula, a Nero, Galba, Otho, Vitellius, Vespasian, a Titus Vespasian, Domitian, this one is called a Silius Brutus, then Agrippa, Marcus Aurelius, another Vitellius, and one more that is unidentified."

"Let me ask you then. Why are you painting me?"

"Why?"

"You have a bust of Aristotle. Why do you want to paint my face as Aristotle's when you have his face right here?"

Rembrandt turned dour. "I like your face better. It looks more real."

"More real than his?"

"Yes."

"My face looks more real as Aristotle's than his does?"

"Yes. Are you blind?"

"How can that be?"

"I know what I'm doing."

"Isn't that dishonest?"

Rembrandt did not see why. "It's only art. What do you care? It's not a portrait."

"It does not sound logical. You're painting a picture of me and you're calling it him. Would you paint a picture of him and call it me?"

"I can call him anybody I want to for this painting. As long as I call him a philosopher. For his five hundred guilders, I feel I can give my Sicilian a picture of a philosopher who is a real person."

"Of me? I'm not a real philosopher."

"I make changes in you. You smile more. I put red in your beard. Look at your clothes."

"Were they his?"

"Are they yours?"

"I don't complain of the clothes. I'm inquiring about this painting of me."

"It's not of you. It's a painting of Aristotle."

"Then I'm glad it will not be in Amsterdam, where people would recognize me and believe I am Aristotle. I must admit that I *like* this picture of me that you will say is of somebody else. But it remains a mystery why you use my face for his when you have his right here. You could dress him up in this same costume."

"His face isn't much."

"He looks sadder and sadder, even as we speak of him. Why do you make him so sad?"

Rembrandt grunted a contented laugh. "Aristotle's face would not look natural between that hat and that robe. By now, yours is the only one that does. Should I ship to my Sicilian connoisseur a painting of the face of one statue con-

templating the bust of another?'' The man laughed too. ''And
sign it 'Rembrandt'?''

''You're moving my pendant again.''

''It isn't yours. I like it better here.''

''You never finish. There's a face on it now. Are we supposed to know whose?''

''Alexander's, naturally.''

''Who?''

''Alexander the Great.''

X-ray studies of Rembrandt's painting *Aristotle Contemplating the Bust of Homer* disclose repeated changes in the
position of the medallion of Alexander and a growth on Aristotle's liver undoubtedly related to the intestinal distress of
which he complained in the year of his death.

To Aristotle, Rembrandt was not in himself an interesting
person or one especially nice, but Aristotle had to wonder
again at his way with light and shadow and somber tones and
his alchemy with gold. All three were charmed with the al-
terations Rembrandt made in the garments worn by the model
when he fitted them on Aristotle in the painting.

''They look better on him,'' said the man, sulking, ''than
on me.''

''I add color to his,'' said Rembrandt. ''I can't put paint
on those clothes you're wearing, can I?''

He scumbled his impasto on the silken robe, added glazes,
and enhanced his chiaroscuro. He turned light into gold in
Aristotle's billowing sleeves, shot golden rays of reflection
through other white areas. He blended more green and blue-
green into the folds and ripples.

He molded the gold chain in full relief with thicker addi-
tions of white paint, and on top of this white he laid glaze
after glaze of yellows, browns, and blacks. That was how
Rembrandt manufactured gold for Aristotle.

''The gold looks almost real,'' said Rembrandt's model.

''It is real,'' mumbled Rembrandt. He did not glance up.
He made changes in the pinky ring, put tiny yellow-white
dots on top of heavy white dots on the surface of the ring and

caused it to gleam, as though he were inventing gold out of paint odors and a slender brush that was a magic wand. "Your gold is fake."

"I don't understand you."

"I've painted pure gold."

"Using black, brown, and white?"

"What you're wearing is plated. The ring, the earring, the rest. The chain is an imitation in brass. Come closer. Look at the chain and look at the picture. Don't you see the difference? This gold is real."

The gold on the canvas looked the more authentic.

"I don't think I want to talk about it," the man said unhappily. "You speak of imitation," he said tentatively, and fell silent, considering whether to say more. "Do you know that Govert Flinck is becoming more and more successful with paintings he did that are imitations of yours, of you and your style?"

"Flinck was my best pupil," Rembrandt answered graciously, nodding. "He already knew much when he came to me. He learned to paint in my manner in less than one year."

The man nodded also. "They say he is more successful now than you are. And that he gets much higher prices now for his paintings like yours."

Putting aside his palette and maulstick with very slow movements, Rembrandt took up a heavy brush, wiping it clean on his tunic, and clasped it with the butt end forward like a sharp weapon. Aristotle feared for his life. Rembrandt looked like a man who might stab him through the chest.

"I don't understand that," he said coldly.

"They say he now gets more money for his paintings than you do for yours."

"For his paintings like mine?"

"For those too."

"That can't be true. How can that be true?"

"It's true in Amsterdam"

"That makes no sense. He gets more for his imitations of my work than I do for my originals?"

"They're more in demand."

"Why should they be? Why should people pay more money to him for his old imitations of my work when they can buy my original paintings from me?"

"They say his are better."

"How can they be better? I don't know what to say. That will be enough for today. What else do they say? Please tell me all."

"Well, since you ask," said the man, as he changed back into his own solemn black attire in preparation for leaving. "They say in your circle that your housekeeper is with child."

"What business is that of mine?" asked Rembrandt.

"They say," said the man, "that the child is from you."

"What business is that of theirs?"

"Good day, my friend. God go with you."

"And God go with you."

Descartes married the maidservant with whom he cohabited. Rembrandt had higher social standards and would not sink that low. He and Hendrickje never married, although he did make mention of her once, in a legal affirmation, as his "late wife."

When Jan Six came later that day to stand for his portrait, Rembrandt wished to know immediately if the report of Govert Flinck's success was true.

Six thought that it was.

"He was my worst pupil!" cried Rembrandt indignantly.

"His reputation gets better," said Six. "As do his connections. Soon he will control all city commissions."

"There is no logic to it!"

"If it's logic you want," said Six, amused, "you should meet with Descartes. Or perhaps you should talk to your Aristotle there. He perfected the syllogism, you know."

Rembrandt did not want to talk of Aristotle! "Flinck gets more for his old Rembrandts now than I get for my new ones? Is that what you are trying to make me believe?"

"I think he does. I don't say it's just."

"But how can that happen?"

"For the usual business reasons, I suppose. People think they're more valuable."

Rembrandt snorted in rage. "I find that amazing. You are saying that people find his imitations of my originals more valuable than my originals? People find them more valuable? That does not seem credible."

"They think they are better."

"But how is that possible? That Govert Flinck, my most stupid pupil, a dunce!—he would paint guilders on my floor that I could tell from a distance were always counterfeit—should paint in my style and command higher prices for his imitations of my work because people think they are *better* than my work? Is everyone mad? Are they out of their minds? Am I out of mine?"

"You speak too slightingly of imitations, my friend," said Jan Six amiably. "In his *Poetics*, you know, your Aristotle there—"

"This is not my Aristotle. This is a painting, not a person."

"Nevertheless, Aristotle states that all great tragedies are imitations of an action. I suppose that here in Holland, because there is no other place like this, our national tragedies can still, perhaps, be original."

"That is not what we mean by tragedies. *Flinck* is a tragedy. What you are telling me does not make sense."

"About Aristotle?"

"About Flinck. I don't care about Aristotle. You are an intellectual man. How can these old paintings of his that are in imitation of my style be superior to mine?"

"His surfaces are smooth, his colors are transparent, his lines define forms, his details are precise."

"That's not my style!" Rembrandt cried out in pain. "Flinck is an impostor! I don't paint that way."

"Then perhaps you ought to," counseled Six with a smile, "if you want to regain your popularity and get prices like his."

"And then," said Rembrandt, with a sneer, "my paintings would be copies of his imitations of my originals, wouldn't they?"

"Exactly," Six agreed. "Especially if he went back to painting like you. Best of all, you would not have to spend time doing any more originals, would you?"

"And what name should I sign to them? Mine or his?"

"You'd make more money, I think, if you signed them with his. Or, if you like, perhaps you can persuade Flinck to sign the name Rembrandt to yours."

"Can he do my signature in my style too?"

"Oh, yes, he does that too. He could even do your signature with a more classical hand than yours."

"Should I start with your portrait?" Rembrandt challenged acidly. "I can begin changing it right now."

"Continue with mine as you have it, please."

"No, let me make it appear like an imitation of what Flinck will do in imitation of me with the commissions he receives for portraits like yours in the style of the one I am doing of Jan Six after people see yours."

"Leave this one alone."

"I can even date it in the future to make it more valuable, to look like a copy by me of the imitation by him of the portrait of you by me."

"I wish you to proceed with ours exactly as you've begun and exactly as we have discussed," said Six. "I did not know, my friend, that you could be so humorous."

"I am not being humorous."

"I admire my face."

"It isn't yours."

"That one isn't Aristotle's. You've changed me a bit, haven't you? You've done much more since I've been here last."

"I'm going to make you look older."

"Harder, I see. Almost ruthless. And you're giving me cuffs, and a turned-up sleeve, and a freshly ironed collar. How did you make me so clean? I wish our laundress could do as well. I like those hands. You've made them all out of nothing, haven't you? Just some strokes and some colors. You let me see that much. Will you let me watch the rest? You use all of your best tricks when I'm not here, don't you?''

"I like the hands too," Rembrandt said grouchily, with a loud puff of pride.

So did Aristotle.

The three were in agreement.

Aristotle took the plaudits from Six with hardly a blush. He had spent many a late and fatiguing hour watching out of the corner of his eye as Rembrandt worked with confidence and a sneaky intensity, using different grades of white to create a sense of dimension in the collar and the cuffs Jan Six had commented on. Smugly, Rembrandt moved a dry brush with yellow gold across the right arm of the figure of Six to suggest a turned-back sleeve at the cuff of his doublet and replied with a noncommittal grunt when Six inquired how he had achieved that glinting fabric, that crisp texture. Aristotle knew that Six would not guess in a million years that Rembrandt had employed the identical stroke to give a touch of bulk to the limp glove Six was holding and had utilized only color and shape for that inconspicuous item of attire that is central to the balance of the whole.

"Are you making me heavier too?" Six wondered now with a semblance of faint distaste. He was not yet thirty-six.

"Older, not heavier," Rembrandt corrected. "More mature, a man of strength and more personal substance. You will not always be that slender, you know, or that young. I will paint you like a man who always makes the right decisions. It's the way you will want to look when you are a regent and a burgomaster."

The conversations always seemed to Aristotle to take a more intellectual turn when Six was there, especially when he talked of Aristotle.

"In his *Poetics*, you know, Aristotle praises you for this portrait of me," commented Jan Six, and Aristotle pricked up his ear. Rembrandt moved in at once with an ebony overglaze and sank the ear back into shadows where it belonged. "Not by name, of course. He talks of painters."

"He doesn't say Rembrandt van Rijn?"

"Nor does he say Govert Flinck. Aristotle instructs dramatists to follow the example of good portrait painters. He says of the good portrait painters that they, while reproducing the distinctive form of the original, make a likeness which is true to life, and yet more beautiful. I think you are doing that with me. I think that your Aristotle seems in a lighter frame of mind today than I have ever seen him. He looks almost cheerful, as though he enjoys hearing me talk about him. Have you changed him again? He looked morbid before."

"He'll look morbid again," vowed Rembrandt. "Sometimes I go too far in one direction and have to go back to the other. I have a question about business that I think you should be able to answer. Among the paintings that I own are more than seventy by me that I can put out for sale."

"Sign them with Flinck's name," joked Six, "and you will be a wealthy man in Amsterdam."

"Should I do that?" inquired Rembrandt seriously.

Six shook his head. "To sell a product for money, says Aristotle, is not the proper use of that product. A shoe, for example, is made to be worn."

That was easier for Aristotle to say, replied Rembrandt crossly, than for any of them to do. With a cloth and his finger, he came back to the canvas and wiped what looked like a smile off Aristotle's face.

Six had been friendly with the poet and historian Pieter C. Hooft, who died in 1647 and for whom Aristotle would be mistaken in London in 1815. He was a dabbling member of the Muiden literary circle. He spoke with Descartes. He was friendly with Spinoza.

And as Aristotle listened that afternoon, he shuddered with the memory of the time earlier that year when, eavesdropping, he suddenly wished he had someplace to hide. Six had been telling of Descartes and Spinoza, and Rembrandt interrupted to ask to borrow a thousand guilders. Aristotle cringed when he offered to pay interest.

"When I lend you the money, my friend," Jan Six chided softly, "it will not be to earn interest."

When Six married, the portrait he commissioned of his wife was not by Rembrandt but by Govert Flinck. And sometime before 1656, Six sold the Rembrandt debt of one thousand guilders at discount to a man who demanded payment, ultimately forcing Rembrandt into bankruptcy.

We don't know why.

Neither Six nor the second man needed money.

Aristotle was no help.

By then he was already in the castle of Signor Ruffo in Sicily, that same Sicily of antiquity to which Athens had sailed vaingloriously to monstrous military catastrophe, from which the glamorous general Alcibiades defected to Sparta sooner than go home to stand trial on trumped-up charges, and to which a misguided Plato ventured three times persistently in quixotic and egotistical expectation, and from which he three times returned abjectly in unhappy frustration and disillusionment.

XI

IMAGINE THAT

22

THE DESTRUCTION OF MELOS TOOK PLACE IN THAT INTERVAL of peace that was known as the cold war.

With the death in battle of the brilliant Spartan general Brasidas, who had opposed peace because of the success and the reputation he had derived from war, and the death in the same battle of Cleon, who had opposed peace because he believed that in time of war people would be less likely to notice his evil doings and more likely to believe his slanders of others, it was possible to bring the war to an end.

An endearing feature of Greek wars then was that people advocating them often died in them.

The Peace of Nicias was negotiated to last fifty years.

It lasted seven.

It might have lasted forever had not Alcibiades decided to play a more active role in the affairs of his nation, to the eventual distress of Athens, Syracuse, Sparta, Persia, Melos, Argos, and Socrates.

If not forever, then for seventy years, until Philip marched down the mainland from Macedonia and subdued all cities there and in the Peloponnese.

Alcibiades went into politics because he wanted glory and money. He went in as a warhawk because that's where the money and the glory are. No one ever captured the imagination of a country by fighting for peace.

In essence the terms of the treaty were simple: Athens and Sparta would recognize each other's boundaries and respective alliances and contend with each other only in the neutral cities of the third world.

One of these cities was Melos, on a small island not far to the south in the Cretan Sea, about an equal distance from Athens and Sparta.

With Mytilene, you know, a city in rebellion, there was a change of heart by Athens at the eleventh hour. With Melos, which wished only to remain neutral, there was no change of heart. The revolt of Mytilene occurred during war in a year of desperate reverses for Athens. The destruction of Melos took place in a calm atmosphere of peace.

The Athenians arrived in Melos with thirty of their own ships, and six from Chios and two from Lesbos, landing twelve hundred hoplites, three hundred bowmen, and twenty mounted archers of their own, and about fifteen hundred hoplites more from the allies and islanders.

The famed Melian debate was brief. The Athenians displayed at the outset that practical intelligence in realpolitik in which they were foremost in intelligence among all Greeks and which, in the modern world, is the trademark of the worldly professional in international relations. The Athenians, having landed troops, took control of the talks with two irrefutable propositions:

1. The hatred of the Melians was more valuable to Athens than their friendship.
2. It is a law of civilization that the strong dominate the weak.

The dialogue was held on the beach outside the city.

The Melian leaders would not permit the Athenians to talk directly to the people, as though there did not exist in the city a legitimate government.

"All right then," said the Athenians. "Since our proposals are not to be made before the people, that they might not hear from us arguments that are seductive and persuasive, let us proceed here. And we will propose a course that is doubly safe for you. We will not make any set speech to you either. We will talk and you will listen. Do not you either expect to make a single speech. But interrupt and reply to any statement of ours that seems unsatisfactory, and we will deal with that before going on to the next point."

Did that seem fair?

Fair enough, said the Melians, were it not for the threat of war the Athenians conveyed: this appeared at variance with the proposal that they should converse and leisurely attempt to instruct one another as to the merits of their position.

"For we see that you yourselves have come to be judges of what is said. And the likely end will be war, if our arguments are right and we refuse to yield, or, if we are not, submission."

If the Melians were going to conjecture about the outcome or talk about anything other than the facts before their eyes, said the Athenians, they might as well end there and waste no more time. The Melians, concerned for the safety of their city, wished to continue.

At the start, therefore, said the Athenians, they would put aside the question of justice. "We will forget entirely about what is fair or what is right and wrong, since you know as well as we that what is just, what is fair, is arrived at in human arguments only between powers of equal strength."

As the world went, the strong did what they could and the weak suffered what they had to.

It was expedient—the Melians were constrained to speak of expediency, since the Athenians wished to ignore the principle of justice—to urge the Athenians not also to rule out the principle of good. Might not the Athenians be injuring their own cause? Would not other neutral islanders, seeing what was happening at Melos, fear the Athenians would attack them too?

"This is precisely what we intend," replied the Athenians. "We put more trust in the fear of others than in their loyalty."

That the Melians were smaller than the others made it all the more necessary that they be compelled to submit. "If we allow you to keep your independence, they believe it is because you are strong, and if we fail to attack you, it is because we are afraid. You would strengthen our reign by being subdued."

The Athenians could not consent to the Melians' remaining neutral.

"Your hostility does not injure us so much as your friendship. Your friendship would be proof of our weakness, whereas your hatred is proof of our power. Thus, by subjugating you now, we would be increasing the size of our empire as well as the security."

All that was necessary to be understood was that the Athenians had come there for the preservation of their empire, and that it would be to the equal advantage of both parties for Melos to submit.

"How could it be as advantageous for us to become slaves as for you to become masters?"

"Because you would have the advantage of submitting without suffering the most horrible fate. We, by not destroying you, will profit by having you as an ally and a subject city."

Surely, mused the Melians, if such great risks as they described were always taken by their subjects to escape their empire and by Athens to keep it, would not they, who still had their freedom, show themselves cowards by yielding what the Athenians themselves would refuse to yield?

No, not if they were well advised and took a sensible view of the matter.

"This is not a fair fight on equal terms, with honor as the prize and disgrace the penalty." The Athenians were speaking realistically. "The question before you is one of self-preservation—to save your lives and your city instead of foolishly offering resistance to those far stronger than you."

"Yet," said the Melians, "we know, as you have learned, that the fortunes of war are sometimes impartial and not always in accordance with the difference in numbers. For us to yield now is at once to give up hope. But if we make an effort, there is still hope that we may yet stand upright as free men."

Hope was an expensive commodity, was the reply by the Athenians. "Hope is indeed a solace in times of danger for those who have other resources to fall back on. Hope may do harm to these, but she does not ruin them. But those who stake all on a single throw of hope find out only when disaster has befallen how prodigal is her true nature. This fate, we beg of you, weak as you are, do not willingly incur. And please do not be misled by a false sense of honor. There is nothing dishonorable in submitting to the greatest city in Greece, when it makes you the moderate offer of becoming its tributary ally, allowing you otherwise to enjoy your liberty and your property."

When allowed to choose between war and security, it hardly made sense to hold out for the worse alternative.

"This is the safe rule," advised the Athenians. "To stand up to one's equals, to defer to one's superiors, and to be moderate toward one's inferiors."

Because their cause was right, the Melians were tempted to put their trust in the gods.

The Athenians had no fear of doing that either, since their conduct and beliefs were in no way contrary to what men believe about the gods, or to the principles the gods practiced among themselves.

"For of the gods we hold the belief, and of men we know, that wherever they have power, they rule. We did not make this law and we are not the first to act on it, but we found it existing before us and shall leave it to exist after us, for all time. All we do is make use of it, knowing that you and everybody else, if clothed with the same power as we are, would do the same. And so far as the gods are concerned, we have no good reason to see ourselves at any disadvantage.''

The Melians might count on help from Sparta.

The Athenians might have thought of laughing out loud. ''We are not at war with Sparta now.''

''Still—''

''We must declare that Spartans are most conspicuous for believing that what they like doing is honorable and what suits their interest is just. We bless your simplicity but do not envy you your folly.''

Self-interest and security went hand in hand, while justice and honor were practiced with danger, said Athens. Was it really likely, while Athens was master of the seas, and while the two were restrained by a peace treaty, that the Spartans would cross over to an island to help a small city that was now no use to them?

''What surprises us most,'' said the Athenians, ''is that in this long discussion, although you announced that you wished to discuss how to save yourselves, you have not yet advanced a single argument that would justify an ordinary man in thinking he could be preserved. On the contrary, your strongest grounds for confidence are merely cherished hopes whose fulfillment is in the future, whereas your present resources for achieving them are too slight for any chance of success when compared with those arrayed against you. You will therefore be showing quite an unreasonable attitude if you fail to come to some decision that is wiser than any you have mentioned so far.''

The Melians conferred when the Athenians withdrew and resolved that they would not give up in a moment the freedom that the city had enjoyed since its founding more than seven hundred years before.

They would trust in the gods and in help from Sparta.

"But we propose that we be your friends, enemies to neither side, and that you withdraw from our country, after making a truce as may seem suitable for both of us."

The Athenians scoffed. "You are unique. For you are the only men who think you can see the future as more certain than what is before your eyes, and who look at what is out of sight as already realized, in your eagerness to see it come to pass. You have staked your all in luck and hope, and with your all you will come to ruin."

Several months later, when the city fell to the Athenian siege, all men of military age were slain. (Exceptions, perhaps, were the treacherous few in the fifth column who helped betray the city from inside.) The women and children were sold as slaves.

Euripides wrote *The Trojan Women*.

The play was selected for public competition in a city already preparing for the invasion of Syracuse, which also took place in that interval of peace that was known as the cold war.

In democratic Athens, there was always a surfeit of that sophisticated political wisdom founded on realpolitik, which in other Greek cities was usually in short supply, and twelve years later, Athens lost the war.

23

FROM ATHENS TO SYRACUSE BY OAR AND SAIL WAS JUST about equivalent to the journey by troopship today from California to Vietnam, or from Washington, D.C., to the Beirut airport in Lebanon or to the Persian Gulf.

Do not make war in a hostile distant land unless you intend to live there.

The people will outnumber you, your presence will be alarming, the government you install to keep order will not keep order, victory is impossible if the people keep fighting, there is only genocide to cope with determined local military resistance.

The general Nicias, one of three commanders chosen for the Sicilian expedition, was moody, conservative, religious, superstitious. He had a strong sense of the obstacles and spoke in opposition to the expedition, although the majority had already voted for it.

The occasion for intervention was a quarrel between cities in Sicily; and the ally, as usual, had lied about the magnitude of the money and popular support it would supply.

The Assembly was convoked to consider the size of the armament needed. Nicias used the meeting to question whether Athens ought to go at all.

"Do not get drawn into a war which does not truly concern us," he warned.

Because Nicias was a wealthy, highly respected member of the peace party, the Athenians, with peculiar logic, and against his wishes, had appointed him one of the generals.

He feared that the war party of the hawks, led now by the youthful Alcibiades, was using the conflict between two cities as part of a vaster plan to conquer all Sicily.

It seemed to him unwise to go off leaving many enemies near home and sailing to Sicily to make new ones.

"The treaty with Sparta is a treaty only as long as we remain quiet. Should we suffer defeat, our foes will attack us. Even if we conquer the Sicilians, there are so many of them and they live so far off that it would be difficult to govern them. It is folly to go against people who, even if conquered, cannot be controlled, and for us to go grasping at a new empire before we have been able to secure the one we already have. The Hellenes in Sicily will be most in awe of us if we do not come at all. If we should suffer a defeat, they would very quickly despise us and join our enemies. We get only grudging obedience from our subjects now, and we rush to the help of Egesta in Sicily, of all places, which we suddenly say is an ally, and which we say has been wronged, and whose interest it is to tell lies and make us believe them. Sicily is not a danger to us. Let us not make it one. And if there be a certain one here now who, elated at being chosen to command, exhorts you to sail, considering only his own interest, how he may get admiration for his fine horses, how he may also get some profit from his command, do not afford this man, at the cost of the state, an opportunity to make a personal display. It is of such youths that I am afraid. And I make a counterappeal for the support of the older men among you. If any of you is sitting next to one of the supporters of this young man's war party, do not allow yourself to be browbeaten and do not fear being called a coward if you do not vote for war. Leave the Sicilians alone to enjoy their own country and manage their own affairs. We should not make allies of people who have to be helped by us but who can do nothing for us when we need help from them.''

In Syracuse, the city in the Greek world second largest to Athens in population, the leaders were urging defiance.

There was no need to be frightened of the daring and power of the Athenians, said the first speaker, even if the rumors of their expedition were true.

''They will not be able to inflict more injury upon us than they will have to suffer.''

There had not been many expeditions, either Hellenic or foreign, that had been successful when sent far from home.

''They cannot come in greater numbers than the inhabitants of this country and our neighbors, and it is not unlikely that things will go wrong with them because of lack of suppliers in a foreign country.''

The Athenians had a great stretch of open sea to cross. Their detachments could be attacked when the rowers were tired. They would grow short of rations.

Said the next speaker, who was leader of the democratic party: ''Only cowards or people with no sense of patriotism are not anxious for the Athenians to prove as mad as they are made out to be, and for them to come here and fall into our power.''

He was less perturbed by the rumors of the Athenian expedition than by the danger that the aristocrats and oligarchs of Syracuse would exploit the emergency to obtain control of the defense and curtail the freedoms of the citizens.

''Some will say that a democracy is neither wise nor equitable, and that those that have property are more competent to rule best. But I say that a democracy is a name for all, oligarchy for only a part; next, that while the wealthy may be the best guardians of property, the wise would be the best councillors. And the many, after hearing matters discussed, would be the best judges.''

Democracy in Syracuse was put in jeopardy by the threat from democratic Athens.

Even if the Athenians brought with them another city as large as Syracuse and planted it down on the borders and made war from there, they would have little chance of survival.

How much less would they have when most of Sicily was united against them, when they were in a camp pitched just after landing and could not venture far from their wretched tents and meager supplies, unable to move in any direction because of the Sicilian cavalry and the other armed forces surrounding them? They would only go back the way they came, *if* their ships survived and the harbor remained open.

The motion in the Athenian Assembly to invade Syracuse to restore order in Sicily was deceitful, corrupt, stupid, chauvinistic, irrational, and suicidal.

It carried by a huge majority.

Most zealous in urging the motion for war was Alcibiades, the young man alluded to by Nicias as one who wished to be admired for the horses he raised. Above all, he was eager to be made general and hoped thereby to subdue both Sicily and Carthage, and at the same time promote his private interests in wealth as well as in glory.

In that period of peace known as the cold war, Alcibiades had spent time fomenting new wars, intriguing with Argos and other independent cities in an anti-Spartan alliance that was beaten decisively in the battle of Mantinea.

Alcibiades called this defeat a glorious victory, and friends in Athens acclaimed him a national hero.

"It's too amusing, too silly," exulted Alcibiades in confidence afterward, "and it is truly impossible to take much of it seriously. I must give you more credit, my very good friend. What you've said to me about democracy, equality, fraternity, and liberty is all of it absolutely true."

"What was it I said to you that you have in mind now?" inquired Socrates.

"That it's thoroughly absurd."

"Was that my word?"

"More than once. Look how they've listened to me and how they've elevated me and made me one of the generals. Only because they feel beneath me, and because they are themselves a herd of snobs. All their talk of equality is hypocrisy. These new middle-class businessmen want to be equal only to us. And they want no one but us to be equal to them."

"And so now they have given you the war in Syracuse you asked for," said Socrates. "I personally cannot see how any good can come of it. Please explain to me," continued the philosopher, after a moment to reflect, "the real reasons you want to go to Sicily to make war."

"I'm not sure that I know them," said Alcibiades.

"If not the real reasons, tell me the good ones. What are the good reasons that truly are convincing to you? By my beard, Alcibiades, if I were much younger, I might find myself upset to go off on a war like this one."

"We will have more men than we need. But we will take them anyway."

"Please give me a clue. Your most powerful motive for wanting this dangerous war in Sicily?"

"Horses, of course."

"I'm at a loss for words."

"It's the first time that has happened in our years of friendship."

"You know my next question."

"Breeding and raising good horses is more expensive than you'd ever believe, my dear Socrates," said Alcibiades, with that air of careless jocularity that was by now his second nature. "And entering seven teams of chariots in the Olympic Games was far from cheap, you know."

"Then why did you do that?" wondered Socrates. "To enter so many has never been done by one man before."

"That's just why I did it. Don't you remember? You used to try to teach me contempt for wealth."

"Did I fail or did I succeed? It's impossible to say from this example you give."

"I wished to attract an enormous amount of attention to myself, to make a magnificent, spectacular, and infuriating impression."

"You have never done anything else."

"I wished to display to the entire Greek world how much wealth I had," explained Alcibiades, "and to make clear, by throwing so much of it away, with such open vulgarity, how little I valued it."

"But when you spoke in the Assembly for your Sicilian war resolution," said Socrates, "you maintained that you entered these seven chariots to demonstrate the glory of Athens."

"Do you think I care more for my city than I do for myself?"

"You were being ironic?"

"You taught me how."

"You would have learned without me."

"I was telling a lie they would adore to hear. And they lapped it up like intoxicating wine. And now that I've squandered my money on my horses with such nonchalant contempt, I need this invasion to make back what I've squandered."

"Tell me. There's a thing I don't know."

"Now I am the teacher?"

"I always professed that I did not know anything."

"While making clear to your listeners that you believed you knew much."

"I do not know how a person serving the state can accumulate wealth for himself by going to war in the service of the state."

"I don't know that either," confessed Alcibiades. "But I do know that I am going to find out"

"You brought back a woman slave last year from the destruction of Melos."

"The spoils of war," Alcibiades said, and added with a

mock frown, "but I made it a point to pay a small price for her anyway. Since the idea for Melos was mine, I felt it my burden to set an example. You've seen her, haven't you? She's beautiful, isn't she? For a woman, I mean."

"Alcibiades, you're incorrigible."

"My wife thinks that too."

"You have put me in danger," chuckled Socrates. "Your enemies blame me for making you the way you are."

"My friends blame you for not making me more so."

"You would not practice the flute when young," Socrates remembered.

"It made my face look ridiculous. I could see what it did to others."

"And now all of the fashionable young men about town refuse to study the flute."

"The flute is for flute girls."

"You exaggerate your lisp. Please don't try to lie to me— I've heard you in your cups and it is scarcely there at all. Now everyone speaks with a lisp. Your son, who was not born with a lisp, studies hard to speak with a lisp."

"I am proud of his lisp."

"He now lisps more lispingly than you do."

"It's the fashion, of course."

"You, Alcibiades, made the fashion."

"Who else would you rather see do it?"

"You go about in a long Persian robe, trailing it in dust, and now all do the same. In the Assembly now they obey you too, as though war policies also were a matter of fashion."

"War is always in fashion, my dear old friend. Look at our history. In our golden age of Athens there is scarcely a period as long as five years in which we have not been at war. We lose most of the big battles and can't hold on to what we win. Yet the city prospers, the economy booms. And now see how unconvincing and feeble poor Nicias appears each time he comes into public to argue for threadbare, ragged, tedious peace. A politician can roar for war. For peace he can only plead.''

"And why, when fortune was good enough to make you a superior man, do you go walking about like an inferior woman?''

"Why, Socrates, did you never kiss me when I was young?''

Here Socrates emitted a burst of laughter. ''You had quite enough of that from other men, my dear Alcibiades. It was my eccentric fancy to develop your mind and your soul.''

"What good would that do?''

"I had hoped to attract you to a life of philosophy.''

"And how much good does that do for anybody?''

"It has kept me busy enough.''

"People want more. Thought is overrated. Look back at history, my dear Socrates, and you will see that all the powerful ideas that have moved men most were simpleminded and superficial, never deep.''

"I suppose I should be grateful for that, since it has left me immune and given me time to think freely. And you surprise me with your political views too,'' said Socrates seriously. "I would have predicted, with your breeding and background, that you would have been pro-Spartan and in favor of peace. Yet you have schemed for a new war against Sparta from the hour the last one stopped.''

"But how else would I stand out in politics?'' explained Alcibiades. "Today there are even democrats and businessmen in politics who want peace with Sparta. Would you expect me to wait my turn in back of them?''

"But why do you agitate so? If you succeed and go to Syracuse to make war, you will destroy the Peace of Nicias with Sparta and we will be back at war there.''

"It's what I count on.''

"Why do you want to?''

"Because,'' said Alcibiades, "it is called the Peace of Nicias.''

"Aha! And if it were the Peace of Alcibiades?''

"I would proclaim it divine. The Spartans have slighted me. They should have insisted on conducting their negotiations with me, Socrates. My family has always been their business agents in Athens."

"You were much too young."

"That makes no difference to me."

Peace was indeed a blessing, preached Alcibiades with levity. Peace brought an opportunity to make war in other places, and a great civilization like theirs would be foolish to waste it.

"We have sworn to help our loyal friends in Egesta, and it is our duty to help them," he had argued with vigor in the Assembly after Nicias finished, saying this to the surprise of many, who had not known till then that Athens was allied with the distant town of Egesta and who, like Nicias, did not believe that military commitments there should be honored even if they indeed existed. Alcibiades was willing to be instructive. "We are forced to plan new conquests, because success has brought us to the point of danger"—success always brings nations to the point of danger—"the danger that we ourselves may fall under the power of others unless we put all others in our power. If we don't keep adding to our empire we risk losing the empire we have. As for the Peloponnesians, never were they more helpless against us. They can invade us only by land—and that they can do even if we do not make this expedition. As for my youth and my lack of experience, I remind you that it was I who brought together the greatest independent powers of the Peloponnese without danger or expense to Athens and forced the Lacedaemonians to stake all against them in a single day at the battle of Mantinea. True, they won; but for us it was a major victory. We spent no money, suffered no casualties. They know what trouble we can make and they do not have firm confidence against us. Consider that our city, if she remains at peace, will, like anything else, wear herself out upon herself, and her skill in all pursuits will grow old; whereas if she is continually at conflict, she will be adding to her experience, and will acquire more by deed the habit of defending herself.''

Nicias hoped to dissuade them with a request for appropriations of staggering size. The result was the contrary. They granted all, for they felt they were getting sound advice from this good, conservative man, and there fell upon all alike an eager desire to sail.

To Socrates, Alcibiades repeated the theory with which he had enticed his audience in the Assembly, the theory of the dominoes. When Syracuse fell, the cities nearest Syracuse would fall, like dominoes, in sequence, then all of Sicily, then Italy, next Carthage, and then, of course, with all these new allies and subjects of Athens attacking, Sparta too would fall.

Socrates was spellbound. ''Will all of that really happen?'' he asked now.

''I really don't know,'' answered Alcibiades frankly, ''and don't care to look that far ahead. I simply want to go now. I'm impatient. I'd rather do it than think about it. Socrates, don't be severe. It is so much easier for me, I know, to find fault in the programs of others than to present one of my own that has none.''

''You have learned the Socratic method,'' Socrates told him with good humor.

Alcibiades smiled too. ''You surely must appreciate, my dear Socrates, that I have gone into politics only for all of the usual reasons: to shine and show off, to wield power, to make money.''

''You say that all so carelessly,'' Socrates said. ''Do you know that you have become a constant embarrassment to me?''

''Oh, please pay no attention to the disapproval of the silly people in this city. They don't like you much either, you know. People hate me and love me and don't know how to do without me. So they elect me a general. Because they fear my audacity, they appoint Nicias a second general as a counterweight, a man who will paralyze us with timidity. For the third general they appoint Lamachus, the only one of us with knowledge for so large a military campaign. But Lamachus is from a poor family, so it is beneath our dignity to heed him. He will want to attack at once, I will want to attract allies in Sicily because I enjoy putting on a show, Nicias will want to go home, and we will probably not do any of these. Will you come along? I would like you with me again as a hoplite, just as an old friend.''

Socrates was shaking his head. ''I have no armor. You know my Xanthippe sold it.''

''Is she opposed to our wars?''

''She's a wife who wants money for our house. She wants me to beg.''

''You could give lessons for pay.''

''I would call that begging.''

''I will give you armor. That robe you are wearing, my friend, is one that on a slave would put a master to shame. I will give you a new one. I will lend you my golden shield.''

''Your golden shield is a scandal too! That gilded shield of yours, with Cupid, of all the divinities, wielding a thunderbolt, is insolent and disgusting and offends many of the older men in the city. Alcibiades, they say you've dressed in female clothes to attend the women's Mysteries.''

''They say I dress in female clothes and conduct my own Mysteries in my house, in a mockery of them all.''

''You received an invitation to dine with Anthemion and rejected it with rudeness.''

''He should have known that I would. He wished to use me to impress his other guests.''

''And then you came by afterward with drunken friends and sent your servants in to walk out of his house with the silver and gold plates from his table.''

''In that way I gave him the impression he deserved.''

''When your wife was in court for divorce, you came in only to throw her over your shoulder and carry her back home, without a word.''

''That is my right under law. A wife must appear in person

expressly so a husband like me can halt a divorce when he does not want one.''

''You did not say that when you did it. You just carried her out. You said nothing.''

''I would not deign to.''

''The jurors were offended.''

''My wife was not.''

''I feel almost endangered,'' said Socrates with a gleam of pride. ''It's a disgrace to me that people believe I taught you.''

''It's a disgrace to me,'' said Alcibiades, ''to have been taught by a husband whose wife empties the chamber pot on his head.''

''You have only heard that!'' cried Socrates, in a tone of mirthful indignation. ''You have never seen it.''

''No, I have not even heard it. I am the person who tells it!''

''Oh, Alcibiades! You'll be the death of me yet.''

This dialogue of Socrates and Alcibiades, which is thought to be spurious, is the last between them that we have.

24

THE SWIFTNESS WITH WHICH THE RUMORS OF ALCIBIADES'
guilt for the mutilation of the Hermae took hold was surpris-
ing even to those who had started them. Normally, it is not
the swashbuckling warmonger who is suspected of impiety
and treason.

Normally, the warmonger is a person with an aura of outspoken piety and an outstanding capacity for blending his
religious beliefs with his secular and who, as was said of the
Spartans by the Athenians, is most conspicuous for believing
that what he likes doing is correct and that what suits his
spiritual and personal wants is always moral and best for the
nation.

The desecration of these public icons occurred almost on
the eve of departure of the expedition to Syracuse.

This city was religious; and the mutilation of these stone
idols did not augur well for the mission. The charges against
him were taken up by those in the city who were most jealous
of him, and they declared that the desecration of the Hermae

had been committed with a view to the overthrow of the democracy.

That it hardly made sense for the general most in favor of the expedition to undertake with friends an act of vandalism that would force its cancellation did not carry much weight in the deductions of those in authority who were not his friends.

Alcibiades had a good sense of smell, and he demanded to be tried at once, to be put to death if found guilty or allowed to sail if not.

Fearing his popularity with the military forces now assembled in the city, his enemies bade him embark for Syracuse as planned. They schemed to procure a more slanderous indictment in his absence and have him brought home for trial when his adherents were abroad.

He left as scheduled.

It was already midsummer when the Athenians set sail.

Most of the allies, together with the ships carrying grain and equipment, were assembling at Corcyra, so as to cross the Ionian Sea in one body.

But the Athenians themselves, and all their allies who were in Athens, went down to Piraeus at dawn on the day appointed and manned the ships for putting out to sea. The rest of the people—in fact, almost the entire population of Athens—citizens as well as foreigners, went down with them to see them off. The sight was inspiring. Those sailing who were natives of the country all had people to see them off on their way, whether friends or relatives or sons, and these came full of hope and full of lamentation at the same time, thinking of the conquests that might be made and thinking, too, of those whom they might never see again, considering the long voyage on which they were going.

At this moment, when parting from each other with all the risks ahead, the dangers became more real to them than when they had voted for the expedition.

Nevertheless they were heartened with the strength they

had and with the sight of the quantities of every kind of armament displayed before their eyes.

Certainly this expedition that first set sail was by a long way the most costly and the finest-looking force of Hellenic troops that up to that time had ever come from a single city. Other forces, which may have been as large, went only on short voyages and were equipped only in the ordinary way. This expedition was planned with a view to its being away for a long time and was equipped for both kinds of fighting, with warships and ground troops. All the ships were staffed with the best crews available. The captains, too, announced extra pay in addition to that provided by the state, and they went to great expense on the figureheads and general fittings, every one of the captains being anxious that his own ship should stand out for its fine looks and speed. As for the land forces, they had been chosen from the best men, and there had been much rivalry and many pains taken by each one on his armor and personal equipment. Thus there was this competition among the Athenians themselves, and to the rest of Hellas it looked more like a display of wealth and power than an undertaking against enemies.

From Corcyra one hundred thirty-four triremes and two fifty-oared ships from Rhodes would cross over the Ionian Sea together and continue to Sicily. A hundred of these triremes were from Athens and the rest came from Chios and other allies. Of hoplites there were fifty-one hundred in all— of these, fifteen hundred were Athenians from the muster roll and seven hundred from the lowest property class, who usually served as oarsmen but in extraordinary cases, as now, went as marines with hoplite armor. There were altogether four hundred eighty archers, eighty of whom were Cretans, seven hundred slingers from Rhodes, one hundred twenty exiles from Megara, serving as light troops, and one horse transport carrying thirty horses.

This was the strength of the first expeditionary force that went overseas to the war.

And for these, thirty food-bearing transports brought supplies, having also bakers, stonemasons, carpenters, and all tools for wall-building; and there sailed also one hundred boats that were pressed into service, along with the transports. But many boats besides, as well as transports, voluntarily accompanied the expedition for the sake of trade.

In Piraeus when the ships were manned and everything had been taken aboard, silence was commanded by the sound of the trumpet, and the customary prayers made before putting to sea were offered up, not by each ship separately but by them all together following the words of a herald. The whole army had wine poured out into bowls, and officers and men made their libations from cups of gold and silver. Then, when the hymn had been sung and the libations finished, they put out to sea, first sailing out in column, and then racing each other as far as Aegina. The ships from Athens made good speed on their way to Corcyra, where the other forces of their allies were assembling.

Plato was thirteen when he saw them depart. He stood on a bulkhead with his uncle Critias.

He did not see them return.

They never did.

In short time, of the three generals, only Nicias remained.

Lamachus was killed in action, and Alcibiades, summoned home to face charges, made his way to Sparta instead, bringing secret knowledge and good advice. In one of the towns in Sicily through which he passed he was recognized by an Athenian.

"Don't you trust your own country to act fairly to you, Alcibiades?" asked the man in reproach.

"Yes, in other things," said Alcibiades. "But where my life is at stake, I would not trust my own mother not to mistake a black pebble for a white one when she casts her vote."

To the Spartans he said: "Democracy is ridiculous. Only take a look at what those democrats have done to me!"

He advised Sparta to send high-ranking military advisers to Sicily, and triremes and troops, and to invade Attica once more and *stay there*, instead of retiring each fall, as they had done before. The surest way to harm an enemy was to find out what form of attack he was most frightened of and launch it.

"You have just found out from me."

The Spartans were leery. "That would violate the treaty and put an end to our truce."

Alcibiades threw back his head in laughter. "Do you truly believe that you and Athens are not making war now when you attack each other's friends and supply each other's enemies? Of course you're at war."

He alarmed them by revealing the theory of the dominoes, and did not tell them the theory was his own. "If you do not fight them in Syracuse now, you will have to fight them in Sparta later, and Carthage and all Sicily will be on their side. Where do you get your grain?"

"We grow most ourselves."

"As for the rest?"

"We obtain it from Sicily."

"You won't have Sicily. The Athenians were foolish to send their forces to Sicily and leave themselves open to you."

He did not tell them the idea had been his.

Sparta followed his advice with excellent results, and Alcibiades won the hearts of his new countrymen by allowing his hair to grow long, taking cold baths, eating coarse bread, and adapting to other Spartan ways with an élan that was dazzling.

Among the hearts he won was that of the wife of King Agis. Her pet name for the child she bore was Alcibiades.

Alcibiades left Sparta just in time and enlisted with the Persian Tissaphernes. Having served with Athens and Sparta, he could advise about both.

In Sicily, by then, Nicias had lost.

But first, before the fighting began, a second armada as large as the first was requested and sent. This gambit by Nicias for the recall of the mission failed. The war went ahead. In the last of the battles in the two years it lasted,

Nicias and his men retreated once more and encamped on high ground.

Their ships had been lost, the harbor sealed.

The next day the Syracusans caught up and attacked them from all sides with missiles until the evening. The fleeing Athenians were in a wretched state too in their need for food and all the other necessities. When the day came, Nicias renewed his retreat, but the Syracusans and their allies kept pressing them hard.

The Athenians pushed on toward the river Assinarus, partly because they thought—attacked as they were on all sides by horsemen and miscellaneous troops—that they would be better off on the other side, and partly by reason of their weariness and their desire for water. And when they reached the river, they rushed down into it, no longer preserving order, but each one eager to be the first to cross. And at the same time, the attacks of the enemy made the crossing more difficult. For, as they had no choice now but to move in a dense mass, they fell and trampled upon each other, and some perished at once, while others became entangled among their trappings and their baggage and were swept away by the current. The Syracusan troops were stationed along the other bank of the river, which was steep, and rained their missiles down upon the Athenians, most of whom were drinking greedily in the deep riverbed. And the Peloponnesians, who had entered the war, of course, came down to the water's edge and butchered them, especially those who were in the river. The water at once became foul, but they went on drinking it, all muddy as it was and dyed with blood, and indeed it was fought for by most of them in their longing to have it.

At length, when the dead now lay in heaps one upon another, and much of the army had perished utterly—part in the river, and that part that crossed cut down at the hands of the cavalry—Nicias surrendered, saying they should do what they liked with him, but to stop the slaughter of his soldiers.

The Syracusans and their allies now brought their forces

together, took up the spoils and as many of the captives as they could, and went back to their city.

Nicias they put to the sword, a man who of all the Hellenes of the time, says Thucydides, least deserved to come to so miserable an end, since the whole of his life had been devoted to the study and the practice of virtue.

The noble Nicias got rich leasing slaves to the city to work in the silver mines.

The Athenians who were prisoners and all their allies were taken down into the stone quarries as the safest method of keeping them.

The prisoners in the stone quarries were treated badly at first. There were many of them, and they were crowded together in a narrow pit, where, since there was no roof over their heads, they suffered first from the heat of the sun and the closeness of the air, while, in contrast, the nights that followed were autumnal and cold, and the change in temperature brought disease among them.

In addition, the lack of space made it necessary for them to do everything on the same spot; moreover, the bodies of the dead were all heaped together on top of one another—those who had died from their wounds or from the change of temperature or other such causes—so that there was a stench that was insupportable. At the same time they suffered from hunger and from thirst. During eight months, the Syracusans allowed each man but half a pint of water and a pint of food a day, and in fact, of all the other ills which men thrown into imprisonment in such a place would be likely to suffer, there was none that did not befall them.

For about ten weeks they lived like this all together. Then all those except the Athenians and the Greeks from Sicily or Italy who had joined the Athenians found release by being sold into slavery.

It is hard to speak with accuracy of the number of prisoners taken, but the total must have been more than seven thousand.

This was the greatest action of this war, the greatest that we know of in Greek history.

To the victors went the most brilliant of successes, to the vanquished the most calamitous of defeats, for they were utterly and entirely defeated. Their sufferings were on an enormous scale, their losses were total: army, navy, everything was destroyed, and out of the many, only few returned. Only one we know of by name survived, and that was Alcibiades.

Rebellions erupted throughout the Athenian empire.

It is almost impossible to believe that Athens struggled on for nine more years.

"Keep them fighting," Alcibiades advised his Persian benefactor, Tissaphernes. Soon he would falsely invoke the name of Tissaphernes to help bring about the overthrow of the democratic government in Athens by an oligarchy. "Give Sparta money for ships, but not too much. Support the weaker side, and let them wear themselves out fighting each other instead of us. Whichever side wins will not be our ally."

In 407 he was elected a general again by the democracy in Athens he had plotted to overthrow. And not long after that, he was blamed unjustly for defeat at the sea battle of Notium and gave it all up and retired to Thrace.

The end for Athens came with Lysander and his victory at Aegospotami: there, one hundred eighty Athenian ships were trapped on the beach, and only nine put to sea and escaped.

The year before, Athens, in brutal rashness, had legislated the measure directing Athenian commanders to cut off the right hand of every Spartan captured at sea. One captain went further and threw overboard every Spartan on two ships he captured.

Lysander retaliated now. He ordered that captain's throat cut. And he executed every Athenian among the prisoners except one man who was known to have opposed the motion in the Assembly. And he began moving with his ships to blockade the harbors.

Tidings of the defeat arrived at night, wrote Xenophon.

A sound of wailing ran from Piraeus through the long walls to the city, one man passing the news to another, and during that night no one slept. All mourned, not for the lost alone but more for their own selves, thinking that now they would suffer such treatment as they had visited upon others, the people of Melos, Histiaea, Scione, Torone, Aegina, and many other Greek peoples.

But Sparta refused to allow the destruction of the city that had done so much for all Greeks, and Spartan allies like Corinth, Thebes, and Elis refused to sign the treaty, denouncing the terms as a giveaway and a sellout.

Athens could keep twelve ships, but the walls had to come down.

Only when all supplies of food were exhausted had Athens finally sent ambassadors to Sparta to sue for peace. As the ambassadors were returning, a great crowd gathered around them, fearful that they had been unsuccessful, for it was no longer possible to delay with so many dying from hunger.

The ambassadors reported to the Assembly the terms on which the Lacedaemonians offered to make peace and lift the blockade. They spoke in favor of accepting. Some people spoke in opposition, but many more were in favor, and it was voted to accept the peace. After this, Lysander sailed into Piraeus, exiles who wanted to return were allowed to, and the Peloponnesians with great enthusiasm began to tear down the walls to the music of flute girls, hailing that day as the beginning of freedom for Greece.

Athenians who listened were stunned that the capitulation of their democratic city was acclaimed by others as the return of liberty for the rest.

In that same year, Alcibiades was murdered by Persian assassins, at the request of Sparta, at the insistence of the

Tyrants in Athens. By then, leaders in all three places had grown sick of him.

The woman in whose arms he lay that night, says Plutarch, took up his dead body, covered it, wrapped it in her own robes, and gave it as decent and honorable a burial as her circumstances would allow.

25

AGING *ENFANTS TERRIBLES* DO NOT WEAR WELL, AND THIS was true of Alcibiades.

There were respectable married women in Athens who also were content with news of the manner of his death. It came as no surprise to Xanthippe, the wife of Socrates. He had gotten no worse than he deserved, she said, and it only went to prove what she had known all along, that he would come to a very bad end.

Socrates said: "That's life."

XII

LITERARY REMAINS

26

THE ATHENIAN CITIZEN IS REPUTED AMONG ALL THE HELlenes to be a great talker, wrote Plato. With the Dutch in general, and Rembrandt in particular, the reverse seems true.

In Rembrandt's literary remains we have just seven letters in his own hand and the translation into Italian by someone unknown of a letter from him to Ruffo. All the letters deal with business. The business is money.

In addition to the letters, there is a short memo by Rembrandt to Ruffo relating to his unfinished *Homer*, which he had enclosed with the *Alexander* in hope he could sell him the third of the three Greek figures he had included in his *Aristotle*. It reads:

> Because each piece measures 6 palms wide and 8
> in height, they are of good size, and the Gentleman
> will not think the price is too high.
> Your respectful servant
> Rembrandt van Rijn.

The seven letters in his own hand went to his first influential admirer, Constantijn Huygens, and are concerned with the final three paintings in the Passion series commissioned by Prince Frederick Henry.

The letter translated into Italian was his reply to objections by Don Antonio to the *Alexander*. Rembrandt's lofty tone and rude independence of mind are clues, perhaps, to his breakups with Jan Six and Constantijn Huygens and with other patrons who had been helpful to him.

Along with the letters are some other statements pertinent now, all short, three written, two spoken to persons repeating them. Almost all the rest heard from him is incorporated in legal pleadings and financial agreements. In these, his pomposity of language is not inconsistent with the puffed-up personality we have come to know, or with the imperious demeanor in the self-portraits executed when his misfortunes were at their worst.

In Amsterdam at twenty-eight he wrote the following as his motto in the album of a German traveler:

An upright soul respects honor before wealth.

Only two times in his life do we find Rembrandt expressing himself with anything like true feeling. The first is an inscription on a drawing of Saskia commemorating their engagement. The second was an exclamation of woe to a maidservant toward the end.

The inscription to Saskia reads:

This is drawn after my wife, when she was 21 years old, the third day after we were betrothed—8 June 1633.

The drawing is executed in silverpoint on prepared paper, a delicate procedure of the early Renaissance. Saskia wears a straw hat with a band and flowers and looks healthy, a trifle seductive, and more than twenty-one. In drawings of her near the end of her life, nine years later, she is wasted with disease and often in bed.

They were married in 1634 in Friesland, where her sister lived with her husband, an attorney and town clerk.

We have no reason to conclude that Rembrandt favored the distant locale to avoid introducing his Catholic mother and plebeian brothers and sisters to the circle into which he was marrying. His father, who probably had gone blind with age, was already dead.

There is no reason for believing he would not have kept them away even had the ceremonies been in Amsterdam.

They were married on the twenty-second day of June.

One month later, on his anniversary date, Rembrandt signed the document giving power to his new brother-in-law, the town clerk and practicing lawyer Gerrit van Loo, to collect those debts in Friesland on Saskia's behalf.

This family of van Loos, into which a sister of Saskia's had married, was to remain involved in Rembrandt's legal entanglements for the rest of his life, and even beyond. Titus married a van Loo; when he died, she was pregnant, carrying another van Loo, who had a potential, prenatal claim to anything of value left by the artist or his son.

Only in the underdeveloped nations of the world do lawyers struggle for a living.

Their first child, Rombartus, was baptized in December of 1635. When he was buried, two months later, Rembrandt wrote the first of the letters to Huygens that survive in his literary estate. And two months after that ensued the first of several lawsuits over Saskia's legacy which Rembrandt and Saskia initiated as plaintiffs.

In all his lawsuits while Saskia was alive, Rembrandt was the complainant; in the lawsuits after her death, he was almost always the defendant. We must note in fairness that court decisions over the Uylenburgh inheritance were always in favor of Rembrandt and Saskia. We can assume, however, that any appetite for litigation Rembrandt had at the peak of his success was more than slaked before his life was over.

In the first of the seven letters to Huygens, Rembrandt says to his lord, his gracious Lord Huygens, that he hopes his lordship will please inform His Excellency, by whom he means Prince Frederick Henry, that he is very diligently engaged in completing as quickly as possible the three Passion pictures which His Excellency himself commissioned him to do: an Entombment, and a Resurrection, and an Ascension of Christ.

Rembrandt's *Raising of the Cross* and *Descent from the Cross* had been done three years before. Of these new paintings, Rembrandt writes, one was completed. The other two were more than half done. Rembrandt concludes this epistle:

> And should it please His Excellency to receive his finished piece at once or the three of them together, I pray you my lord to let me know concerning this matter so that I may serve the wishes of His Excellency the Prince, to the best of my ability.
>
> And I also cannot refrain, as a token of my humble favor, from presenting my lord with something of my latest work, trusting that this will be accepted as favorably as possible. Besides my greetings to your lordship, I commend you to God in health.
>
> My Lord, your humble and
> devoted servant
> Rembrandt

Had His Excellency wanted the three paintings together, he might have had to wait three more years, until Rembrandt bought the house and was scrambling for cash.

We know the painting was shipped and that it was received with some disappointment, for Rembrandt offers in his *Second Letter* to go to The Hague to see how his *Ascension* "accords" with the previous pictures. There is also, for Rembrandt, the sensitive matter of money:

> As far as the price of the picture is concerned, I have certainly deserved 1200 guilders for it, but I

shall be satisfied with what His Excellency pays
me. My lord, should your lordship not take this
liberty amiss I shall leave nothing undone by which
I can repay it.

The best place to show it is in the gallery of His
Excellency since there is a strong light there.

Rembrandt was paid the same six hundred guilders he had
received for the first two. Three years passed before his famed
Third Letter. The interval was not without its excitements.

There was that lawsuit over Saskia's inheritance in April
of 1636, in which Rembrandt, Saskia, and her brother Idsert
triumphed over a Dr. Albert van Loo and others in litigation
relating to an estate in Friesland belonging to all of the
Uylenburghs.

In March of 1638 Gerrit van Loo, Rembrandt, a brother-
in-law, François Coopal, another brother-in-law, Dr. Joannes
Maccovius, and the brother Idsert all brought suit, and won,
against another brother, Dr. Ulricus Uylenburgh, and one
other person in respect to the sale of a farm.

In that year a daughter was born in July and buried in
August, and in that same July, the libel suit was filed by
Rembrandt and Saskia and came to trial in Friesland.

The plaintiffs charged that Dr. Albert van Loo, a losing
defendant in one of the previous lawsuits, and his sister
Mayke had stated, and had continued to state, that Saskia
had "squandered her parents' legacy by ostentatious display,
vanity, and flaunting."

We cannot be sure the defendants knew about Rembrandt's *Self-Portrait with Saskia,* although they seemed to
know about Rembrandt and Saskia.

Rembrandt's words in his affidavit of complaint were in
part as follows:

The plaintiff and his wife were quite well off and
were blessed richly with a superabundance of

earthly possessions (for which they can never be
sufficiently grateful to the good Lord).

And because this offense was, praise God, entirely contrary to the truth, Rembrandt could not let it pass and asked
for damages in the form of an apology and payment of sixty-
four gold guilders for the offense against his name, and for
sixty-four gold guilders for the offense against Saskia, claim-
ing especially the payment of legal expenses.

Dr. van Loo replied that neither he nor his sister had made
any such statement as was alleged against them. Should com-
pensation be in order, however, the defendant offered the
plaintiffs, who were "a mere painter and his wife," eight
gold guilders, which should suffice for any offense against
their name.

In this legal action objecting to allegations of extravagance
directed against him and his wife, Rembrandt was not victorious. Each side was ordered to pay its own costs, and six
months later Rembrandt extravagantly bought the house.

With the purchase of the house, Rembrandt's written output suddenly resumed in a flurry of creative activity that also
witnessed the completion of the last two paintings in the
Passion series, paintings he had described three years before
as half done and with which he had depicted himself as being
"very diligently engaged in completing as quickly as possible."

Only nine days after he bought the house, and after a silence of three years, he wrote his *Third Letter* to Huygens
and had it delivered by hand on January 12, 1639.

Because of the great zeal and devotion which I exercised in executing well the two pictures which His
Highness commissioned me to make—the one being where Christ's dead body is being laid in the
tomb and the other where Christ arises from the
dead to the great consternation of the guards—these
same two pictures have now been finished through
studious application, so that I am now also dis-

posed to deliver the same and so to afford pleasure
to His Highness, for in these two pictures the greatest and most natural emotion has been expressed,
which is also the main reason why they have taken
so long to execute. . . .

And as my lord has been troubled in these matters
for the second time, a piece 10 feet long and 8 feet
high shall be added as a token of appreciation,
which will be worthy of my lord's house. And wishing you all happiness and heavenly blessings,
Amen.
    Your lordship, my lord's humble and
    devoted servant
    Rembrandt
    This 12th January
    1639
My lord I live on the Binnen Amstel. The house is
called the sugar bakery.

Huygens did not want the gift of this painting, perhaps
construing it as a bribe. But Rembrandt dispatched it anyway, with an accompanying letter that again broached near
the end the touchy matter of remuneration:

I have read your lordship's agreeable missive of the
fourteenth with extraordinary pleasure. I find there
your lordship's good favor and affection so that I
cordially remain obliged to you to repay your lordship with service and friendship. Because I wish to
do this, I am sending this accompanying canvas,
against my lord's wishes, hoping that you will not
take me amiss in this as it is the first token which I
offer my lord. . . .

. . . I would request you my lord that, whatever
His Highness grants me for the 2 pieces, I may
receive this money here as soon as possible, which
would at the moment be particularly convenient to
me. If it pleases my lord I await an answer to this

and I wish your lordship and your family all happiness and blessings besides my regards.
    Your lordship's humble and
    affectionate servant
    Rembrandt

In haste this 27th January 1639

My lord hang this piece in a strong light and so that
one can stand at a distance from it, then it will
sparkle at its best.

In such haste was Rembrandt to receive his money that
these two new paintings were shipped before they were completely dry. Fresh layers of paint did not bond with those
beneath, and Rembrandt's *Entombment* and *Resurrection*
have been from the start a steady source of income to
restorers.

Rembrandt's covering letter is brief:

My Lord,
It is then with your permission that I send your
lordship these 2 pieces which I think will be considered of such quality that His Highness will now
even pay me not less than a thousand guilders each.
But should His Highness consider that they are not
worth this, he shall pay me less according to his
own pleasure. Relying on His Highness' knowledge and discretion, I shall gratefully be satisfied
with what he says. And with my regards I remain
his
    Humble and devoted servant
    Rembrandt

What I have advanced for the frames and crate is
44 guilders in all.

We learn from Rembrandt's next letter, the sixth in his
slender oeuvre of written work, that he did not get the thousand he'd asked for.

Honored Lord,
I have confidence in the good faith of your lordship
in everything and in particular as regards the remuneration for these last 2 pieces and I believe your
lordship that if the matter had gone according to
your lordship's pleasure and according to right,
there would have been no objection to the price
agreed upon. And as far as the earlier delivered
pieces are concerned, not more than 600 carolus
guilders have been paid for each. And if His Highness cannot in all decency be moved to a higher
price, though they are obviously worth it, I shall be
satisfied with 600 carolus guilders each, provided
that I am also credited for my outlay on the 2 ebony
frames and the crate, which is 44 guilders in all.
So I would kindly request of my lord that I may
now receive my payments here in Amsterdam as
soon as possible, trusting that through the good
favor which is done to me I shall soon enjoy my
money, while I remain grateful for all such friendship. And with regards to my lord and to your lordship's closest friends, all are commended to God
in long-lasting health.
    Your lordship's humble and
    affectionate servant
    Rembrandt

   The payment was authorized immediately, but Rembrandt
didn't know and didn't get it, for the paymaster general, with
the instinct of all paymaster generals to retain the use of other
people's money, informed him dishonestly that the fund from
which the money would come was not complete.
   By frantic inquiry Rembrandt learned the truth.
   It is interesting to compare the *Seventh Epistle* of Plato
with the *Seventh Letter* of Rembrandt. Both are querulous,
wordy, and self-serving. But Rembrandt's is a beggarly re-
minder and complaint:

My Lord,

My noble Lord, it is with hesitation that I come to trouble you with my letter and I am doing so because of what was told me by the collector . . . to whom I complained about the delay of my payment. . . . And this being the true state of affairs, I pray you my kind lord that my warrant might now be prepared at once so that I may now at last receive my well-earned 1244 guilders and I shall always seek to recompense your lordship for this with reverential service and proof of friendship. With this I cordially take leave of my lord and express the hope that God may long keep your lordship in good health and bless you. Amen.

    Your lordship's humble and
    affectionate servant Rembrandt.

I live on the Binnen Amstel in the sugar bakery.

But Rembrandt's *Seventh*, unlike the Plato *Seventh*, is genuinely a letter; whereas the Plato *Epistle* was a vanity piece written for publication to put himself in an excellent light with contemporary readers and with future generations like ours.

And Rembrandt's did produce the money he wanted. Coincidentally, it marks the last time we know of that he and Huygens took notice of each other, although Rembrandt lived thirty years longer, and Huygens lived past ninety and was prolific with diaries.

In July of 1640, Saskia gave birth to another daughter, who died the next month, and on the thirtieth day of the month she died, Rembrandt appointed a lawyer to collect a legacy due Saskia from an aunt who had died six years before.

In September of 1641 Titus was born.

Nine months later Saskia died.

Naming Titus sole heir in the new will drawn several days before her death, she made Rembrandt sole guardian and gave to him the use and the income of her property, on condition he bear the cost of rearing Titus and as long as he did not remarry.

Rembrandt did not remarry, as Geertge Dircx could testify. In 1649 she sued for breach of promise, alleging that:

> . . . the defendant made oral promises to marry her and gave her a ring as a pledge thereof. Furthermore, that he slept with her more than once. She therefore demands that she may be married to the defendant, or otherwise be supported by him.

Rembrandt's written reply, while doubtless influenced by his attorney, was more contemptuous than conciliatory:

> The defendant denies having promised to marry the plaintiff, and furthermore declares that he is not obliged to admit that he slept with her. The plaintiff herself raised the point and will have to come with proof.

The commissioners satisfied neither: they compelled Rembrandt to pay the two hundred guilders annually for her support, but they did not order him to marry her.

Two hundred guilders was forty more than he had offered.

In April of 1650 Geertge gave power of attorney to her brother. And in July her brother joined with Rembrandt in committing her to a house of correction in Gouda. So deftly was this done that Geertge's friends did not know what had become of her until Rembrandt overreached and sought testimony from them to confine her for at least twelve years.

Geertge was released after five years, in late 1655, when Rembrandt was trying desperately to stave off bankruptcy.

In 1655 and 1656, when so much was going against him, Rembrandt nevertheless found time to try to have Geertge recommitted, to have her brother legally detained for a debt of one hundred forty guilders, to have Titus draw a will, and to finish his *Anatomy Lesson of Dr. Jan Deyman*; *Jacob Blessing the Sons of Joseph*; *Christ and the Woman of Samaria*; *Titus at His Desk*; *Titus Reading*; *An Old Woman Reading*; *Hendrickje Bathing*; *Hendrickje at an Open Door*;

two paintings of Joseph accused by Potiphar's wife; two paintings of Alexander (neither the one for Don Antonio); one self-portrait; and, perhaps self-consciously and symbolically as another self-portrait, his *Slaughtered Ox*; and more drawings and etchings than are necessary to catalogue to demonstrate that his fecundity as an artist was no more diminished by adversity in these years of desperation than was his unscrupulous behavior with money and brazen irresponsibility with others.

Rembrandt's *Aristotle* was commissioned in 1652 and finished in 1653, and his literary output for 1653 consists largely of signatures by him to borrow money and collect money.

Between January and March of 1653, he signed a promissory note for 4,180 guilders for a loan from Cornelius Witsen, a prominent political official, who eventually received all the money due him, a promissory note for 1,000 guilders, interest-free, for a loan from Jan Six, who got some of his money back by selling the note at discount, and a note for 4,200 guilders at five percent from an acquaintance, Isaac van Heertsbeck, who got none of his money back.

Twice that year he signed powers of attorney to collect debts, and he also signed his first name to his painting *Aristotle Contemplating the Bust of Homer*. Rembrandt was the first Dutch painter we know of to sign his works with just his first name.

In June the following year, when Aristotle was packed for his passage to Sicily, Hendrickje Stoffels, who was five months pregnant, was about to be summoned by the consistory of the Calvinist Church of Amsterdam to defend herself for having practiced whoredom with the painter Rembrandt.

Rembrandt received a summons too. He threw his away.

He was not a member of that or any other church.

Hendrickje was.

"You would let me go there alone?" she asked, with Aristotle, hammered inside his crate, as witness.

"They don't seem interested in me," said Rembrandt. They had said nothing about his having committed whoredom with her, he pointed out. "There is really nothing they can do to you."

Except excommunicate her.

Church records recount her admitting she "had stained herself by fornication with Rembrandt" and that she was admonished to penitence and excluded from the Lord's Supper.

Three months later she delivered the daughter, Cornelia.

All in all, Aristotle never wavered in his negative assessment of Rembrandt as a human while admiring him as an artist, still treasuring the flashy gold jewelry he wore and still dumbfounded by Rembrandt's layering and glazing and his magical versatility with those shades of red, brown, and black in the muted palette with which he was at his best.

Visitors traveling great distances to watch Aristotle contemplating the bust of Homer in the Metropolitan Museum of Art still whispered compliments. Aristotle noted in darkening dejection that they no longer came hurrying for the sight of him in crowds as numerous and as enthusiastic as at first. He moped. With wounded pride, he convinced himself that he did not approve of large museums as permanent places for paintings of such high quality as his, where masterpieces, such as they were, were commonplace. He frequently appeared on the verge of tears. He felt underappreciated.

He often hoped that somebody nice would kidnap him.

From the year after Hendrickje was excommunicated, we have testimony of sayings by Rembrandt to a woman named Trijn Jacobs, a friend of Geertge's, who told him she was on her way to Gouda to try to effect Geertge's release.

"I would not encourage you to do that," Trijn Jacobs swears he said, pointing his finger at her and adding in a threatening manner: "You will be sorry if you go there."

Upon arriving at Gouda, she was surprised to discover that the magistrate already had received a number of letters from Rembrandt urging that Geertge's detention be continued. These letters do not survive.

When Geertge was freed, she revoked the power of attorney to her brother and made claim against Rembrandt for money owed her for support that year.

Rembrandt was not successful in having her recommitted. We know she soon died.

And in the year she was released, Rembrandt completed the touching Rotterdam canvas *Titus at His Desk*, a painting, jokes Schwartz, that might aptly be called *Titus Writing His Will* but for the simple reason that Rembrandt wrote the boy's will for him.

Titus was fourteen and had less reason for resenting Saskia's family than Rembrandt did. The will named Rembrandt universal heir, excluded any relatives on his mother's side from participating in the estate, and prohibited any third party from interfering with the legacy.

Since the authorship of this will by Titus cannot be authenticated as Rembrandt's, the document is outside the canon of his written work.

Late that year, Rembrandt began taking steps certain to arouse consternation in those from whom he had borrowed money two years before that he had vowed to repay in one.

He rented a hall and began to dispose of possessions in a series of public sales. We do not know what he sold or how much money he obtained. We do know he used none of this money to reduce his debts on the house.

In May of 1656 he transferred the house to Titus.

In thinking to safeguard the house from creditors in the financial collapse he saw coming, he naively underestimated the political power of the burgomaster Witsen to persuade the Insolvency Court to overrule the Chamber of Orphans and sell the house, and to pay him in full before allowing the remainder of the proceeds to be frozen in the interests of Titus.

Just two months after transferring title to the house, Rembrandt applied for a *cessio bonorum*, that is, a voluntary assignment of his assets to creditors, writing that "losses suffered in business as well as damages and losses at sea" were his reasons for insolvency. For Rembrandt this was a fiction. A business bankruptcy was a more honorable form of bankruptcy and afforded greater personal protection. He was safe from jail but penniless.

It is fantastic to recall that in a year of such wrenching experiences, he completed not only his *Anatomy Lesson of Dr. Jan Deyman* but his mesmerizing *Jacob Blessing the Sons of Joseph*, in which powerful construction and exquisite, infallible tonalities meld into a perfect mood of ineffable serenity. No father's son has ever looked more sweetly devoted than Rembrandt's Joseph; blind Jacob, his hand guided by divine providence, gives the blessing to the younger son, Ephraim, while the older Manasseh, and Asenath, Joseph's Egyptian wife, complete the verticals in the geometrical grouping.

The theme of the scene is inheritance.

It was completed in the year of his bankruptcy.

The Anatomy Lesson of Dr. Jan Deyman, unlike the *Dr. Tulp*, is the real thing, in which Rembrandt blends into his own vision the contrasts of Caravaggio with the free brushwork and atmosphere of Titian and other Venetians. Some say Leonardo and Raphael are present too.

The grisly colors are ideal. The dead man looks straight out. The ventral cavity has been opened and emptied. The cap of the skull has been sliced off neatly. Much of the painting has been burned away. What remains unharmed is the cadaver of a man executed the day before for attempting the robbery of a draper's shop, and drawing a knife to resist arrest.

In Amsterdam a man could be executed for stealing a coat and invited to city hall after stealing a fortune.

The inventory of Rembrandt's possessions for the public auctions mandated by his bankruptcy includes among hundreds of items his busts of Homer, Socrates, Aristotle, and sixteen Roman emperors; paintings and drawings by dozens of masters; three shirts, six handkerchiefs, twelve napkins, and three tablecloths; and some collars and cuffs said to be at the laundry. There were more than seventy paintings of his own on sale and hundreds of his drawings.

The auctions took place during the worst recession anyone could remember.

His whole collection, including the seventy paintings and hundreds of drawings by him, brought 2,516 guilders. Six hundred came from his drawings, leaving just over 1,900 for his seventy paintings and all of the rest, less than four times more than he had received for just the *Aristotle*.

Shares in the Dutch East India Company plummeted too.

The house went up for auction in 1658, the same year he completed the majestic self-portrait now in the Frick Collection in New York, in which, lushly attired in a fur mantle and a gown of gold, he sits in a chair as though filling a throne, rests his fingers around a silver-topped cane that could be a scepter, and looks as regal, perhaps, as Mr. Henry Clay Frick, of the steel industry, did himself, as baronial, perhaps, as Frick, Cornelius Vanderbilt, Henry Ford, John Pierpont Morgan, and Lorenzo de' Medici rolled into one.

You would not guess you were looking at a bankrupt.

Four paintings by Rembrandt put up as collateral for a loan of one hundred sixteen guilders were ordered sold by the court and brought just over ninety-five.

A guild rule barred an artist who liquidated his paintings from ever again dealing in artworks in Amsterdam.

Rembrandt found a way around that one, using Titus and Hendrickje, with a written contract designating him an employee of an art-dealing company formed by the two: in return for board and lodgings and small sums of money advanced for living expenses, which could *not* be used for the retirement of debts, he would act as adviser and give to the firm all new works produced in his lifetime.

They lived in the house on the Rozengracht in the Jordaan, where the rent was two hundred twenty-five guilders a year.

We do not know how the second commission from Don Antonio Ruffo originated. But in 1661 the *Aristotle* was in Messina when Rembrandt's *Alexander* arrived.

Never in his lifetime had Aristotle heard such ferocious cursing! The air rang wildly with disgusting obscenities and horrifying threats of Sicilian vengeance. For several days men walked around armed. A fiery nephew with a rapier looked wickedly at Aristotle in a glittering temper and shouted he would like to cut off his balls too.

Signor Ruffo recovered from his shock eventually and called in a scribe.

Of the more than two hundred paintings in his collection, which consisted of pieces from the best masters in Europe, he dictated softly, straining to keep calm, no other painting was put together like this one out of four pieces of cloth sewed together. The seams were frightful. Clearly, the painting was originally a head which Rembrandt decided to make into a half-length by sewing on pieces.

To compensate for this disservice, Signor Ruffo would be willing to keep the *Alexander* and take the proposed *Homer* for two hundred fifty guilders, not the five hundred asked. Otherwise, he threatened to return the *Alexander*, for a person was not obliged to keep a painting so expensive that was nevertheless so faulty.

Rembrandt, whose paintings in forced sales had averaged well under thirty guilders each, was anything but humble in reply to this patron contracting to pay five hundred. This last written work we have by Rembrandt has come down to us only in translation.

> I am greatly surprised by the manner in which they report of the Alexander, which is done so wonderfully well. I believe there cannot be many art lovers in Messina. In addition Your Lordship complains about both the price and the canvas, but if Your Lordship wishes to send the piece back, at your expense and at your own risk, I will make another Alexander. As regards the canvas, I found I had too little while painting, so that it was necessary to add to its length, but if the painting is hung in the proper light, no one will notice this at all.

Should Your Lordship be satisfied with the Alexander this way, everything is in order. Should Your
Lordship not wish to keep the said Alexander, the
lowest price for a new one is 600 guilders. And the
Homer is 500 and the cost of the canvas. The expenses are of course for Your Lordship's account.

Should you wish another piece to be executed,
would you be so kind as to send me the exact mea-
surements for the dimensions you desire. I await
your reply for my guidance.
Rembrandt van Rijn.

In the end, Don Antonio caved in, sighing loudly, rolling
his eyes, and gazing helplessly at Aristotle, to whom he said:
"Who can argue with a madman like that?"

Aristotle looked aside in inexpressible sympathy.

Ruffo kept the *Alexander* (today we wish we knew where
it was) and ordered the *Homer*, paying five hundred guilders.

Rembrandt appeared unconquerable.

In 1661 he did his *Portrait of the Artist as the Apostle Paul*,
in which he is wearing a brimless baker's cap and reading
what is unmistakably a facsimile of *The Wall Street Journal*.

The painter most in demand in Amsterdam in this period
had been Govert Flinck, who died in 1660. For the new town
hall, numerous artists had been asked to contribute paintings. Rembrandt was not among them. To Flinck had gone
the commission of grandeur: twelve paintings for the main
gallery at a thousand guilders each, most portraying the revolt against the Romans of the Batavian people, from whom
the Dutch were said to descend.

When Flinck died while preparing his drawings, the town
fathers selected Rembrandt for just the first, *The Conspiracy
of Claudius Civilis: The Oath.*

His huge painting was rejected and was returned to him
after a year.

See it in Stockholm and you will understand why. It is
anything but decorative. In ochers and umbers laid on with

a palette knife, he offered the community and visitors to the town hall a very good view of the one blind eye in the grizzled face of the primitive leader which we know from Tacitus is correct historically.

Rembrandt received nothing for it but the canvas. Probably, he was disappointed.

The work was huge, the largest ever painted by Rembrandt, the original measuring almost nineteen feet in one direction and almost nineteen feet in the other. To make it more salable and to make use of the canvas—we assume with safety—Rembrandt himself cut down by nearly four-fifths a work that would have ranked in epic scale and overwhelming impact with Raphael's *School of Athens* as one of the majestic masterpieces of Western painting.

The year after that he sold Saskia's grave. The price is unknown.

Probably, he was disappointed.

Hendrickje was ailing.

In 1662, the same year he sold Saskia's grave and worked on the *Homer* for Ruffo, he completed the great group portrait *The Sampling Officials of the Clothmakers' Guild*, which is as often called *The Portrait of the Syndics of the Clothmakers' Guild*, and in this year too, perhaps, he did another of the great paintings of his final years, his glorious and mystifying *The Jewish Bride*.

The *Syndics* is certainly among the greatest group portraits in the world. Alongside this Rembrandt, Leonardo's *Last Supper* fades away.

Keep in mind that when we talk of a great painting we are not really talking about anything great. We are talking of only a painting.

In Rembrandt's great painting *The Syndics of the Clothmakers' Guild*, the ingenious composition is made complete only by eye contact with the staring spectator, at whom the unsmiling officials in the painting stare right back. We have interrupted them. They do not like us and want us to go. Try to imagine these officials unobserved in the Rijksmuseum and it is hard to imagine them doing anything but their work.

They work to make money.

In *The Jewish Bride*, almost everything seems wrong in a picture that is absolutely right.

The man and woman look funny. We don't know who they are, or the year the painting was completed, or why it is called *The Jewish Bride*. They are not thinking of each other. Neither relates to the viewer. The infinity of glazes and layers and daubs on the right sleeve of the man could not possibly be copied by any hand other than the one that painted the left sleeve of the woman too and united both figures in that stunning embrasure of radiant color. His hand on her breast is a startling intimacy in a scene with no others. They are lost in thought in worlds apart. No interpretation yet advanced of this enigmatic monument in pictorial art makes sense. We don't know who these two people are, or who they are supposed to be, or what they are doing there. We don't even know that they are married, and neither the man nor the woman looks any more Jewish than you or I.

More popularly recognized than these two paintings is Rembrandt's unforgettable masterpiece *The Man in the Gilt Helmet* in West Berlin, which is not by Rembrandt. Now that we're told it is not by Rembrandt, it does not seem like much of a painting.

In the 1920s more than seven hundred paintings were attributed to Rembrandt. By 1969 the number had fallen to four hundred. Studies from Wall Street predict that by the end of this century, there will be *no* Rembrandts left, and not much interest in books about the most eminent Dutch painter of the seventeenth century of whose works we have none and who, conceivably, might never have painted.

Hendrickje died in 1663, around the age of forty, probably from the plague. She was buried in a rented grave. We do not know what the rent was.

What little she had she left to Cornelia, naming Rembrandt guardian.

One year after she passed away, New Amsterdam was surrendered at the start of the Second Anglo-Dutch War to an approaching body of fewer than two hundred Englishmen and was renamed New York.

It was surrendered without a struggle by the Dutch director general of New Netherland, Peter Stuyvesant, who had a wooden leg and was a bigot, fostering the religious persecution of Catholics, Jews, Anglicans, and Protestant dissenters of all denominations differing with the teachings of the strict Calvinists there.

He gave up Wall Street.

Try getting it back now without a fight.

From the number of sites, organizations, and institutions in New York City named after Peter Stuyvesant you would assume they were commemorating a figure in history with more to his credit than surrender and bigotry.

In September of 1665 Titus attained his maturity and received the 6,952 guilders left of his mother's bequest. God knows what became of that money, for the year after that they were behind with the rent.

Titus married in 1668 and moved out.

Titus died.

He died less than a year after he married, while Isaac Newton was constructing his reflecting telescope and the Dutchman Antony van Leeuwenhoek, looking at human blood under another of his microscopes, was providing the first accurate description of red corpuscles.

His young widow, Magdalana van Loo, soon was alleging that Rembrandt was misappropriating assets left by Titus that legitimately belonged to her and her infant child.

The last words by Rembrandt we know of were said to a housemaid:

"I have to draw on the savings of Cornelia to cover our living expenses."

Luckily for both, he did not live much longer.

Rembrandt died in 1669, a year after Titus, at the age of sixty-three.

The widow of Titus was buried thirteen days later.

Surviving Rembrandt were Cornelia, who was fifteen, and the granddaughter, Titia, seven months.

In his house at his death were four unfinished works, and twenty-two others described as both finished and unfinished.

It is delightful to report that news of his death brought a shock of remorse to a country that had forgotten he was alive, and that the sudden increase in the value of the paintings in his estate was sufficient to provide comfortably for his daughter and his granddaughter for the rest of their lives.

But it isn't true.

Constantijn Huygens does not even mention his death in a copious diary in which you will find noted the deaths of other Dutch artists you won't hear of again.

The guardian of Titia filed legal action against the guardian of Cornelia on grounds she was illegitimate and excluded from sharing in anything of value that might remain.

Rembrandt did not own even that one mina which Socrates offered at his trial in exchange for his life.

Cornelia married the son of her guardian and moved to Batavia in the Dutch East Indies, where she bore two children, a boy and a girl. The one she named Rembrandt, the other Hendrickje.

The year Rembrandt died, the Venetians lost Crete to the Turks, the last of their colonial possessions.

XIII

PLATO

27

THAT PLATO DID GO TO SICILY WE KNOW FOR CERTAIN FROM his thirteen *Epistles*, of which five, and perhaps all thirteen, are spurious.

The Greek physician and writer Galen, living in Rome in the second century after Christ, reports that libraries there were already paying high prices for manuscripts by illustrious figures from the past, creating a market with rich rewards for spurious documents by skillful forgers.

The document in which Galen says this may be spurious. The avarice of man is insatiable, says Aristotle.

In Sicily Plato did not have much personal rapport with the free-living, pleasure-loving, self-indulgent Greeks among whom he had come as a man of wisdom and something of a savior. These were people, he complained later in his *Seventh Epistle*, who ate full meals twice a day and never slept alone at night.

In Athens, he was something of a joke for his gravity and self-importance, and he was the frequent target of the comic poets, and of taunting barbs by such as Diogenes, who found him pretentious and his lectures, he said, a boring waste of time.

When Plato read his dialogue *On the Soul*, says Favorinus, Aristotle alone, of all in the audience, stayed to the end, while the rest stood up and walked away.

Plato said of the soul, which he decided was immortal, that by transmigration it put on many bodies and had a numerical first principle. The body, on the other hand, had a first principle that was geometrical.

Aristotle was not positive this made sense to him.

The soul, said Plato, was vital breath diffused in all directions.

Aristotle was not positive this made sense either.

Plato said also of the soul that it is self-moved and tripartite, the rational part of it having its seat in the head, the passionate part about the heart, while the hungering part was placed in the region of the navel and the liver.

He said more of the soul than anyone else has ever said of the soul. It exists before we are born and outlives the body after we die. It is older than all created matter, older than the universe.

From the center outward, the soul enclosed the body on all sides in a circle, was compounded of elements, and, being divided at harmony intervals, formed two circles that touched each other twice, and with the interior circle, which was slit six times over, made seven circles in all.

The interior circle of the soul moved by way of the diagonal to the left, and the other, the outer circle, moved by way of the side to the right. Thus, the one was supreme, because it was a single circle, while the other interior circle was divided. The supreme is the circle of the Same, the latter is the circle of the Other, by which he meant to say, said Plato, that the motion of the soul was the motion of the universe together with the revolutions of the planets.

When Plato talked of the soul, Aristotle's mind often wandered to jewelry and girls.

Of the two universal principles of God and matter, Plato

held that matter was without form and unlimited, that composite substances arose from it, and that it was all once in disorderly motion but, inasmuch as God preferred order to disorder, was brought together in one place. This matter, Plato said, was converted into the elements of fire, water, air, and earth, of which the world and all things in it are formed.

Plato said of these four elements that the earth alone is not subject to change, and only because of the peculiarity of its constituent triangles.

In the other three elements, he explained, the geometric figures employed are homogeneous, the scalene triangle out of which they were all put together being one and the same. Whereas for earth a triangle of peculiar shape had been employed. The element of fire was a pyramid, of air an octahedron, of water an icosahedron, but of earth a cube. Hence, earth was never transmuted into the other three elements, nor the other three into earth.

Everything was geometric.

Aristotle often was numb.

Plato was the first to introduce arguments by means of question and answer, the first to explain the method of solving problems by analysis, the first who employed the terms "antipodes," "element," "dialectic," "quality," "oblong number," "plane superficies," and also "divine providence" in philosophical discussion, and the first to study the significance of grammar.

Plato's faith in the superiority of pure thought over inductive reasoning enabled him to absorb the wishful thinking of Orphism into his speculations on the immortality of the soul and on the unchanging world of ideas and the spirit.

Orphism derived from the tale of Orpheus, one of several pre-Christian resurrection stories found in Greek mythology, the tales of Persephone and Adonis being others.

Orpheus of course never lived.

Orphics maintained that there was a soul and that it was

of divine creation, and that it was imprisoned in our bodies, which tend to defile it and are therefore unworthy of it.

The struggle in life is to keep the soul pure in this world to inherit blessedness in the next. After death, said the Orphics, the pure go to eternal bliss, the incurably evil to eternal suffering, and the rest suffer purgatorial pains, atoning each sin ten times over until the time comes around to be reincarnated and born again.

They were vegetarians.

Plato absorbed much of this, and his Theory of Ideas, with his introduction of a spiritual life, and his insistence on the supremacy of the spiritual life over the corporeal, is considered possibly the most important contribution ever made to the philosophy of religion.

This is not saying very much.

It is stated of Plato that by his Idealism, by his sense of an unchanging real world behind the visible world of the senses, and by his conception of God and the relation of religion to morality, he exercised a profound influence on Cicero, Quintilian, St. Augustine, Spenser, Addison, Coleridge, Shelley, and Wordsworth.

For all of these he may be forgiven too.

When young, Plato wrote love poems to young men and young women that were dreadful.

He wrote a play he intended for the city competition but consigned it to flames after meeting Socrates. He so feared the tender effects of music that he restricted its presentation in both of the prison states he projected as ideal.

That Plato could recognize a joke is clear from the multitude he gave to Socrates. In his *Laws*, there is no Socrates and there are no jokes.

Plato the teacher defined man as animal, biped, and featherless, and was extolled for this illuminating description.

Diogenes plucked a chicken and brought it to Plato's next lecture, saying, "Here is Plato's man."

Plato added to his definition "and having broad nails."

We have it from Diogenes Laertius that Socrates, on hearing Plato read his *Lysis*, exclaimed: "By Heracles, what a number of lies this young man is telling about me!"

About systems of government, Plato found out early what the rest of us learn later: All are sooner or later deficient. So he invented one of his own. It stinks.

Plato's *Republic*, that work in which Socrates, of course, is the genial personality throughout, is a literary account in dialogue form of a conversation occupying about four hundred pages that ostensibly took place one evening in 421 B.C., approximately fifty years before publication, when Plato was just seven.

His ideal republic was a communist state in which a fascist corps of guardians maintained order for a governing elite of philosophers, notwithstanding that all the philosophers known to him and his friends, they agreed, either were unscrupulous rogues or were held by the world to be useless.

Property and wives were owned by the community and shared in common. Children would be separated at birth from their natural mothers and reared in community groups, and no mother in this perfect world would know her own child, no father be sure he was one.

Plato thought more of women than Aristotle ever did and believed they should be given the same duties and education as men.

"Should we let them go naked on the wrestling ground as men do?" he has Socrates say. "This might seem absurd at the start, especially to see old women exercising with old men, but we can get used to it."

Plato was at the trial, or has Socrates *say* he was there in the *Apology* Plato wrote, and if he had lied, there were literary rivals like Xenophon to expose him.

It is impossible to overestimate the feelings of rivalry that could exist between one Greek philosopher and another, between gifted teacher and gifted pupil.

It is easy to picture the relish with which Aristotle noted at the outset of his *Nicomachean Ethics* that, while Plato had been dear to him, he loved truth more. Or the exasperation that might rack him upon learning that the impact of Plato on future generations was greater than his own.

Aristotle has been called the father of logic, psychology, political science, literary criticism, physics, physiology, biology and other natural sciences, aesthetics, epistemology, cosmology, metaphysics, and the scientific study of language, and. he had more to say on the subject of ethics than anyone else.

It stands to reason Plato would have the wider appeal.

Christian Fathers in the Middle Ages, writes Hamilton, said they found in the first sentence of Plato's *Timaeus* a foreknowledge of the Trinity. The first sentence, spoken by Socrates, reads as follows:

"One, two, three, but where, my dear Timaeus, is the fourth of those who were yesterday my guests and are to be my entertainers today?"

Plato at the trial heard Socrates, found guilty and granted a last opportunity to plead for a lesser penalty than death, say:

"Why should I?"

Since Socrates did not know if death was a good or an evil, he did not fear it. And since he was convinced that he had never wronged another, he would assuredly not wrong himself by proposing any penalty that would be an evil.

"Shall I say imprisonment?"

Why should he live in prison and be the slave of the jailers of the year—of the official Eleven?

"Or shall the penalty be a fine, and my days spent in prison until the fine is paid?"

That would be the same, because money he had none in any substantial amount and would have to lie in prison anyway. If, on the other hand, he did have the money, he remarked trenchantly, he might suggest a fine he could afford to pay, and then be not much the worse off for the crime of which he had been found guilty.

"Or should I say exile?"

This might possibly be the punishment they would most likely accept and the one they expected him to request.

But he would not let them off that easily.

He did not wish to go anywhere else. "I must indeed be blinded by a desperate love of life if I am so irrational as to expect that when you, who are my fellow citizens, cannot endure my discourses and words, and have found them so grievous and odious that you will have no more of them, others are likely to endure me. No, indeed, men of Athens, that is not very probable. And what kind of life should I lead, at my age, wandering from city to city, ever changing my place of exile, and always being driven out? For I am quite sure that wherever I go, there, as here, the young men will flock to talk to me. If I drive them away, their elders will drive me out at their request; and if I talk to them freely, their elders will drive me out for their own sakes, as you wish to do now."

Could he not simply hold his tongue when he went somewhere else?

No, he could not.

"Now, I know I may have great difficulty in making you understand this. For if I tell you that this would be a disobedience to God, and that therefore I cannot hold my tongue, you will not believe that I am serious. And if I say again that daily to discourse about virtue, and of those other things about which you hear me examining myself and others, is the greatest good of man, and if I say that the unexamined life is not worth living—you are still less likely to believe me. And yet what I say is true, although it is hard to persuade you."

He had gone about the city questioning people, hoping to find a man wiser than himself. He thought this would not take long, for he knew that he himself had no wisdom, small or great.

"And I swear to you, Athenians, by the dog I swear!—for I must tell you the truth—the result of my mission was this: I found that the men most in repute were all but the most foolish; and that others less esteemed were wiser and better.''

He went first to one with a reputation for wisdom, a politician whose name he would not mention, and he could not help thinking that the man was not really wise, although he was thought wise by many, and thought still wiser by himself.

"So I left him, saying to myself: Well, although I do not suppose that either of us knows anything really beautiful and good, I am better off than he is, for he knows nothing and thinks that he knows, whereas I neither know nor think that I know."

Then he went to another with still higher pretensions of wisdom, and his conclusion was the same.

"Whereupon I made another enemy."

Politicians resented finding out from him that they could not talk wisely about the policies they advocated.

Gifted poets also could not talk well about their best passages or explain the source of their inspiration.

"I took them some of the most elaborate passages in their own writings, and asked what the meaning was, thinking they would teach me something. And will you believe me? There is hardly a person present here today who would not have talked better about their poetry than they did themselves."

Yet because they were known to be poets, they believed themselves to be the wisest men in other things in which they were not wise.

The artisans he spoke to suffered that same defect in intelligence, which overshadowed their virtues. They did indeed know many things of which he was ignorant, and in this they were certainly wiser than he was. But even the good artisans fell into the same error as the poets—because they were good workmen and knowledgeable in one thing, they believed they also were knowledgeable in all sorts of high matters, and they had the conceit that they knew things that were beyond them.

And Socrates conceived himself superior to all of them in one singular respect: Socrates knew that he did not know.

"And these investigations have led to my having many enemies of the worst and most dangerous kind, and have given occasion also to many calumnies. For my hearers always imagine that I myself possess the wisdom which I find wanting in others."

Whereas his wisdom consisted in knowing that his wisdom was worth nothing and that only God was wise.

What penalty could he recommend as being most just?

"Clearly, that which is my due," he said. "What shall be done to the man who never had the wit to lead a quiet life and has been careless about the things most men care about: wealth, and a comfortable home, and family interests, and military offices, and speaking in the Assembly, and magistracies, and political plots, and secret party organizations? Reflecting that I was really too honest a man to be a politician and live, I did not go to where I could do no good to you or to myself, but went about privately and tried to persuade every man among you to look to himself and seek virtue and wisdom before he looks to his private interests, and to look to the character of the state before he looks to its interests. What shall be done to such a man if that's the sort of person I am? Doubtless some good thing, O men of Athens, if the penalty proposed is really to match my deserts, and the good should be of a kind appropriate to my condition. Well, what would be a reward suitable to a poor man who is your benefactor and who desires the leisure that he may continue to instruct you?"

Nothing could be more fitting for a person such as himself, he told them, than maintenance by the city on an exalted scale usually bestowed upon victors at Olympia. This is what he proposed, and this reward of free maintenance in the Prytaneum was one he asserted he deserved far more than the citizen who had won the prize in the Olympics in the horse or chariot race.

"I need it more. I am in want, and he has enough. And

he gives you only the appearance of happiness. I give you the reality.''

Earlier he had told them right out: "O men of Athens, I say to you, do as Anytus bids or not as Anytus bids, and either acquit me or not; but whichever you do, understand that I am not going to alter my ways, even if I have to die a hundred deaths—men of Athens! Do not interrupt, but hear me! I thought there was an understanding between us that you should hear me to the end. I have something else to say at which you may be inclined to cry out, but I believe that to hear me will be good for you. I would have you know that if you kill such a one as I am, you will injure yourselves more than you will injure me.''

At the end, he condescended to pay a fine of the one mina he thought he could afford.

Then he added: "But my friends here, Plato, Crito, Critobulus, and Apollodorus, want me to say thirty minae, for which they will be the guarantors, so let the penalty be thirty minae, for which sum they will be ample security to you.''

Clearly, this was not the cringing plea for clemency expected by a complacent jury of five hundred one men who might be predisposed to grant it.

He was found guilty by a vote of two hundred eighty to two hundred twenty-one. A shift of thirty, he said, would have made the difference.

He was surprised only by the tally, he said. As he'd committed no crime, he gibed without fear, he'd been certain the margin for conviction would be larger.

The vote for death was larger: three hundred sixty to one hundred forty-one.

Eighty jurors voted he be put to death for the crimes they believed he had not committed.

28

THE LARGER MAJORITY FOR THE DEATH SENTENCE FOR SOC-
rates was not helpful to the pleadings of the tanner Asclepius
at his own trial one month later. The vote was a precious
freedom in Athens, Anytus scolded at the pretrial examination. Asclepius had twice wasted his by being in the minority
and voting to exonerate a criminal whom the bulk of his
fellow citizens had first found guilty and then ordered executed.

So far as Asclepius could judge, nothing at the trial at-
tested to the guilt of Socrates for any of the crimes with which
he had been charged.

What difference did that make? Anytus snapped. What
mattered was that most people thought him guilty, wanted
him guilty, and voted him guilty, and Asclepius had not. The
integrity of the system was at issue, not the life of one man
of seventy.

And the system had worked.

Asclepius admitted under oath that he had never lent a

cock or any other fowl to Socrates or provided him with any goods or services of equivalent value.

Maintaining his innocence in the face of so much that was incriminating was proof to his prosecutors of an unwillingness to admit guilt.

Why had Socrates said he owed a cock to Asclepius if indeed he did not?

"Maybe," ventured Asclepius uncertainly, "he was referring to the god of healing and talking about a sacrifice."

"Why would a man on the point of dying owe a sacrifice to the god of healing?"

That did not make much sense to the suspect either.

"Is it possible he was joking?" he suggested lamely.

"After drinking the hemlock?"

The tanner was at his wit's end.

He vaguely remembered that Socrates at his trial had said he was not afraid of dying and therefore may have been jesting. The others had no recollection.

There was nothing in the record.

Plato had not yet published his *Apology*.

The record did show that Plato and others known to be associated with Socrates had prudently withdrawn temporarily from Athens after the execution, in fear, probably, of a bloodbath.

Asclepius, however, had not, arousing curiosity over his complacency, as though he'd not just been implicated by the last words of a prisoner.

Asclepius answered that since he had done nothing wrong, he took for granted he had nothing to fear.

There were guilty people in Athens committing criminal acts every day who knew they would not be punished.

What right had anyone innocent to assume he was safe from the law?

The penalty demanded was death.

29

PLATO LIVED ANOTHER FIFTY YEARS. HE WROTE HIS BOOKS. He founded his Academy. And he gradually abandoned hope in the potential of men and societies to improve themselves.

Every existing community was misgoverned, he wrote in his *Seventh Epistle*, if his *Seventh Epistle* was indeed written by him. If the *Seventh Epistle* was not written by Plato, it was written by someone as good as Plato at writing like Plato.

All states, said Plato, were governed by the selfish interests of the ruling class. And the reform of existing institutions was therefore no less difficult than the establishment of new ones.

Convinced that knowledge is virtue and that all knowledge is innate in all men and could be uncovered through untiring search, he vested his faith for a model community in the concept of a "virtuous tyrant," a man with absolute power who was altruistic enough to become his philosopher king. And three times he went to Sicily when deluding himself into believing he had one.

His first time in Syracuse, the tyrant-ruler there vacillated, it is said, between having him killed and selling him into slavery, and decided on the latter. He was rescued from slavery, goes the tale, by a fortuitous coincidence of Aristotelian dramatic recognition of very low caliber, and by a generous ransom from a benefactor to gain his release.

The next time he went, the father was dead and Dionysius II was installed, and Plato had a powerful sponsor in the new ruler's uncle; the powerful sponsor was exiled on suspicion of importing the philosopher to warp the ruler's brain with philosophy and seize power for himself.

Plato was old when summoned the third time and went against his better judgment. He found himself under house arrest for months and was released only after appeals by intellectuals from other parts of the island.

Returning to his own country, says Diogenes Laertius, he thereafter refrained from meddling in politics ever again, although his writings showed a continuing interest in the measures and institutions of government.

Having been born in the eighty-eighth Olympiad, on the seventh day of the month Thargelion, he was now about seventy.

At seventy, he explained his failures in Syracuse by writing that no city could remain in tranquillity under any laws whatsoever "when men think it right to squander all their property in extravagant excesses, and consider it a duty to be idle in everything else except eating and drinking and the laborious prosecution of debauchery."

Completing his Sicilian mortifications was that Dionysius II, when overthrown and exiled, fancying himself an expert in philosophy now, published a book elucidating Plato's.

It was in tart reaction to this travesty that Plato asserted surprisingly in his *Seventh Epistle* that there neither was nor ever would be a treatise of his on the doctrines to which he devoted himself. Unless, of course, Plato was indeed not the author of his seventh letter. In which case, it is conceivable he never set foot in Sicily at all.

His kind of knowledge could not be communicated in words, he wrote, but was kindled in one soul suddenly like a flame of belief that leaped to it like light from another soul.

These are strange words from a man who taught with words until the day of his death.

He died after a wedding party. It was not from overeating.

One regrets that he did not live long enough to finish the *Laws* and rewrite for coherence and clarity these garrulous instructions by an elderly Athenian Stranger to two listeners for a Model City in which the only freedom was the freedom to obey, and in which Plato himself would have been prohibited from making that same discourse, and all his earlier ones.

All power in his new community of the *Laws* would be vested in the elderly, said the elderly Plato, because the elderly were conservatives.

There were slaves.

There were twelve tribes, and in each tribe there were four classes of people, and, as in the ancient Athens of Solon, the classes were determined by property. Excessive wealth was banished, the pursuit of gain forbidden; husbandry and trade were forbidden too. Yet the ruling Senate would contain only men from his twelve tribes who had property and rank.

Denouncing wealth, he gave power to the wealthy.

And here was classical Greek oligarchy again, which always comes triumphantly to the fore, no matter what else you name it. Aristotle was probably the first to observe in writing that property is the chief means to political power under all constitutions. And it therefore followed, he stated in his *Politics*, that the granting of extra privileges to non-ruling citizens without property does little to strengthen their power and a great deal to keep them contented.

Voting is one of those extra privileges that hardly ever have much effect on public policy or the redistribution of property or political power.

Said Cornelius Vanderbilt, whom some biographical dictionaries still, archaically, call an American capitalist of the nineteenth century: "Law? What do I care about the law? H'ain't I got the power?" Lacking higher education, Cornelius Vanderbilt nevertheless formulated into simple English the principle of political science known everywhere now as Vanderbilt's First Law of Government.

Today in America there are no longer any capitalists: they are industrialists, small businessmen, developers, financiers, promoters, and philanthropists.

We forget the name of the prominent American family whose financial dynasty began with the selling of rotten meat to the government during the Civil War. Or the other who sold blankets contaminated with smallpox disease to tribes of American Indians. Or the other who gave cattle salt to lick and water to drink before bringing them in to be weighed in the meat markets in New York. We remember the name of the man who financed the sale of condemned muskets to the Union Army. It was J. P. Morgan.

Today sound business decisions of that kind are made by blue-chip corporations.

Maritime states are unstable and given to the pursuit of gain, said Plato, and added that cities of merchants and shopkeepers would be unfriendly and unfaithful, to other nations and to their own citizens.

After World War II, in 1947, the U.S. Department of War, an institution of American government since 1789, was abolished and subsequently reconstituted as the Department of Defense; the Secretary of War was renamed the Secretary of Defense.

And from that day to the present, the United States of America was never again in danger of war.

It was in danger of defense.

A city armed against its neighbor, says Plato, could not but cause a neighboring city fear, could not but incite it to arm in its own defense, could not, therefore, but make real the peril it feared, or avoid generating an unending arms race that was likely to lead to the war it started out to deter.

It was William Henry Vanderbilt, the son of Cornelius,

who in 1882 laid the foundation for the study of political science as an academic discipline with the dictum now known universally as Vanderbilt's Second Law of Government:

"The public be damned."

In totalitarian countries like China and Russia the public is damned by decree, regimentation, police, and terror.

In the industrial democracies it is damned by neglect.

And favoritism.

In Plato's *Laws*, which seeks to remedy all ills, there are prescriptions by the score, and there are prescriptions for the punishment of those who flout them.

"You have a low opinion of man," observes one of his listeners.

Human affairs are hardly worth serious consideration, says Plato's Athenian Stranger, whose audience of two can scarcely get a comment in edgewise throughout all twelve books of meandering observations of equal antipathy and malignance.

In comparison to the Plato of the *Laws*, Jonathan Swift is Santa Claus.

Human affairs may not be worth consideration to Plato, but among the classes of religious criminals he marks out for severe punishment are those who believe, as Aristotle did in his *Metaphysics*, that the gods take no heed of human affairs.

The Plato of the *Laws* was more severe than the juror-judges who had sentenced Socrates to death for impiety and indicted Aristotle later on that same charge.

Anybody teaching Homer or any other work in which the gods were not always just, moral, and benevolent to men and to each other would be imprisoned for five years for a first offense. For a second he would suffer death without burial.

Hesiod and Homer, said Plato, told lies of the worst sort. He does not say who told lies of a better sort.

All children would be educated in a uniform manner: if they played the same games under the same rules in the same conditions and had pleasure from the same toys, they would be alike in adult life and have no taste for novelty and no wish to change the laws and customs of the state.

At festivals there would be three choruses, one of children, another of youths, a third of men of thirty to sixty, and they would voice this same refrain:

"Virtue and happiness are inseparable."

The law was supreme, of course. Guardians were watched by Scrutineers, and the Scrutineers observed by a Nocturnal Council, but all the rulers were merely the ministers of the law, which was perfect and unchangeable.

Plato still thought more of women than Aristotle did. He believed they could learn, and women would receive the same education as men, in order to cease being the useless burdens they had always been.

His citizens would number five thousand forty.

This constitution he was outlining would not be the best of all constitutions, Plato's Athenian Stranger regretted with some pique and vexation. The best, the communism of his earlier *Republic*, would be abandoned as unsuitable for citizens reared as his would be.

His citizens would not be good enough for his communism of the *Republic*.

Now men would have to have their own wives and children, and each man would be given an equal allotment of land.

The left hand would be trained to be equal to the right.

Children would not be permitted to walk during the first three years of life, to safeguard their tender limbs from deformity caused by too early exercise. However, they would be carried about by nurses without stop, for motion had magical properties salutary to the constitution of humans.

Motion was no less beneficial to the soul, Plato's Athenian Stranger knew, quieting fears and promoting courage and cheerfulness.

No usury and no dowries were permitted.

And any head of a household who disgraced his family by peddling for profit would be imprisoned for one year the first time, two years the second, and so on.

The state was to be virtuous not wealthy, for both at once no state could be.

Cities constructed on his model would be distant from the coast to avoid the import-export activities of unnecessary products that threaten a state with the flood of gold and silver which is always fatal to noble and just habits of life.

Retailing—that contemptible but indispensable practice of buying products at one price and selling them at a higher one, selling them despicably, so to say, for more than their true value—was restricted to foreigners and resident aliens. And those who were more than a little successful at making money and accumulated wealth would not be tolerated.

Plato had already noticed in his *Republic* that people in business were commonly those who were weakest in bodily strength and therefore of little use for any other purpose.

Like motion, numbers too had sacred metaphysical properties, and all of the proportions and ratios he specified were inviolate. His five thousand forty citizens must never be allowed to increase or diminish. He gave more ways than we want to know for stabilizing the population at five thousand forty.

People would rise early and keep busy, for the sleeping man was no better than the dead man, and nature has shown that we do not need as much sleep as we enjoy getting.

Aristotle going through these unedited and unrevised literary remains of his mentor found more laws about trade and marketing than he could keep track of, and laws even for the posting of new laws regulating commerce, money, and profits.

Hunger, thirst, and sexual excitement, three needs and desires innate in man, were morbid conditions, Aristotle read with lingering incredulity; and Plato would keep them in check with the three greatest forces affecting human behavior—fear, law, and true reasoning.

Life in his state was to be good, not pleasurable.

Emigration was allowed only for colonization when the population of citizens exceeded five thousand forty. No one under forty could travel to a foreign country, and no one over forty could ever go in a private capacity.

There were three prisons: one near the market for the average criminal; a second near the assembly room of officials of the Nocturnal Council, which held nightly assemblies; and a third, situated in the middle of the country, in the wildest and loneliest spot possible.

Peace is better than war, said Plato, and conciliation better than conquest. But he would arm his state in that same way which could not but cause fear in a neighboring state and lead it to arm for war.

Men would train for war continually, and not just in wartime but while they were living in peace. Every month, for not less than a whole day, the state must carry out a march, paying no heed to cold weather or hot, in which all would join in—men, women, and children.

No one under fifty could compose a speech of praise or censure for public ceremonies, and no one anytime could sing an unauthorized song.

In Plato's *Laws* the soul must be duly honored as the most divine element of man's nature.

Mendicant priests who offered for any kind of fee to intercede with the gods to win the favor of Heaven, and to bring up the dead from Hades, would be imprisoned during life. Never again would they hold intercourse with their fellows, and when they died their bodies would be cast beyond the borders without burial.

Such were the conclusions in the mature writings of this pagan Greek philosopher who provided a philosophical rationale for Western religions that did not have one before, and have not found a better one since, and whose hatred of mankind was a match for his own.

"It is the incurable wickedness of man that makes the work of the legislator a sad necessity," declared Plato.

For the incurable wickedness of the legislator he gave no efficacious remedy.

Rich friends of Solon used inside knowledge to make themselves richer.

The oracle at Delphi was known to take bribes.

XIV

ARISTOTLE

30

ARISTOTLE WAS PRACTICALLY ALMOST POSITIVE THAT Alexander probably had really not had very much to do with the assassination of his father. About the mother, Olympias, he could not be that definite.

Between the two, resistance to the idea of Alexander as king did not last long.

It took him only days, with strong help from his mother, to accomplish the necessary murders and executions of nobles opposed to his succession, and but a few months longer to quell the rebellions in Greek cities reluctant, at first, to accept the continuation of Macedonian hegemony.

Olympias herself disposed of the most appealing of his rivals, the infant son of Philip's newest young favorite, Cleopatra, a different Cleopatra from the notorious voluptuary of the Nile who, three hundred years later, became the paramour first of Julius Caesar and then of Mark Antony. Olympias murdered the child in the lap of his mother. Next she forced the young queen to hang herself.

The name Cleopatra is Greek and ancient enough in Hellenic lore to appear in Homer, as well as in the legend of Jason and the Argonauts, and traditional enough in Macedonian culture to persist in Egypt through all the generations of the first Ptolemy, Alexander's friend and officer, and to include Cleopatra VII, that paramour of Caesar and Antony.

It is an error to think of any of the Cleopatras as other than Greek.

In keeping with Egyptian custom, the Cleopatras tended to marry their full brothers, who assumed the name and role of Ptolemy, and the married couple usually set right to work murdering each other's children, each other, their own children, and their own parents.

The widowed Cleopatra II was left with a son by her brother when her brother died. She married another brother, Ptolemy VIII, upon his promising to rule jointly with the boy and supply protection to both. He murdered the boy on their wedding day.

Next, he also married his wife's daughter, Cleopatra III, his niece, whom he came greatly to prefer in this incestuous *ménage à trois*.

When Cleopatra II objected to this arrangement and proclaimed her first son by him king, the father murdered his son, dismembered the corpse, and sent the head and hands to the mother.

In the end they put aside their quarrels.

Cleopatra III inherited the throne by agreement and was murdered by one of her sons, who desired to take it away from her.

A Cleopatra Thea killed one of her sons when he resisted her efforts to control him and was poisoned by another son as she prepared to poison him.

The legitimate descendants in this line expired with a Cleopatra Berenice and a Ptolemy XI. He murdered Cleopatra Berenice and was in turn murdered by the Alexandrians.

The throne passed to an illegitimate son, Ptolemy XII, whose sons were Ptolemy XIII and Ptolemy XIV and whose daughter was Cleopatra VII, the Cleopatra known to us from

Plutarch and Shakespeare, she of the barge like a burnished throne.

When Caesar came along, she was married to one of her brothers, who was killed in a civil war against the two, and when Caesar had gone, she was married to the other brother, to whose murder she had already attended by the time Antony arrived.

In such ways did the descendants of Ptolemy contrive to keep power in the family.

It was the open boast of Alexander's mother that he, Alexander, was not the progeny of King Philip of Macedonia but of someone more illustrious: he was the bastard son, she claimed, of the great god Zeus, who had come to her bed on her wedding night in the form of a snake. Olympias bragged spitefully that Philip had lost vision in the eye with which he had peeked through the keyhole to watch the woman and the god copulate.

Aristotle did not believe her.

Alexander did.

Frictions between the father and son were exacerbated by Philip's rejection of Olympias and by the obstacles this foreboded to his succession.

They squabbled frequently at the evening drinking debauches customary at the court in Pella. At the party for Philip's wedding to Cleopatra, Alexander reacted belligerently to a toast by the bride's uncle. An enraged Philip staggered drunkenly toward his son with drawn sword, tripped over the blade, and slid to the floor.

Alexander laughed. "See there," he taunted, looking down at his father, "how the man who prepares to cross out of Europe to invade Asia is overturned so easily as he tries to cross a room."

Alexander was then about nineteen.

By the time he was twenty-two, he had put down revolts in the north as far as the Danube, razed the city of Thebes, and compelled the Federation of Corinth to declare him ruler of all Greece. He had assembled an army of thirty-two thousand infantry and five thousand cavalry, supported by a navy of one hundred sixty ships, and already had crossed the Hellespont into Persia for the mission of far-ranging conquests on which he would spend the remaining eleven years of his life.

Aristotle did not go along. He ranked this decision among the most astute of his career. He recommended his nephew Callisthenes.

Also on the expedition went a number of young scholars associated with Aristotle, who diligently sent back historical reports, and descriptions, drawings, and even specimens, when feasible, of the animal and vegetable life they encountered that was alien to Greece. Aristotle added these to his museum of natural history and included them in his catalogues of phylum, genus, and species, biological classifications of his own invention, and otherwise kept himself busy establishing and expanding his Lyceum, revising his earlier foundations for the theory of music, and ceaselessly augmenting his ideas for his *Physics*, *Logic*, *Metaphysics*, *Politics*, *Posterior Analytics*, *Prior Analytics*, and *Nicomachean* and *Eudemian Ethics*, and perhaps (we have no conclusive documentation for this) the *Magna Moralia* too, along with such shorter works as his *Topics* and *Sophistical Refutations*, to which he intermittently returned, and of course, his *Poetics*.

His nephew Callisthenes, a philosopher and historian, was an officious pedant, with a tendency to interrupt, an inability to listen, and an unwillingness to defer. Alexander had him put to death.

From Olympias nagging letters came regularly to Alexander, invariably letters of complaint, mainly about his regent, Antipater, and the restraints he placed upon her.

Alexander was abnormally attached to his mother and never wanted to see her again.

She was asking a high price for the nine months she had housed him in her body, he groaned once to his boon companion, Clitus the Black, who had rescued him from death in the early battle of Granicus and whom Alexander, while in a drunken fury he would regret remorsefully, soon would kill with a spear hurled into his chest at very close range.

"Will I never be free of this nuisance of a mother?" Alexander wondered out loud.

Clitus the Black shook his head. "Only another Olympias would help you with that."

When news came to Greece that Alexander had died, among the several steps taken by his mother to seize power for herself was to murder his half-witted half-brother, Philip's last surviving son.

She celebrated a brief triumph, which lasted about one year, with an orgy of killing and was murdered in turn by relatives of her victims.

31

IN 332 B.C. ALEXANDER MOVED DOWN FROM BABYLON AND Syria through Palestine into Egypt to make himself Pharaoh there, and word trickled back to Athens of a Hebrew Bible encountered along the way that contained in its first paragraphs a theory of the creation of the universe. Aristotle heard the details and knew it would have to be suppressed.

The account was so simple he was furious he had not thought of it first. Let there be light, and there was light. What could be easier?

There it all was, in a handful of paragraphs.

In the beginning God created the heaven and the earth.

Why hadn't he said that? So much clearer than the Unmoved Mover or Unthinking Thinker or the Prime Unmoved Mover of his own intricate cosmology. And so much shorter.

He had to give credit to those Jews, whoever they were, and he resented them too. How long could he keep the secret from his students?

A middle-aged man with a theory to which he has long been attached, he knew, grows less interested in whether it is true and more obsessed that it be accepted as true, and that he be honored for it in his lifetime.

Now here was this damned Jewish Bible coming along at the worst possible time.

Against this Jewish Bible, he did not think his *Metaphysics* would have a chance.

He had more cause for gloom than Plato ever did.

He had better reason to be anti-Semitic.

Aristotle's *Metaphysics*, with its theory of being, was the key to his whole philosophy, and anyone wishing to understand him as a philosopher would have to begin with a knowledge of that work.

Avicenna, the great eleventh-century Arabian scholar, is said to have read the *Metaphysics* forty-one times without understanding a word.

Aristotle went through a prolonged depression over the Bible and talked about it to almost no one. Traces of this harrowing trauma are still clearly visible in the face painted by Rembrandt.

Like all scrupulous men of letters, Aristotle never wished to see any of his work go to waste, bad or good, right or wrong. Even had he guessed of a Shakespeare to come, he would have stuck by his *Poetics*. Copernicus, Galileo, and Newton might have given him pause; yet he still would have publicized his thoughts on the heavenly bodies, for they were the best that he had and sounded more plausible than any others around.

About slaves and women he might reconsider, although his phrasing was as smooth as anything in Plato.

"Even a woman may be good, and even a slave," he had written in his *Poetics*, while discoursing on characterizations in tragedy, "though the woman may be said to be an inferior being, and a slave quite worthless."

That was liberal enough from a conservative like him.

Critics forgot that he had loved two women, his wife and his mistress, and had, on his death, freed his slaves, which was more, he believed, than could be said of Abraham Lincoln.

He had written too much. Aristotle himself could compile a long list of foolish statements he had made, and he was glad that nobody he knew of wanted to.

One swallow, he had written, did not a summer make.

He hardly ever was congratulated for that one, although the figure of speech, he knew, was already an ancient cliché at the time he put it into his *Ethics*.

"You cannot deceive all of the people all of the time," he said in his *Politics*, and few Americans recalled that these words originated with him.

There are no known absolute moral standards, he said, and always proceeded as though he knew there were.

Aristotle had no problem with the theory that in the beginning God created the heaven and the earth and had divided the sky from the land and directed the waters to go to one place. The initial community was small. The man and the woman lived in a garden with everything needed at hand. They were free to spend all day contemplating. That was heaven.

What did it matter that there was no proof? There was none for his *Metaphysics* either, or for Plato's Soul or Ideas.

"If we demand a proof for everything," he had said, "we shall never be able to prove anything, since we shall not have a starting point for any proof. Certain things are obviously true and do not require proof."

"Prove it," his nephew Callisthenes had said. Aristotle was glad Callisthenes had gone off with Alexander. He was not sorry to learn he'd been killed.

Obviously, Aristotle saw, it is impossible to prove that anything is obviously true.

Even that.

He enjoyed the paradox.

Aristotle remembered wryly in New York, a city he had come to abhor, that the Sophist Gorgias could prove that there was nothing any man could know, that if he did learn something he would not understand it, and that if he understood it, he would be unable to communicate it.

The Sophist Protagoras had said: "About the gods I cannot know that they exist or that they do not exist or what is their nature."

In the *Critias* he remembered reading that nothing was certain except that birth leads to death.

From Metrodorus came his favorite: "None of us knows anything, not even whether we know or do not know."

Aristotle back then was a man who knew that he knew.

For Aristotle any *polis* of more than one hundred thousand people would lack common aims and a sense of community and be confused in its efforts to govern itself. Slaves were essential for happiness. Women too. In Aristotle's perfect community, the aristocratic communism of Plato was discarded, but Aristotle's citizens too would be forbidden to engage in trade or husbandry. His people would be up before daybreak, for such habits, he said, contribute to health, wealth, and wisdom. Aristotle was up before daybreak one morning and concluded that women have fewer teeth than men.

Today we are inclined to believe they probably have the same amount.

Aristotle permitted himself a twisted smile each time he contemplated Homer and recalled that nearly all Greeks writing in democratic Athens, a culture in which poetry, drama, science, philosophy, and animated debate flourished, were antidemocratic, including himself, and filled with articulate scorn for the democratic society in which they were free to write so critically. Odd, too, that they should affect to prefer the regimented aristocracy of Sparta, in which there was no writing and no music, science, or art.

It was not love of Sparta that inspired these sentiments but a loathing of the common and the commercial in democratic Athens.

Because Socrates had never written and Plato in his dialogues never spoke, Aristotle took care not to criticize Socrates by name for Plato's assaults on private property in the *Republic*, for the suggestion that communism would do away with all the evils of human nature, for the view that, just as the hand moves at the wishes of the brain, so must the individual move at the wishes of the state.

More modest than Plato, more scientific and less dogmatic, Aristotle had come to think of himself as a more serious writer with more of value to say. Plato, said Aristotle, had proved that the good man was the happy man. But Aristotle knew when he wrote it that Plato was not a happy man. Today we know there is hardly ever such a thing.

"What I would need to begin with," explained Plato, before he gave up on this world, "is a virtuous tyrant."

"He would have to be young?" Aristotle guessed.

"He would have to be young," agreed Plato, "and possess virtue, intelligence, and absolute power. Let him enjoy his absolute power long enough to grow bored with it. Let him have virtue and intelligence enough to envision a just society and let him employ this power to create it."

"And what would you do with him?" Aristotle inquired.

"I would educate him in philosophy. I would instruct him in goals and ideals."

"And then? How would he rule?"

"Virtuously."

"What does that mean? What would he do?"

Plato looked at Aristotle with dismay. "He would read my *Republic*, of course."

"And after that?"

"He would create that republic."

"With philosophers as rulers? Not himself?"

"There would be better philosophers then," said Plato indulgently. "You might qualify too."

"With all property owned by the community? And all wives and children too?"

"Naturally. That would be for the best."

"For whom? For the rich?"

"There will be no rich."

"For the other citizens and the slaves?"

"For all."

"How would they know? Why is it best?"

"Because I say that it is."

"For him?"

"My tyrant will be happy to give up his rule and let his power wither away."

"Why," wondered Aristotle, trying his hardest to puzzle it out, "would a ruler with absolute power, and those around him who allow him to have it, agree to surrender it?"

"Because he is virtuous. Because I will tell them to."

"Will the rest of the population want to comply?"

"They would have to comply, whether they want to or not. In my virtuous communist republic, it will be the role of the individual to do the bidding of the state."

"And if people don't agree?"

"They will be oppressed, for the good of the state. The Guardians will make them."

"Who will make the Guardians obey?" inquired Aristotle. "Where is the stronger force to compel them?"

"What difference does it make?" said Plato, vexed. "What people do in this world is of no consequence."

"Then why are you bothering? Why are we talking? Why did you write your *Republic*?"

"Let me think about that. Because I wanted to."

"Why should we read it?"

"Where are you going?"

Aristotle walked away from Plato to count the legs on a new beetle he had found.

He did not say to his teacher that he could think of no city on earth so badly managed, not even Athens, whose members would not prefer what they had to what Plato proposed.

Or that common ownership of property and families went against the nature of humans and the nature of the state; or that property owned in common by all of the people is owned by none of the people but belongs to the government, and that governments typically have no concern for the well-being of the people they govern; or that the role of the state, in his opinion, which differed from Plato's opinion, was to provide the conditions necessary for the happiness of its citizens. In a community that had the happiness of all members as a goal, even Aristotle's slaves would have to have slaves.

He was unblessed in timing, born too late or too soon.

He was writing of tragedy when the theater was dead, reforming the *polis* when the Greek city-state was no longer viable. Alexander was Pharaoh of Egypt and considered himself divine. In Italy the Romans captured Naples from the Samnites.

While Heraclides, another disciple of Plato's, was speaking of a heliocentric universe, Aristotle was describing the heavens as though he, Adam, and Eve dwelt in a world in which the stars, sun, moon, and planets shined and rotated just for them.

Aristotle never had imagined that cities would unite into provinces like Holland, provinces grow into states like New York, and states merge into nations unimaginably large that would be always ungovernable and always untrustworthy and unfriendly, not least of all to their own citizens.

He was belittling money when everywhere around him there was no attraction more powerful. He was bewildered in Amsterdam that he was the official philosopher of Calvinism, and he could not comprehend why a culture committed to an orthodoxy of commerce, capitalism, profit, and financial acquisition should glorify an ancient Greek philosopher whose scientific speculations were crumbling and who had argued that excess capital has no use and is unnecessary, that the virtuous man does not make money for the sake of making money, and that it is undignified and unappealing for a man who is well-off and of good social standing to run after money.

Money answers all things, said that Bible.

Aristotle ground his teeth.

"It was just my luck," he wrote in the mammoth autobiography he did not live long enough to complete, of which just that opening fragment of his first sentence survives.

XV

THE LAST
LAUGH

32

It was the fortune of Rembrandt's Aristotle to begin his travels with a journey from Amsterdam to Sicily in 1654 and to conclude them in America in 1961 with a triumphant debut at the Metropolitan Museum of Art on Fifth Avenue in New York, three centuries short six years after the island of Manhattan was ceded to the English, the Dutch deciding that they would not fight to hold what they could not keep and administer.

In actuality, the painting had crossed the Atlantic soon after the turn of the century, in time to avoid the dangers of the First World War and the perils of crossing the Atlantic at any time. On the night of April 14 in 1912, the unsinkable British ocean liner the *Titanic* sank after colliding with an iceberg, with a loss of lives of over fifteen hundred of the twenty-two hundred people aboard, the same year U.S. troops occupied Tientsin, China, to protect American interests there, U.S. Marines landed in Cuba to protect American interests there, and U.S. Marines were landed in Nicaragua to protect American interests there too after rebels had massacred Nicaraguan soldiers, and the First Balkan War broke out.

Because the *Titanic* was unsinkable, there were insufficient lifeboats.

On May 7, 1915, the British liner *Lusitania* was sunk by a German submarine, with a loss of eleven hundred ninety-five, of whom one hundred twenty-eight were American citizens. Two years later, following a narrow presidential election, the U.S. entered World War I under Woodrow Wilson, who is still remembered as an idealist, a reformer, and an intellectual.

By then the Rembrandt painting was safely across the Atlantic, having traveled to New York in 1907 from the dealer Duveen to the American purchaser and collector Mrs. Collis P. Huntington. In that same year, the *Lusitania* set a world speed record on its maiden voyage from Queenstown, Ireland, to New York City, and it is possible the *Aristotle* was aboard.

Nobody knows how many Rembrandts perished in the First World War because nobody knows how many Rembrandts were painted by Rembrandt, his collaborators, and his counterfeiters.

It was the fate of the *Homer*, scorched, repainted, and reduced by fire to almost half the original size, to make its way to the museum of the Mauritshuis in The Hague, where, presumably, like the *Aristotle* at the Metropolitan, it will stay forever, until the end of time.

It was the fate of the Ruffo *Alexander* to be lost. If found, it will be worth a fortune.

In the meanwhile, a golden opportunity exists for a gifted forger to create the original Rembrandt painting of the Ruffo *Alexander*, the only stipulations being that it conform in dimensions with those in the contract, be made of four pieces of canvas sewn together with seams so "frightful, it is difficult to believe," and that it be done with pigments old enough to stand the tests of time as measured by advanced technological procedures. The chances to succeed will be enhanced if the face of Alexander resembles the face in the two Rembrandt *Alexander*s we do have.

Don Antonio too admired the work if not the workman, and in his will he included his three Rembrandts in a list of one hundred paintings to go intact to the oldest son in each generation after him as a collection never to be separated, sold, or disposed of in any other way.

At his death the collection passed in succession as bequeathed until it reached his great-grandson Don Caligoro Ruffo in 1739. In 1743 this newest heir died in the plague, as did all his brothers, and the collection went to another branch of the family.

In 1750 the Ruffo family divided into the "Principi della Scaletta" and the "Principi della Floresta," with the first, it is thought, inheriting the collection and moving much of it to Naples. From that year on, what became of the "hundred paintings" bequeathed to remain together forever is anybody's guess.

We do know the following:

In 1783 the Ruffo castle in Sicily was damaged by an earthquake. Perhaps there was fire.

In 1818 the right of primogeniture was abolished in Sicily.

And in 1848 the Ruffo villa outside Naples caught fire, and much of the art there was destroyed or damaged. We don't know what was there.

One of these fires might be the blaze in which sections surrounding the center of the *Homer* were burned away so fortuitously. If not, no art historian has guessed convincingly at another conflagration that destroyed large peripheral areas of the painting and left the principal subject so hauntingly and tragically alone, with only a pen and part of a hand belonging to someone else for companionship.

But even before 1848, a year of widespread republican revolutions and reforms in Europe, we know that Don Antonio's wishes were disregarded and his collection had been broken up, for in 1815, another pivotal year in the history of Europe, Aristotle was on display in London, having survived, miraculously, the First Northern War, the Second Northern War, the War of Devolution, the War of the Grand Alliance, the War of the Spanish Succession, the War of the Polish Succession, the War of the Austrian Succession, the Seven Years' War, the First Silesian War, the Second Silesian War, the War of the Bavarian Succession, the Russo-Turkish War, the French Revolution, the Turkish-Polish War, the Swedish-Danish War, the Swedish-Russian War, the Franco-Austrian Prussian War, the War of the First Coalition against France, the French-Dutch War, Napoleon's Italian Campaign, the British-Spanish War, Napoleon's Egyptian Campaign, the War of the Second Coalition against France, the Rebellion of the United Irishmen against Britain, another British-Spanish War, the Russian-Persian War, the War of the Third Coalition against France, the Prussian-French War, the French-Portuguese War, Napoleon's triumphal invasion of Russia and disastrous retreat, the Congress of Vienna, and the battle of Waterloo, pulling through these and other perilous occurrences and arriving unscathed in London in ways we do not know.

He could hardly be recognized.

"I wonder who he is?" a bewhiskered gentleman inquired from a distance in the gallery in which he was on exhibition.

His companion, an elegant woman with auburn hair and a rolled-up parasol, answered: "He looks just like the Dutch poet and historian Pieter Corneliszoon Hooft, doesn't he?"

"You're right, by Jove!" said the gentleman happily, reading the identification.

Aristotle was shaken.

The painting belonged to Sir Abraham Hume of Ashridge Park, Berkhampstead, Hertfordshire, and Aristotle, when not on exhibition as Pieter Cornelisz. Hooft, did his contemplating in comfortable surroundings in Hertfordshire on the family estate of Sir Abraham and his heirs. Aristotle felt more at peace in the country home of this established landowning family than with any of his owners since.

No one knows how he went so far, from Ruffo's Messina

in Sicily to Sir Abraham Hume's Hertfordshire and London, although we know much about him since.

No one knows the tortuous route traveled by the damaged *Homer* from the Ruffos in Italy into the collection of the Bridgewater Gallery of the Earl of Ellesmere in England by 1885, but there can be no doubt that the scarred *Homer* of Rembrandt, like the blind Homer in legend, had a harder time than the *Aristotle*.

Life has always been easier for the sons of professional men in the upper class than for artists who start at the bottom, especially poets.

In 1894, in battered and grimy condition, the *Homer* was for sale in London by the art-dealing firm of T. Humphrey Ward and Son as an anonymous *Portrait of an Old Man*, where it was spied, recognized, identified, and purchased by the pioneering Dutch Rembrandt scholar Abraham Bredius.

T. Humphrey Ward and Son was asking twenty-four hundred pounds for this damaged fragment by an unknown artist that had sold for eighteen shillings only nine years earlier.

The head of the man looked familiar to Bredius—it resembled the head on the bust in the Rembrandt portrait of P. C. Hooft, which had changed hands in London the year before. There remained legible as a corroborating clue the letters "andt" from the artist's signature and the date, "f. 1663." The broad technique and subdued palette were familiar to him also. It was a work that Bredius himself could now authenticate as a painting by Rembrandt.

In Sicily back in 1664 Aristotle too had recognized the face in the painting as the one on the bust he had been contemplating on Ruffo's wall the previous ten years. With Homer's arrival, the cursing in the castle at last stopped. The *Alexander* was forgiven. The Greek triptych of three great figures from the Hellenic past, already present *in nuce* in the *Aristotle* of 1653, was complete. And this time the artist had not scrimped.

There were even *two* scribes.

Aristotle could tell at first glance that to the ground of a light shade of yellow and pink, consisting of much chalk mixed with a little ocher, Rembrandt had added preparatory layers of a rather darker tone of reddish brown. Aristotle had learned much more about painting in his two years with Rembrandt. These basic layers of the ground consisted in the main of chalk, ochers, and umbers mixed with a little white lead. On top of these layers he spread a dark grayish-brown underpainting of mysterious and subtle effect that appeared in various places in the cloak, the head, the beard, and the background, into which umber and a great deal of coarse white lead had been worked. Rembrandt put only a lighter top layer in the shadowy areas of the head, the cap, and the beard, making sure that the tone of even the dark areas of the figure was tinged by the grayish-brown layer of umber and white lead underneath. The brown, red, and yellow pigments in the cap, face, and beard were ochers, while the yellow ribbon across the forehead was of lead-tin yellow mixed with more white lead.

There was no red lake pigment used, not even in the flesh tones or areas of shadow.

In a color scheme restricted almost wholly to shades of brown, white, and dim gold, Rembrandt had conceived a blind old poet in a dark-brown cloak with wide sleeves and with a golden-yellow shawl over his cloak. Homer is wearing a poet's fillet on his brow, and on his head Rembrandt put an odd cap. Homer leans on his stick, his mouth open. His sightless eyes are open too.

He was almost human.

Aristotle was tormented by the thought that more work, and more paint, had gone into this painting than his own, although the price was the same. He did not feel cordial. He tried hard not to be envious. Aristotle was better-looking. Homer was blind.

He convinced himself he was much better off: he would rather have eyes and look like a foreigner than be blind like Homer and find his way with a staff, and by the time Homer came into the picture, the Ruffos had found out who he was and looked up to him as Aristotle, the great philosopher of antiquity, and knew he was not Albertus Magnus or some nameless phrenologist. They were all the more vain for his presence in their household.

In the *Homer*, as in the *Aristotle*, the hands were weakly modeled.

In Sicily in 1664 the bard was in an elaborate architectural setting and was dictating or teaching his verses. He looked placid and content with his lot.

When Bredius found him, the surroundings had been burned away and he was alone. Bereft of place and audience, and of the company of other humans, he is forsaken and destitute, bewildered.

For all that we know, he could be gasping with loneliness when we watch him today.

He looks like a man who has forgotten more than his lines.

The *craquelure* of the painting is just what we would expect, varying from fine cracks to wide grooves, some filled with brown varnish. There are coarse grains of pigment in the background, which are not Rembrandt's. There are no striking *pentimenti*.

The twenty-four hundred pounds asked by T. Humphrey Ward and Son was a great deal of money back then.

Bredius bought him for eight hundred, and this was a small fortune too.

But Bredius had inherited a small fortune.

His family manufactured gunpowder.

Bredius had the painting restored and gave it on loan to the Mauritshuis. When he died in 1946, he bequeathed it to that museum, where the solitary poet hangs now, an isolated figure of a lonely, blind, poor old man, shrunken in size by unsung hardships.

Put the *Homer* and the *Self-Portrait of the Artist Laughing* together and you might find more pathos than your heart can bear, if you're a person inclined that way.

Before Bredius identified him in London, there was a span of about a hundred thirty-five years in which nothing more of the *Homer* is known than was known to the Greeks of the Homer of ancient Ionia.

We deduce the poet from the poetry.

We deduce a Creator from a universe moving like clock-work, although we now know that our universe is a fire and our planet an ember.

Soon there will be no more people left.

Life is more than half over.

With the *Aristotle*, there was a disappearance of some sixty-five years before he turned up in London in 1815 as P. C. Hooft, the possession of Sir Abraham Hume. Sir Abraham died in 1838, and after his death Aristotle remained for much of the rest of that century with the family at Ashridge Park, his successive owners being:

John Hume Cust, Viscount Alford, Ashridge Park, 1838–1851;

John William Spencer Brownlow Cust, 2nd Earl Brownlow, Ashridge Park, 1851–1867;

And Adelbert Wellington Brownlow Cust, 3rd Earl Brownlow, Ashridge Park, 1867–1893.

With the death of Adelbert Wellington Brownlow Cust in 1893, Aristotle's idyll at Ashridge Park, for reasons we don't know, came unfortunately to an end.

Except for Rembrandt, art dealers, and one young American heir, all the owners we know of kept the painting their whole lives.

He was sold in London, where Bredius saw him, and within four years was in Paris, the property of the extraordinary collector Rodolphe Kann. One offer of $5.5 million for just the better part of his collection, which included a dozen Rembrandts, was spurned by Kann's executors. After Kann died in 1905, the painting was bought by the dealer Joseph Duveen, and the stage was set for the completion of the journeys of the *Aristotle*, from their commencement in Amsterdam to their termination in New York, and for his continued descent from the aristocracy of the old world into the middle class of the new.

In 1897, when Kann acquired the painting, the Dreyfus Affair was a raging scandal in France, and Emile Zola would soon flee to England to escape imprisonment for his blistering published attack on anti-Semitic members of the high military caste who were concealing their acts of treason with forged papers incriminating the innocent and unprepossessing Jewish captain condemned to Devil's Island for crimes of espionage for Germany of which they themselves had been guilty.

In 1907, when the steamship *Lusitania* set her speed record after Dreyfus had already been released, Duveen sold the *Aristotle*, for "six figures," he reported, to Mrs. Collis P. Huntington of New York City, the first of its American owners.

Mrs. Huntington, the former Arabella Duval Yarrington Worsham of Alabama, was the widow of the eastern railroad millionaire Collis P. Huntington, who was born in the state of Connecticut, lived in New York, and was instrumental in the construction of the Central Pacific Railroad across the Sierra Nevada Mountains and eventually consolidated virtually all transportation in the West into the Southern Pacific Railroad Company, of which he was the principal owner, as he was of the Chesapeake & Ohio and other railroads, and she would soon become Mrs. Henry E. Huntington by marrying the nephew of her former husband. The real story behind this marriage to her deceased husband's nephew is undoubtedly intriguing, but not to us.

Mrs. Huntington thought Duveen's asking price high, and Aristotle agreed. But she wanted a Rembrandt.

"Do you know who the man in the painting is?" she inquired. "I have always wanted a painting of the poet Virgil."

"It's a portrait of the poet Virgil."

Rembrandt's *Portrait of Virgil* crossed the Atlantic and was installed in Mrs. Huntington's home at Fifth Avenue and Fifty-seventh Street, Number 2 East.

Rembrandt's painting of P. C. Hooft has not been heard of since.

And in the same year Aristotle passed customs and was admitted to America, President Theodore Roosevelt barred the Japanese from immigrating to the United States, the Dutch completed the occupation of Sumatra by defeating the Achinese people there, and John Pierpont Morgan halted the run on banks in the United States by importing $100 million in gold from Europe.

Morgan could now do with a pen and some words what the government of the United States could not.

This great American financier, the first J. P. Morgan, was a renowned collector of art and rare books, a devout Episcopalian, and a committed anti-Semite. He was famous for his philanthropies.

Mrs. Huntington kept the painting until she passed away seventeen years later, in 1924, when Adolf Hitler was in prison in Munich writing the first volume of his *Mein Kampf*.

She left the *Aristotle* to her son, Archer M. Huntington, who sold it back to Duveen in 1928, twenty-one years after the dealer had parted with it. Duveen shipped the painting back across the Atlantic to be cleaned by a master restorer in The Hague, and next to his London or Paris establishment, where he had it examined by the noted Dutch Rembrandt scholar F. Schmidt-Degener. Only then did Duveen find out that this Rembrandt he owned was the *Aristotle* described in the Ruffo family archives.

Rembrandt's celebrated *Portrait of Virgil* then went the way of the celebrated Rembrandt *Portrait of Pieter Hooft*.

By November of that year, Aristotle was back in New York, and Duveen sold the painting to Mr. and Mrs. Alfred W. Erickson, of 110 East Thirty-fifth Street. Mr. Erickson owned an advertising agency and was later a founding partner of the firm of McCann-Erickson, which grew to become, and probably remains, one of the largest advertising entities in the world.

The price was $750,000.

We are surprised that the owner of an advertising agency back in 1928 could spend $750,000 for a painting.

Aristotle wanted to cry out from the canvas that no painting on earth was worth $750,000 in aesthetic value, and that no artist on earth would disagree.

"Of course," said the suave art dealer, later Lord Duveen of Millbank, to Mr. and Mrs. Erickson, "I am really losing money by selling it so cheaply now, for certainly it soon will be worth very much more."

Money *has* no worth, Aristotle could have told all three of them repeatedly until he was blue in the face, but knew he would not be believed.

There was a boom now in art-buying in America too, fueled in large part by art dealers and interior decorators profiting from it, and Aristotle was pained by his depreciation as a philosopher in contrast to Rembrandt's appreciation as a painter. He would listen despondently as Duveen extolled the virtues of Rembrandt. Duveen never said much about Aristotle's philosophy.

Rembrandt was more illustrious than he was.

So were previous owners. Not least among the rare beauties of the painting stressed by Duveen was the ownership by Mrs. Collis P. Huntington, who had kept it until her death.

Aristotle sometimes longed for the days when he was P. C. Hooft and lived with Sir Abraham Hume in Hertfordshire. Plato might have laughed, sardonically, to see him so coarsely retailed, and as a part of the sales package with the lesser appeal.

The sale to the Ericksons was contracted on November 12, 1928, only a few days after Herbert Hoover was elected thirty-first president of the United States the same year the Kellogg-Briand Pact outlawing war was signed in Paris by more than sixty states; Benito Mussolini published an autobiography titled *My Autobiography*; Walt Disney, in California, produced the first Mickey Mouse film; Franz Lehár composed the operetta *Frederika* in Berlin; Alexander Fleming discovered penicillin; Amsterdam was host to the Olympic Games; and the first machine for boning and cleaning kippers, which are herring, male salmon, and sea trout that are cured by splitting, cleaning, salting, and smoking, was given its initial run in Fleetwood, England.

In the Summer Olympic Games of 1928 the U.S. led all other nations with one hundred thirty-one points.

The sale was completed with a final payment by Mr. Erickson in January of 1929.

In October of 1929 the stock market crashed. The Great Depression followed and spread through the world.

The second J. P. Morgan, the son of the first one, poured out hundreds of millions of dollars in a futile attempt to stabilize the uncontrollable market.

There was no stopping the decline.

People still don't explain why the stock market had to crash and the Great Depression had to follow.

On November 12, 1930, two years to the day after the purchase, Erickson sold the *Aristotle* back to Duveen for $500,000, a quarter of a million less than he had paid.

"You assured me," said Mr. Erickson, grimly, when Mr. Duveen named his price, "that the work would increase in value."

"These are difficult times now, Mr. Erickson," responded Duveen. "We are living in the Great Depression."

"I think I know that."

Duveen could not find another buyer in these years, although there are indications he tried. He put the work in exhibitions in London, and even in Worcester, Massachusetts, an industrial city in the central part of that state that is not likely ever to see it again.

In February of 1936, his financial health restored, Mr. Erickson reacquired the painting from Duveen for $590,000, the difference of $90,000 representing charges for interest and the New York sales tax, and Aristotle moved out of the storage room back to the Erickson home at 110 East Thirty-fifth Street the same year Edward VIII became King of England and abdicated to marry the woman he loved, Mrs. Wallis Warfield Simpson; Italy invaded and annexed Ethiopia; Stalin continued his lethal purge trials in Russia; Hitler won elections in Germany with 99 percent of the vote; Franklin Delano Roosevelt won reelection here, with 98.7 percent of the electoral vote; and Margaret Mitchell published *Gone With the Wind* while the American Negro Jesse Owens was winning four gold medals in the track and field events of the Olympic Games in Berlin, frustrating and enraging Hitler, and the U.S. national debt was increasing to $34 billion because of expenditures for relief programs instituted by Roosevelt's New Deal.

Henry Ford, who was having his problems with union organizers, admired Adolf Hitler and his Nazis, and Hitler admired him.

There were no union problems in Nazi Germany.

There were no union problems in Russia either, but there were no Henry Fords.

Between 1920 and 1922, Mr. Ford's newspaper, the *Dearborn Independent*, had published in ninety-two consecutive issues articles of virulent anti-Semitism, most relating to the contents of a nineteenth-century pamphlet, *The Protocols of the Elders of Zion*, which was known to consist of spurious transcripts of conversations that had never taken place, and whose republication and distribution Ford financed.

Young Hitler kept a photograph of Henry Ford in his room for inspiration.

Shortly before World War II, Chancellor Hitler awarded Henry Ford the Grand Cross of the German Eagle, the highest award to a foreigner that the Third Reich could bestow, and Ford was honored to accept. Ford would not allow his company to fulfill a contract to manufacture engines in this country for Britain's Royal Air Force.

Shortly after the war, it was told of Mr. Ford that he wept repentantly at pictures of the death camps. This is another one of those stories that seem too good to be true.

On November 2 of 1936, nine months after Mr. Erickson repurchased the painting, he died. He left the *Aristotle* in trust to his wife, Rita, together with the rest of the works in his collection, and the painting was with her until her death twenty-five years later, in February of 1961.

The months February and November figure conspicuously in the history of the Ericksons as it relates to the *Aristotle*, a phenomenon that may carry cryptic significance to those who make much of coincidences.

Before her death, Mrs. Erickson was solicited many times by dealers seeking to sell the picture and curators hoping to be given it. After her death, the trustees of her estate decided her testamentary desires would best be fulfilled by a public sale of the paintings, and an auction was announced for later that year at the Parke-Bernet Galleries at 980 Madison Avenue in New York.

It was an open secret, said *The New York Times*, that the auction houses of Sotheby's and Christie's were also vying for "the plum." Because the Erickson sale involved twenty-four pictures expected to bring at least $3,000,000, it was understood that the gallery commission was a negotiated figure instead of the standard rate.

When asked, a spokesman for the gallery said Parke-Bernet was satisfied with the arrangements.

As it happened, the Erickson collection brought $4,679,250, which was a record.

Included in the pictures offered was the Dutch painting *Man with a Herring* by Frans Hals.

The auction was held that autumn between the Berlin crisis and the Cuban missile crisis that brought the former allies Russia and the U.S. to the brink of war again. In less than three years, U.S. troops would be sent to Vietnam to protect American interests in an area that had none except these U.S. troops.

As many American military men were killed in combat in Vietnam as in World War I, more than fifty thousand.

The country was shepherded into both these wars by presidents from the Democratic Party who campaigned as liberals with promises of peace. In the first eighty-eight years of this century every war in which the United States was engaged began with a Democratic president in office. Only one Democratic president this century, Jimmy Carter, did not move the country toward war.

He was not reelected.

The auction of the *Aristotle* took place on November 15. It was over in four minutes. The check for the purchase was dated November 17, and on November 18, with great fanfare and much self-congratulation, Rembrandt's painting, now world-famous, went on display in the Great Hall of the Metropolitan Museum, which acquired the work in a quick but competitive auction with a winning bid, delivered by signals, of $2,300,000.

The price was the highest ever paid for a painting in any public or private sale.

It was the first painting in history to command an opening bid of $1,000,000.

The bid for a million was transmitted secretly to Mr. Louis J. Marion, the auctioneer, at lunch by a clergyman acting for a private collector who preferred remaining anonymous. Mr. Marion related afterward that he had that bid in his pocket when he put the painting on the block.

"There was ten to twenty million dollars in that room to bid on it," he told news reporters.

Twenty-five years later, in 1986, the American owner of a lesser Rembrandt sold the painting at auction in London for $10.3 million, to a buyer rumored to be Taiwanese. This confirmed to Aristotle that money had no value and was useful only as a medium of exchange.

But here in America in 1961, ten to twenty million dollars seemed a large amount. The auction attracted widespread attention. In a three-day exhibition of the painting before the sale, twenty thousand visitors viewed the painting at the Parke-Bernet Galleries.

That works out to almost seven thousand a day.

For the event itself, nearly two thousand people came to the gallery as spectators, most waiting on line in the street for an hour or more.

Prospective buyers—collectors, agents of collectors, representatives of museums—were admitted to the main hall of the gallery, in which the auction would be conducted. Those attending as spectators were seated in three other galleries and witnessed the proceedings on closed-circuit television.

Many months of secret preparations had preceded the auction. Museums electing to try for the painting had to round up the money that would give them a chance. Among these, of course, was the Metropolitan Museum of Art, whose purchase of the painting was made possible by a "war fund," to which several trustees and more than a hundred private individuals contributed.

The director of the museum, Mr. James J. Rorimer, explained:

"*Aristotle* is one of the great paintings in the world, and it would have been heartbreaking, with Wall Street so close, to have lost out on it."

There was applause from the audience in all four galleries when the *Aristotle* was brought onstage for the start of the sale and spotlights transformed those sleeves of his white robe into folds of Rembrandt gold.

There was a louder ovation four minutes later when the auction was over and the auctioneer announced that the prize had been won by an "eastern museum."

The day on which the painting first went on display, a Saturday, forty-two thousand people came to the Metropolitan Museum. Aristotle was mounted against a large background of red velvet, just a few paces from the Sphinx of Queen Hatshepsut, which had been reconstructed from fragments found at her mortuary temple at Deir el Bahari, dating back to around 1490 B.C. The Sphinx drew scant attention.

Aristotle was overcome by the commotion and the ranks of people surging forward to see him.

He wondered if the bust of Homer was as impressed as he was.

He wondered what Rembrandt would say if he could see him now.

Probably, he would say that he had sold him too soon.

For the next day, Sunday, when the museum would be open just four hours, officials forecast hopefully an attendance of fifty thousand. If that many materialized, the record for a single day for the museum, which had exhibited the Mona Lisa and the Vatican *Pietà* of Michelangelo, would be exceeded by nearly seven thousand.

More than eighty thousand showed up!

Long lines formed early at the main entrance and at three supplementary entrances, one from the parking lot behind the museum, another at Fifth Avenue and Eighty-first Street, and the third at Fifth Avenue and Eighty-third Street, and when the four-hour day was over, officials announced that 82,629 persons had attended.

That many in just four hours divides into some 20,650 people an hour, 344 people a minute, or slightly more than 5.7 people every second. Even if this figure is a lie, it is a very impressive lie.

They would have had to step very lively to come one at a time.

However, they approached in groups. At no time were there fewer than eighteen people at the guardrail in front of the masterpiece, and a constant mass of hundreds more stretched patiently behind them to the opposite wall.

For Aristotle those days were the most thrilling he could recall. There were people who had heard of Aristotle and people who had heard of Rembrandt, but there were not many, until they read of the auction, who had known that the two had once been closely associated. Not in either of Aristotle's lifetimes had he been the idol of so much curiosity and veneration.

Some men bared their heads as they neared, as though uncovering for the flag, and many men and women put hand over heart as they paid him homage.

One woman chewed noisily on a salted pretzel.

One gentleman observed with authority that it had cost a lot of money, but he could see now that it was worth it.

Now and then in the chorus of general praise a discordant voice inquired why the money could not have been spent to feed hungry families.

Aristotle knew why.

There is never any shortage of hungry families. But great paintings by great painters come rarely on the market. And a great painting of Aristotle was practically unique.

"I waited longer on line than I did for the Mona Lisa," a mother explained to her young daughter. "This one is better."

"He looks like Pieter Hooft," the little girl answered.

By the end of that week Aristotle was the most famous philosopher in New York. Rembrandt was the most talked-about painter.

Homer was hardly mentioned.

Paperback editions of works by Aristotle appeared on bestseller lists, and publishers', underestimating demand, ran out of stock.

The Getty Foundation and the MacArthur Foundation both made haste to announce they would have wanted the painting had they been in existence.

The governments of Iran, Brunei, and Kuwait were short of cash.

In Washington, a spokesman said the president would have endeavored to raise money to buy the painting for the White House had anyone in his administration known of the sale.

There are people willing to pay a great deal to own the most expensive painting in the world. They will not pay as much for one that costs less.

In the first seven weeks, attendance at the museum was a record 1,079,610, and it is reasonable to assume that almost all came to look at least once at the picture of Aristotle.

He had hardly a moment to himself.

But in the weeks that followed, the numbers inexorably declined, and he began inexorably to feel neglected. He was moved from the Great Hall into an ordinary gallery. People strolled in who did not even know he was there.

He was gloomier than ever. He missed the hurrying crowds with beaming faces that no longer flocked to see him. He even missed the company of the Sphinx of Queen Hatshepsut from the mortuary temple at Deir el Bahari. He hung in a room with a bunch of other somber Rembrandts, of which he quickly grew tired. How he longed for a splash of sunlight, for a touch of the gay color, smiling faces, pretty women present in other paintings with which he had occasionally spent time in other places. He would pay almost anything for a Renoir or a Picasso.

He found himself trembling in fear of his own authenticity each time the attribution of one of the other Rembrandts in his room came into question or was said to be spurious. There were two, a man and a woman, about whom he harbored doubts from the first day he saw them, and he eyed them dejectedly with anxiety and hostility. They did not look to him entirely like the Rembrandt he knew. He was nervously aware that he was several centimeters smaller than he had been originally, and that some specialists did not accept normal shrinkage as a credible explanation.

In 1987 a painting of sunflowers by Vincent van Gogh in which the chrome-yellow pigment had turned muddy was sold for $39.9 million to a Japanese insurance company that did not care about the chrome yellow. Hundreds of millions of people in countries all over the world did not rush to see it. Later in 1987 a different painting by van Gogh brought $53.9 million.

Rembrandt's *Aristotle* was overshadowed.

Aristotle had a lump in his throat. The more he thought about it, the more he wished he were a van Gogh. He envied the paintings in the tidier Frick Collection farther downtown, which itself was a work of art. There, with the Titian and the Goyas, the Velázquez and El Grecos, the Holbein *Thomas More*, and, as a worthy companion piece to himself, the magnificent Rembrandt self-portrait of 1658, in which Rembrandt looks like a man who will throw you out if he does not like your manner or breeding, Aristotle would be with his peers in the company he deserved, and make a much stronger impression in what everyone knew was a smarter museum, despite the repellent Fragonards and the peculiar *Polish Rider.*

Aristotle also preferred the better location of the Frick. It was nearer the zoo.

As for the auction itself, there fell near the end a dramatic silence of some ten seconds that seemed like ten hours in which it appeared that the Cleveland Museum of Art was going to acquire the painting with a bid of $2,250,000.

The wife of one of the trustees of the Metropolitan was in such terror that Mr. Rorimer, bidding for the museum, had fallen asleep that she was on the verge of shrieking to her husband to call out another $100,000.

But Mr. Rorimer was not asleep. Bidding secretively in the code prearranged, he fingered his lapel and moved his eyes to the right, signaling $50,000 more.

The dealer bidding for Cleveland had reached the maximum authorized and could go no higher.

There were no other contenders.

The Metropolitan had the painting.

The sixty-nine-year-old expert representing the Cleveland Museum had predicted months before that a bid of $1,500,000 had no chance, a bid of less than $2,000,000 might have a remote chance, $2,000,000 would have an outside chance, and $2,250,000 was a respectable bid that might get the picture—but that it might go higher.

He was as accurate as any oracle.

The Metropolitan Museum would not say how much higher it was prepared to go.

The third highest bid was $1,950,000 and was traced to the Carnegie Institute of Fine Arts in Pittsburgh, which had the support of a benefactor, Mrs. Sarah Mellon Scaife, who had allotted personal funds of a little over $2,000,000 for the purchase of the Rembrandt.

In small consolation for the loss of the Rembrandt, Pittsburgh came home with the *Man with a Herring* for $145,000.

The fourth highest bidder was a nobleman in Switzerland of German descent.

In 1972, without hullabaloo, the Metropolitan Museum changed the name of the painting to *Aristotle with a Bust of Homer*. Not until 1980, however, was the change reflected in the wall label, and ever since, Rembrandt's *Aristotle Contemplating the Bust of Homer* has been in danger of going the same way as his *Portrait of Pieter Hooft* and *Portrait of Virgil*. If ever assembled and exhibited together, this triad of invisible Rembrandt masterpieces would comprise a priceless and inimitable display.

Within a few days of the auction, Mr. Rorimer felt obliged to take exception to an editorial in *The New York Times* that alluded to the vulgarity of the event. The newspaper spoke of "a persistent feeling of discomfort, even of distaste, with the price," and asked if that amount of money could have been better spent. Mr. Rorimer, defending the museum, explained to the press that the cost was of no importance.

"Money is only a medium of exchange."

There were people of good character in the vicinity of the painting willing to swear under oath they heard Aristotle snort.

XVI

LAST
WORDS

33

THE TRIAL OF SOCRATES WAS A FOREGONE CONCLUSION. It was one of those events whose outcome precedes its beginning and whose ending inspires its start. As Anytus said in demanding the death penalty, he should not be prosecuted if he were not going to be found guilty and they should not find him guilty if they were not going to kill him.

There would be no happy ending.

All good tragedies have happy endings.

What would have happened had Jesus not been crucified?

The trial of Socrates was a fair one. There was no manufactured evidence, no lying witnesses. There was *no* evidence, *no* witnesses. All in the jury knew that. A lucky thing about the rule of law in the democratic society Anytus had helped restore was that charges against a person no longer had to be proved. They had only to be convincing. Due process was observed. Justice was done.

Even Socrates did not complain.

He eschewed a speech of great flair written by a friend with expert rhetorical skills and considerable courtroom experience, counting it more forensic than philosophical and therefore unsuitable for him. There was concern in his circle that he prepare an adequate defense.

"Don't you think that I have been preparing all my life for my defense?" he answered. "In constantly doing what was right and avoiding what was wrong, and in striving ever to make my companions better, don't you think I have been preparing the best defense?"

"It will not be enough," warned his friend Hermogenes. "Don't you see, Socrates, that our juries *like* to be misled by argument, and they often put to death the innocent and acquit the guilty?"

"Do you find it so strange," he replied in good mood, "if it seems better to God that I die now rather than later?"

"Do you think it is God that puts you on trial?"

"Do you think that makes a difference to me? To this day, Hermogenes, I would not acknowledge that any man I know of has lived a better or pleasanter life than I. If I am to die unjustly, they who kill me will bear the shame of it. What shame is there to me that others decide to act unjustly to me?"

Lycon the orator rubbed his hands with malice. "I knew the old fool had too much good character to employ the tricks of a speech written by someone else."

Meletus exulted too. "He will try to talk sense to those five hundred jurors. They will grow restless and annoyed when he fails to entertain them."

Both knew what to say to undermine the credibility of Socrates at the start.

"I was especially astonished at one of their many misrepresentations," Socrates said, when his accusers had finished. "I mean when they told you to be careful not to let me deceive you—the implication being that I am a skillful speaker. This was particularly brazen of them, since they must know that it will soon become obvious that I have not the slightest skill as a speaker—unless, of course, they mean one who speaks the truth. If that is what they mean, I would agree that I am an orator, though not after their pattern.''

Anytus was the most serious and businesslike of the three, and it was not just for the fun of it that he brought Socrates to trial but for something much worse: principle. From men motivated by moral certitude, history teaches, no lasting good ever comes.

At the beginning of the rule of the Thirty, Anytus had been a contented conservative supporter of the moderate fascist Theramenes, until Theramenes was liquidated by the better fascist Critias. Till then it had not occurred to him that he too could be exterminated.

In the democracy he had helped restore, he was conspicuous as one of the leaders of a moral majority demanding a return to traditional Athenian virtues in which the old family values prevailed, although he could not say what these family values were or when they had prevailed.

''There goes a man,'' remarked Socrates of Anytus after the trial, speaking to friends as he awaited the representatives of the Eleven to take him into custody, ''who is filled with pride at the thought that he has accomplished some great and noble end in putting me to death, because, seeing him honored by the state with the highest offices, I ventured to say to him that he ought not to confine his son's education to hides.''

''What is hardest to bear,'' cried his friend Apollodorus, as members of the Eleven approached with their wrist chains, ''is that you should be put to death when you don't deserve it!''

''Would you rather I were put to death because I did deserve it?'' answered Socrates. He held out his hands to the men with the chains.

The dreaded Eleven of Athens, who managed the prisons and saw to the executions, were slaves owned by the government.

Under the new constitution of the free city of democratic Athens, the rights to freedom of speech and thought were sacred, unlimited, and irrevocable; and people could be ruined or put to death for exercising them.

"Shall no one in our democratic free society ever be allowed to hold an unorthodox view?" Socrates inquired of Anytus during the pretrial inquisition.

"Of course," the answer came back. "There is full freedom of expression. An unorthodox view can be expressed, provided it is an orthodox unorthodoxy. One can be pro-democrat or pro-oligarchy or pro-tyranny, but nothing else, and nothing in between. One has to be pro-something. One can be pro-war or pro-peace, but nothing else, and there must never be any discussion to confuse these simple issues." He spoke to soft applause and murmurs of approval from colleagues on the panel. "You yourself have said, Socrates, or at least it is so reported, that you would eject or censor Homer, Hesiod, and other poets, and musicians and other artists in your ideal republic because of the harmful effects such people can produce on the emotions, thoughts, and resolution of the people."

"Until we have my ideal republic," said Socrates, "I would keep them."

"What we will not allow," said Anytus frankly, "is cynicism, skepticism, secrecy, atheism, conspiracy, abortion, opposition, subterfuge, deceit, and false pleading. How will you defend yourself when we say you are an atheist and are guilty of rejecting the gods acknowledged by the state and of believing in strange deities?"

"I will ask you to name the gods and the deities, and I will ask you to explain how I can be an atheist and still believe in those deities."

"You are being subtle and cynical, I see. And what will you answer when we say you are guilty of corrupting the youth?"

"I will ask you to name and produce the people I have corrupted."

"And that," said Anytus, "is exactly the kind of hair-splitting and false pleading that the state of Athens is no longer going to tolerate."

And at the trial itself, Socrates did say: "If it were a fact that I am corrupting some of the young, and have succeeded already in corrupting others, and if it were a fact that some of the latter, being now grown, had discovered that I had ever given them bad advice, surely they ought to come forward now to denounce me and take their revenge; unless they have been so corrupted by me that they do not know I have harmed them. And if they did not do this themselves, you would expect some of their families to remember now if their own flesh and blood had suffered harm from me. Certainly a great many of their fathers and brothers and other near relations have found their way into this court today. Here is Adeimantus the son of Ariston, whose brother Plato is present; and Aeantodorus, who is the brother of Apollodorus, whom I also see here on this side. And you know Chaerephon, of course, a friend of mine from boyhood, and a good democrat who played his part with the rest of you in the recent expulsion of the Tyrants—Chaerephon is dead, but his brother is here in court. I can see many more besides, whom Meletus might have produced as witnesses in the course of his speech. If he simply forgot to do so, then let him do it now—I am willing to make way for him. And let him state if he has any testimony of that sort which he can produce." Socrates paused courteously, prepared to yield the rostrum to his accuser.

Meletus, who is described by Plato as a scrawny man with a sparse beard and a beaky nose, hung back in silence with a stormy countenance and produced no one.

"On the contrary, Athenians," Socrates resumed, "the very opposite is the truth. You will find that all I have named are prepared to bear witness on behalf of me—of me, the corrupter, the injurer, and the evil genius of their nearest and dearest relatives, as Meletus and Anytus call me. Not just the corrupted youth but their uncorrupted elder relatives. As for their relations of mature age, what other reason can they have for helping me except for the sake of truth and justice? And because they know that I am speaking the truth and that Meletus is a liar.''

It was at the end of his defense that Socrates called the attention of the jurors to what they were certain to notice: although he had three sons, one almost grown up and the other two only children, he would forgo the customary tactic of producing his infant children in court to excite the maximum sympathy with pitiful appeals to the jury.

''Such conduct,'' Socrates explained, ''would be discreditable to myself, and to you, and to the whole state. One who has reached my age ought not to demean himself with these methods, and not one with my reputation—which may be true or may be false. The view is held that I am different from the common run of mankind. Now if any of us who are supposed to be distinguished for wisdom or courage or any other virtue are to behave this way, it would be a disgrace. I have seen men of great reputation, when they come up for trial or have been condemned, behaving in the most extraordinary manner: they seemed to fancy they were going to something dreadful if they died, and that they would be immortal if you only allowed them to live.''

If they the jurors had the smallest regard for the reputations of themselves or the city, they must make it clear for the future that anyone staging such pathetic scenes was more likely to be condemned for doing so.

''There seems to be something wrong in asking a favor of a juryman, and procuring an acquittal that way, instead of by informing and convincing him. For a judge sits not to make a favor of justice but to give judgment where justice lies; and he has sworn an oath that he will judge according to the laws, and not according to his pleasure. And we defendants ought not to encourage you in this habit of perjury—there can be no piety in that. Do not then require me, even to save my life, to do what I consider dishonorable, especially now when I am being tried for impiety on the indictment of Meletus. If I tried by entreaties to prevail upon you to go against your oath, I should be teaching you contempt for religion; and by that defense I should be exposing myself as having no religious belief. But that is very far from the truth. I have a more sincere belief, gentlemen, than any of my accusers. And I leave it to you and to God to judge what is best, best for me and for yourselves."

To the dismay of Plato, Crito, Critobulus, and Apollodorus, Socrates shunned any plea for his life that was humble and conciliatory, and the jury did not get from him that contrite supplication they felt was their due in exchange for the leniency they were prepared to grant.

He took with an equanimity most remarkable, as Plato describes it, the sentence of execution.

There were many reasons, he said, why he was not grieved at the vote of condemnation. Frankly, he did not care a straw for death. He had risked death in war, had risked it in the democratic Assembly by refusing to put to a vote the motion to condemn the generals of Arginusae as a group, braved it under the Tyrants by ignoring the order to arrest Leon the Salaminian.

To those who had voted to condemn him he had some warning words of prophecy: "Not much time will be gained, O Athenians, in return for the evil name which you will get from detractors of the city, who will say you killed Socrates, a wise man. For they will call me wise, even though I am not wise, when they want to reproach you. I am about to die, and in the hour of death men are gifted with prophetic power, and I prophesy to you who are my murderers that immediately after my departure a punishment far heavier than you have inflicted on me will surely await you. Me you have killed because you wanted to escape the accuser, and to avoid giving an account of your lives. But that will not be as you suppose. For I say that there will be more accusers of you than there are now, and as they are younger they will be more inconsiderate of you. If you think that by killing me you can prevent someone from censuring your evil lives, you are mistaken."

And to those who had voted to acquit him he had words of consolation: "Friends who have acquitted me, I would like also to talk to you about the thing which has come to pass, while the magistrates are busy with closing the matter, and before I go to the place at which I must die. Please stay then a little, for we may as well talk with one another while there is time. I should like to tell you of a wonderful circumstance."

The prophetic voice to which he had become accustomed, he informed them, his divine sign, which had opposed him in the past even in minute things, had not opposed him that morning when he left his house to face his trial, or when he was taking his place there in court, or at any point in any part of his speech. And from this he concluded that what was happening to him now was a blessing and that all were mistaken in supposing death to be an evil.

Death could be but a dreamless sleep. "If so, would that not be an inexpressible gain? For if any person here were to pick out the night on which he last enjoyed a sleep that was undisturbed, even by dreams, and then, after due consideration, count up how many days and nights in his life he has passed more pleasantly than that one, I think that any man— I will not say just a private man but even the great king of Persia—would have to say that they were very few."

If death were not the dreamless sleep that even the great king himself would cherish, then perhaps it was, as people said, a change of place and a migration of the soul from this world to another.

"And if death is the journey to another place, and a place where all the dead abide, what good, O my friends and judges, can be greater than this? What would not a man give if he might converse with Orpheus and Hesiod and Homer? If this be true, let me die again and again. I shall have a wonderful interest in meeting there with Palamedes, and Ajax the son of Telamon, and any other ancient hero who suffered death unjustly, and there will be no small pleasure in comparing my suffering with theirs. What would not a man give,

O judges, to be able to examine the leader of the great Trojan expedition, Agamemnon, or Odysseus, or Sisyphus? In another world, I presume they do not put a man to death for asking questions, for assuredly, besides being happier than we are, they will be immortal, if what is said is true. Wherefore, O judges, be of good cheer about death.''

And for these reasons he was not, he said, angry with his condemners.

"They have done me no harm, although they did not mean to do me any good, and for this I may gently blame them. And now we go our separate ways, I to die, and you to live. Which is better is known only to God.''

To grieving friends he had earlier offered this solace: ''The law of God does not permit a better man to be harmed by a worse, and know of a certainty that nothing bad can happen to a good man, either in life or after death.''

And there he baffled them.

And Aristotle in exile too.

Would it follow, Aristotle speculated morbidly, knowing he was not well, that nothing bad could happen to a bad man either, since the same things happened to all?

He decided he did not want to follow that up.

Aristotle in exile in the last year of his life had leisure to wonder about much while he prepared his last will and testament. He was a good man, he thought; yet much that was bad had been done to him by Athenians driving him out for impiety seventy-six years after disposing of Socrates on that same pretext. His museum and library were abandoned when he fled. He mourned their loss. His intestinal disorders were growing more critical steadily. He did not know there was blood in his stool. Upon examining the X rays of Aristotle in the Rembrandt painting, Dr. Abraham Bredius, the art historian who gave the painting its present name, spied the growth on his liver and saw a right-side bowel tumor also. Immortal Aristotle was only human.

34

THE TRIAL OF ASCLEPIUS WAS THE ONE THAT EXCITED CURIOSITY. A leather merchant of modest affluence, he was not a person to whom the people supposed they would ever have to give much thought. His outward life was one of undistinguished conformity. As far as neighbors could tell, he seemed a model citizen, obedient to convention, who took as truth the mythology of the past and the folklore of the present. It was as shocking to others as it had been to him that Socrates had uttered his name in an incriminating way.

Asclepius did not deny that he knew Socrates was called a philosopher. He could not define what a philosopher was. He could not prove that he had never committed a crime. A search of his home and business premises turned up nothing.

It was all too pat.

Was there an outside chance he was telling the truth?

They had never been seen together in public.

That raised questions too.

The jailer testified that Socrates had said at the end that he owed Asclepius a cock and wanted him to be paid. Asclepius did not deny that the name was his.

What made the case worse for him was that everyone in Athens considered Socrates, once dead, a truthful and courageous figure who would not lie to save his life.

"I don't know why he said what he did," Asclepius repeated in his deposition during the examinations before trial. "I can only believe he meant someone else."

There was only himself and the deity of medicine.

"Put yourself in our place," persisted Anytus reasonably. " 'Crito, I owe a cock to Asclepius. Will you remember to pay the debt?' Be fair-minded. Which is more likely? That a man would die with a lie on his lips or that you would lie to save yourself?"

Asclepius began to believe he might indeed be lying.

But why?

He racked his brains.

To these sober judges of Athens it was inconceivable that a man would joke with his last breath. Why would Socrates say that he owed Asclepius a cock if he did not?

"Make a guess."

"I don't know," Asclepius answered wretchedly, and then unwittingly spoke the words that ensured his indictment. "The only thing I know is that I know nothing."

This was practically the same statement of Socrates a few weeks earlier!

Yes, it did sound familiar. No, he had never done business with Socrates.

Why, then, had he either conspired in code with a man who owned nothing or loaned him a chicken?

When Asclepius denied under oath that he had ever done either, there was added to the charges against him the crime of perjury. Because his physician father had named him for a deity and he had never changed his name, there was added the charge of impiety.

In contrast to Socrates, who spoke for himself, he retained a noted speechwriter who prepared for him a brilliant defense to read that did not sound the least bit like him, or like anyone else.

In contrast to Socrates, he introduced into the proceedings his wife, his children, his parents, his wife's parents, and a number of aged slaves to wring pity from the jurors and elicit a verdict of innocence or a nominal penalty.

He was shouted down in contempt. They threw heads of lettuce at him. Fresh in the minds of the jurors was the valiant bearing with which Socrates had shunned all such lawyer's tricks for himself and denounced their use by others.

Asclepius was found guilty by acclamation in a roar so overwhelming that any present inclined to his side recoiled from breaking the silence when the opportunity came to vote nay.

The vote was declared unanimous. There was no objection to the death penalty.

Athenian justice normally was swift. In the space between the trial of Asclepius one day and his execution by hemlock at sundown the next, Anytus found time to berate him in prison for his despicable behavior as a defendant and exhort him to be the man that Socrates was when the time came to die.

"It was an honor," said Anytus with austere pride, "to put a man like Socrates to death."

Asclepius asked but one question when the jailers entered with the cup of hemlock on a silver tray.

"What will you do to me if I refuse to drink it?"

The procedure was spelled out in the penal code. "We will force open your jaws and pour it down your throat. Experience has taught us that, when given the choice between choking to death and swallowing poison, the human animal will invariably choose to swallow the poison. Then we will cut off your head and perhaps crucify you too, if the citizens decide."

Asclepius chose the easier course.

He made but one statement as the poison overpowered

him, the meek confession that he was no longer sure he believed in capital punishment.

Anytus pronounced him a disgrace to the leather profession.

The comic playwright Aristophanes told friends it was a pity that Asclepius had not said with his dying words that he owed a cock to Anytus.

35

THE EXECUTION OF SOCRATES WAS POSTPONED A MONTH BY the coincidence of his trial with a sacred holiday celebrating the ancient exploit of Theseus against the Minotaur of Crete and the deliverance of Athens from the funereal burden of sending each year seven Athenian youths and seven maidens to be sacrificed to the fatal ravages of that mythological beast. In annual remembrance, a state galley was garlanded in the Greek month of Thargelion, our May, and sent to Apollo's isle of Delos, fulfilling the oath of Theseus. In religious thanksgiving for the lives spared since, no public executions were performed in the purified city while the ship was away.

Socrates would be killed when the ship returned.

The jailer was kind. He put Socrates in leg irons only at night.

His friends thought of escape.

Socrates awoke one morning before dawn and found old Crito already there, sitting on a stool in a cell almost dark but for the light from a little oil lamp. Socrates was surprised. Crito by now was known to the warders, who admitted him without fuss. Besides, Crito confessed, he had shown to the keeper of the prison a small kindness, a friendly bribe.

"Then why did you sit and say nothing, instead of awakening me at once?" asked Socrates.

"You were sleeping so comfortably—I would not have roused you for the world. I wish I were not so sleepless and depressed myself." Crito frowned. "I have envied you before for your disposition. But I marvel more than ever when I see you in your present misfortune and when I see how easily and placidly you put up with it. Never in my life did I see anything like the tranquil manner in which you bear this fate."

Socrates smiled. "Well, really, Crito, when a man has reached my age, it is hardly suitable to be repining at the approach of death, is it?"

Yet other people his age resented it bitterly when they found themselves in similar misfortunes, Crito was saying when the jailer, hearing their voices, came in, apologetically. He went to Socrates and took off his chains. Socrates massaged the marks they had left. The man seemed ashamed.

"Is there news?" inquired Socrates. "Have you orders for me today?"

"I have orders," said the jailer, in a voice lowered furtively. He stared at the ground.

"What are they?"

"My orders," said the jailer, "are to look the other way if you attempt to escape from the prison and make your way down to the port to the boat that everyone knows will be waiting to carry you away safely."

"And if I do not try to escape?" asked Socrates.

"My orders then are to tell you that a boat can be waiting for you at Piraeus and that we are ordered all to look the other way if you attempt to escape."

"He is a good fellow, Crito," said Socrates, as the jailer departed. "Did you notice—he cannot face me without his eyes filling with tears, poor man."

"Socrates, make up your mind," said Crito sharply. "You

have heard him and you have heard me. The whole thing must be carried through tonight. Or else it will be too late.''

"Has the boat come in from Delos already?''

"There are reports. It seems certain that the boat will be here today. Tomorrow, Socrates, if you don't decide now, will be the last day of your life.''

"In that case, Crito, I hope it may be for the best, if such is the will of the gods.''

"You will not go tonight?''

"No. All the same, my belief is that there will be one more day, that the boat will not arrive on this day that is just beginning, but on the day that follows. Am I right in thinking that I have to die on the day after the boat arrives?''

"That is what the authorities say.''

"I do not think the ship will be here until tomorrow. I had a dream.''

The dream did not matter to Crito. The extra day made no difference either.

"The meaning of your dream may be clear, but oh, my beloved Socrates, let me entreat you once more to take my advice and escape while it is still not too late. Your death means a double calamity for me and your other friends. If you die, we shall not only lose a friend who can never be replaced but people will believe we might have saved you had we been willing to spend the money.''

"But my dear Crito,'' said Socrates, seeing his friend grow agitated, "why should we pay much attention to the opinion of the many? Good men, and they are the only ones with a claim to be considered, will think of these things as they truly occurred.''

"But that does not save you,'' said Crito. "Please tell me, Socrates, that you are not acting out of regard for the risk or the cost to me and your other friends in helping you get away. Are you afraid that we may find ourselves in trouble with the paid informers for having stolen you away? And that we may lose either the whole or a great part of our property, or that even a worse evil may happen to us? If so, be at ease, for in order to save you, we ought surely to run this or even a greater risk. Be persuaded then and do as I say."

"Yes, Crito, there is that one fear which you mention. But that is by no means the only reason."

"Then let me relieve you of that fear," said Crito. "There are persons who are willing to get you out of prison and out of the city at no great cost. And as for the government informers, they are far from exorbitant in their demands and are cheap to buy off. If you have a scruple about spending my money, there are foreign gentlemen here now willing to give you the use of theirs who won't be in danger. And one of them, Simmias the Theban, has brought a large sum of money for this very purpose. And Cebes and a number of others are quite prepared to spend their money to help you escape. They will leave Athens when you do and be out of danger. We are quite entitled to run what risks we want to in saving you."

"All that you are saying is much in my mind," said Socrates seriously, "and very much more besides."

"Then take my advice and be reasonable," said Crito. "And, indeed, I am already really very much ashamed, both on your account and on ours, when I reflect on all that we have let happen so far and that the whole business will be attributed to our want of courage. First there was the way you came into court when it was quite unnecessary—that was the first act. The trial need never have come or might have been managed differently. Why didn't you leave Athens then? Next there was the conduct of your defense—that was the second. And finally, to complete the farce, there is this last act of crowning folly. It begins to appear that we are going to lose you through some lack of courage and enterprise on our part, because we might have saved you if we had been good for anything, and because you didn't save yourself, when it would have been quite possible and practicable."

"My dear Crito," said Socrates, when Crito ended, "I appreciate your warm feelings very much. Your zeal is invaluable, if you are right. But if you are wrong, the greater the zeal, the greater the danger.''

"Then take my advice now and argue with me afterward. For if you are the one who is mistaken, you will not have a second chance. Nor must you feel any misgivings about what you said at your trial. Do not say, as you did in court, that you will have difficulty in knowing what to do with yourself anywhere else. For men will love you in other places to which you may go, and not in Athens only. There are friends of mine in Thessaly, if you choose to go there.''

"In roistering Thessaly? Is that where I fit?''

"They will value and protect you, and no Thessalian will give you trouble. They will be honored to talk with you.''

"And what will I teach them about virtue and honor and wisdom when I am a fugitive from Athens, from the city in which I have lived all my life, in which I am raising and educating my children, and which I never left except for military service? How I broke the laws and escaped when they turned against me? Is that the contract that I had with the city, that I would hold the laws sacred when they were misused against others and repudiate them only when they were misused against me?''

"Socrates, I cannot believe that you are at all justified in betraying your own life when you might be saved. You are doing your best to play into the hands of your enemies, who are hurrying your destruction. You treat yourself the same way your enemies would in seeking to ruin you.''

"And so now you would like me to run away into exile instead, and to obtain by violating the law the same banishment that I probably could have obtained properly at my trial by requesting it. I ask you, Crito, don't you think that this is a sound enough principle, that one should not regard equally all the opinions that people hold but only some and not others? What do you say? Is that not a fair statement?''

"Yes, it is,'' said Crito.

"In other words,'' Socrates continued, "a person should regard the good opinions and not the bad?''

"Yes."

"The opinions of the wise being good, and the opinions of the foolish bad?"

"Naturally," answered Crito, with failing confidence.

"Then I should like very much to proceed from this premise to inquire into this question with you," said Socrates, and Crito felt his heart sink, for he knew where the examination would end, although he did not know how they would get there. "If it turns out that I am clearly right in trying to escape without the official consent of the Athenians, then I will make the attempt; but if not, I of course must abstain. For then the people who are paying money and the others who agree to rescue me will be acting as wrongly as ourselves in arranging my escape. And if it becomes clear that such conduct is wrong, I cannot help thinking that the fact that I am sure to die ought not to weigh with us at all in comparison with the risk of doing wrong. Don't you agree that the important thing is not just to live, but to live well?"

Crito answered yes.

"And that to live well means the same thing as to live honorably and correctly? And that when one does not live honorably and does the wrong thing, he is injuring himself along with whomever else he harms? I want you to consider very carefully whether you share my views and agree with me. If you have formed any other opinion, say so and tell me what it is. If, on the other hand, you stand by what we have said, listen to my next point."

"Yes, I agree with what you say, Socrates. But I wish you would consider quickly what we ought to *do*."

"Then consider the logical consequence. If we leave this place without first persuading the state to let us go, are we, or are we not, doing it an injury, and doing it in a quarter where it is least justifiable? Are we or are we not abiding by our just agreements?"

"I cannot answer your question, Socrates. I am not clear in my mind."

"Let us look at it together, my dear fellow. I am anxious

to obtain your approval for the course which I have in mind. I don't want to act against your convictions. Now will you give your attention to the starting point of this inquiry and answer my questions to the best of your judgment?"

"Of course," Crito promised. "Well, I will try."

And in a very short time they concluded that they ought not to render evil for evil to anyone, whatever evil they may have suffered from a person, and that in no circumstances must one do wrong, not even when one has been wronged.

They were in accord that agreements should be fulfilled and that injuries are wrongs, and that in running away now Socrates would be attempting to injure and destroy, so far as he had power, the laws without which the city could not exist. He, whose arguments were always that goodness and integrity and institutions and laws were the most precious possessions of mankind, would be violating an agreement with the community for reasons indefensibly personal.

Was there not substantial evidence that he was satisfied with the laws of Athens? He begat his children there, he had never gone out of the city, either to see the games or to visit any other place unless sent there on military service. At the trial he had made a noble show of indifference to death and his preference of death to banishment.

He asked Crito to imagine what the laws of the city would say if they could come to him and talk:

"At the trial, Socrates, you might, if you had liked, have fixed the penalty at banishment. The state, which refuses to let you go now, would have let you go then. But no, you pretended that you preferred death to exile, and that you were not unwilling to die. You said bravely that you did not fear death, which might prove to be a blessing. And now you have forgotten these fine sentiments and pay no respect to us, the laws, of whom you now wish to be the destroyer, and doing what only a miserable slave would do, running away, when you could have done with the sanction of the state what Crito is now urging you to do without it. And in Thessaly, where there is great disorder and license, what will you talk to them about? Will you charm them with tales of the ruses you used to escape from prison, with the ludicrous particulars of how you were wrapped in a goatskin or some other disguise in the manner of runaways? Socrates, do not make yourself ridiculous by escaping now.''

If he did not like the laws, he had always been free to attempt to persuade his fellow countrymen to change them. If he could not persuade them, he was free, as was every Athenian, to take his property and go wherever he liked. Although the oligarchies of Sparta and Crete were his favorite models of better government, he had chosen for all of his seventy years to praise them from Athens rather than move to either.

And then, where would be all the fine statements about virtue and justice he had made in his life?

''Ought a man to do what he admits to be right, or ought he to betray what he knows to be right?'' asked Socrates.

''Socrates, he ought always to do what he thinks is right, of course.''

''And in my old age, Crito, will there be no one to remind me that I was not ashamed to violate the most sacred laws from a miserable desire for a little more life? As that is how my opinion stands at present, I warn you it will be useless to urge a different view. However, if you think you will do any good by it, say what you like.''

''What of the man,'' Crito suggested, ''who believes it is right to do wrong?''

''I am not that man.''

''Is it right to disobey a law that is evil?''

''Our laws are not evil.''

''I am asking philosophically.''

''I have no more time for that.''

''I have nothing to say.''

''Leave me then, Crito, to fulfill the will of God and follow whither it leads.''

36

PLATO WAS HOME SICK ON THE DAY SOCRATES DIED, PLATO wrote, and employed, as in the *Symposium*, an indirect narrator to give the eyewitness details of what he himself did not see.

"Were you there with him, Phaedo, when he was executed, or did you hear about it yourself?"

"Yes, Echecrates, I was there myself," Phaedo answered.

"Then what did he say in his last hours, and how did he meet his end? We were informed that he died by taking poison, but no one knew anything more." They were talking in Phlius, a little town in the Peloponnese. "We in Phlius do not go to Athens now, and it is a long time since we have had any visitor from Athens who could give us any definite information, except that he was executed by drinking hemlock. I wish you would be kind enough to tell us the whole account, all that passed, as exactly as you can—unless you are pressed for time."

"No, Echecrates, not at all," said Phaedo, "and I will try to gratify you. To be reminded of Socrates is always the greatest delight to me, whether I speak myself or hear another speak of him.''

"Well, Phaedo, you will have listeners here who feel the same. Please tell us as carefully as you can.''

"In the first place," Phaedo began, "my emotions were quite extraordinary. At no time could I believe I was present at the death of a friend, and therefore I did not pity him, as you might have expected I would at the deathbed of someone very dear to me. He seemed quite happy, both in his manner and in what he said. He died without fear, and his words were noble and gracious. All of us who were there felt the same curious blend of pleasure and pain and were affected the same way. We were laughing and weeping in turns, especially one of us, the excitable Apollodorus—do you know that sort of man? Apollodorus quite lost control of himself, and I and all of the others were greatly moved by him.''

"Who were the others with you?''

"Of the native Athenians," Phaedo recounted, "there were, besides this man Apollodorus, Critobulus and his father, Crito, and then there were Hermogenes and Epigenes and Aeschines and Antisthenes. Oh, yes, and Ctesippus of the deme of Paeania, and Menexenus, and some others. From outside Athens there was Simmias the Theban, with Cebes and Phaedondes, and Eucleides and Terpsion, who came from Megara. Plato, if I am not mistaken, was home ill. I think these were nearly all.''

On that last morning they assembled earlier than usual but were kept waiting.

The jailer explained: "The Eleven are now with Socrates, and while the chains are taken off, they are giving the orders that he is to die today.''

When they were let inside, the wife of Socrates, Xanthippe, was already with him, with one of the smaller of their little boys in her arms. When she saw them come in, said Phaedo, she uttered a cry and broke out with the sort of remark they might expect from a woman, that this was the last time Socrates and his friends would be able to talk together. Xanthippe, who'd been known to fly into a temper because he spent so much time with his friends, was now distraught that he would do so no more.

She was crying hysterically. Socrates turned to Crito and requested that someone take her away, and she was led out, crying and beating herself.

When the room was quiet, Socrates sat up and massaged soothingly the swollen red mark left on his leg by the chain.

It was known from previous visits that he had been putting certain of the fables of Aesop into poetry, and Evenus the poet had sent word that he was eager to know why Socrates, who had never before written a line of poetry, was putting things into verse now.

"Tell him the truth," said Socrates lightly, "that I did not compose them to rival him—which I knew would not be easy." He was only trying by that means to discover the meaning of certain of his dreams. "Tell him this and bid him farewell from me, and tell him, if he is wise, to follow me as quickly as he can. I shall be going today, it seems. Those are my country's orders."

"What a piece of advice for Evenus!" Simmias exclaimed in a comic manner that made the rest laugh. "From what I know of him he will not be at all willing to follow you."

"Why, is he not a philosopher?" asked Socrates.

They agreed that Evenus was.

In that case, Socrates was sure he would have no fear of dying, although he would hardly do himself violence, because he would know that suicide was illegitimate.

Here Cebes was puzzled. "Socrates, why do you say that a man ought not to take his own life, although as a philosopher, he will be willing to follow a friend who dies?"

"Have you and Simmias never heard about these things?"

"Never anything definite, Socrates."

"Well," said Socrates, and he left off massaging his leg and sat up, and during the rest of the conversation he remained sitting. "My information is based only on things I have heard, but I don't mind telling you what I have heard.

As one who will soon be leaving this world, I suppose there is no better subject than thinking and inquiring into the nature of the pilgrimage I am about to make and trying to imagine what it is like. What better way can I have to spend the time between now and the setting of the sun? But you must first let me hear what Crito wants. He has long been wishing to say something to me.''

"Only this, Socrates," Crito said when given the chance. "The attendant who is to give you the poison has been telling me, and he wants me to tell you, that you are not to talk much. Talking, he says, increases body heat, and this is apt to interfere with the action of the poison. Persons who excite themselves sometimes have to take a second or even a third dose."

"Then," said Socrates, "let him be prepared to give the poison twice or even three times if that becomes necessary."

And in the hours left, he proselytized about the soul, immortality, and a future life of which he had never talked much before, although he provided no factual reasons for believing that what he said was true. He knew it was true because he wanted it to be.

Simmias and Cebes were hard to convince.

"Well, you, Simmias and Cebes, and all other men," said Socrates, when they were finishing the conversation, "will depart on this same journey at some time or other. As for me, already, as a tragic poet might say, the voice of fate calls even now. Soon I must drink the poison. I think it is time I took my bath. I would not want the women to have the trouble of washing my body after I am dead."

When he had done speaking, Phaedo related, Crito said: "And have you any commands for us, about your children and anything else? In what way can we serve you?"

"Only as I have always told you, Crito. If you take care of yourself and walk according to the rule of life as I have always prescribed, you may ever be rendering a service to me and mine and to all of us."

"We will do our best," promised Crito. "And in what way shall we bury you?"

"In any way that you like," answered Socrates with a laugh. "But you must get hold of me first and take care that I do not run away from you." Turning to the rest he said: "Crito fancies that I am already the other Socrates whom he will soon see as a dead body—and he wants to know how he shall bury me. I want you to guarantee to Crito the opposite of what he guaranteed for me at the trial: he was surety to the judges that I would remain, you must be surety to him that when I have drunk the poison I will go away. Then he will suffer less at my death and not be grieved when he sees my body being burned or buried. Be of good cheer then, my dear Crito, and say that you are burying my body only, and do with that whatever is usual and what you think best. By then I would have slipped away from you through your fingers, for you will not be able to catch and hold me."

When he had spoken these words, Phaedo related to Echecrates and the others in his audience, Socrates arose and went into the chamber to bathe. Crito followed, asking the others to wait.

Socrates was like a father of whom they were being bereaved, said Phaedo, and they felt they were about to pass the rest of their lives as orphans.

When he had taken his bath, his children were brought in to him—his two young sons and the elder one. And the women of his family also came, and he talked to them and gave them a few directions about his wishes, in the presence of only Crito. Then he sent them away and returned to his friends.

Now the hour of sunset was near, for they had talked long and a good deal of time had passed while he was within. Fresh from his bath, he sat down again, but not much more could be said before the jailer, who was the servant of the Eleven, came in and walked up to him.

"To you, Socrates," he said—and the man looked stricken, as though choking back sobs, "whom I now know to be the noblest, gentlest, and best of all who ever came to this place, I will not impart the angry feelings of other men, who rage and swear at me when I bid them drink the poison. I am sure that you will not be angry with me, for others, as you are aware, not I, are to blame. And so—you know my errand—fare you well, and try to bear lightly what must needs be.''

He burst into tears as he turned to go out.

''I return your good wishes,'' Socrates said to him, ''and will do as you bid.'' He revealed to the others what a kind and charming man he had found the jailer to be. ''Since I have been in prison he has always been coming to see me, and at times he would talk to me, and was as good as he could be. And now see how generously he sorrows on my account. We must do as he says, Crito. Therefore, let the cup be brought if the poison is prepared. If it isn't, let them make it ready.''

''Not yet,'' said Crito. ''The sun is still upon the hilltops. I know that many here have been permitted to take the draught late, and after the announcement, they have eaten and drunk and enjoyed the company of those they love. Do not hurry. There is time left.''

And Socrates said: ''Yes, Crito, and it is natural that they of whom you speak should act that way, for they think that they will be gainers by the delay. And it is just as natural that I should not, because I do not think that I shall gain anything by drinking the poison a little later. I should only be ridiculous in my own eyes for sparing and saving a little longer a life that is already forfeit and has nothing more to offer. Please then do as I say. Don't refuse me.''

Crito made a sign to a servant who had been standing nearby. The man went out. After he had been absent for some time, he returned with the jailer, who was carrying the cup in which the poison had been prepared.

Socrates spoke cordially. ''You, my good friend, who are experienced in these matters, give me directions and tell me how to proceed.''

"Drink the poison," the man answered. "You have only to walk about until your legs grow heavy. Then lie down, and the poison will act."

And at the same time he handed the cup to Socrates, who, as Phaedo described it, took the cup in the easiest and gentlest manner and, without the least fear or change of color or feature, looking at the man with all his eyes, asked if he might make a libation out of the cup to any god.

The man replied that there was only enough poison in the cup as they deemed enough.

"I think I understand," Socrates said. "Then I may and must ask the gods to prosper my journey from this world to the other, even so, and so be it, according to my prayer."

Then, after these words, raising the cup to his lips, quite readily and cheerfully, he drank off all the poison.

Till then, most of them had been able to control their sorrow. Now, however, when they saw him drinking and saw too that he had emptied the cup, they could do so no longer. And in spite of himself, Phaedo's own tears came flowing fast, so that he covered his face and wept.

Socrates seemed almost displeased. "What, are you crying for me?" Socrates chided. "Phaedo, are you sorry?"

"I am crying not just for you. I am weeping at my own calamity in having to part from such a friend."

Nor was Phaedo the first to show such emotion. For Crito, when he found himself unable to restrain his tears, had gotten up as though to go out, and Phaedo began to follow. And at that moment Apollodorus, who had been weeping all the time, broke out in a loud and passionate cry that made cowards of all the rest of them. Socrates alone retained his calmness.

"What is this strange outcry?" he objected. "What a way to behave! I sent out the women that they might not carry on this way, for I have been told that a man should be allowed to die in peace. Be quiet then, and patient."

When they heard these words they were ashamed and did what they could to restrain their tears.

Socrates walked about until, as he said, his legs began to fail, and then he lay down on his back, as he had been told to do.

The man who had given him the poison followed him to the bed and now and then tested his feet and legs. And after a while he squeezed his foot hard and asked him if he could feel. And Socrates said no. Then he did the same to his leg, and so on upward and upward, and let the rest of them feel that Socrates was cold and numb. And again he touched Socrates and then he said: "When the poison reaches his heart, that will be the end."

Socrates lay with a cloth over his face.

"He was beginning to grow cold about the hips," Phaedo related, "when he uncovered his face but for one moment and said—they were his last words, I remember—he said: 'Crito, I owe a cock to Asclepius. Will you remember to pay the debt?' "

"The debt shall be paid," said Crito. "Is there anything else?"

There was no answer. But in a minute or two a movement was heard beneath the cloth. When the jailer uncovered him now, his eyes were set. Crito closed his eyes and mouth.

"Such was the end, Echecrates, of our friend, concerning whom I may truly say, that of all men of our time whom I have known, he was the wisest and justest and best."

37

THERE ARE OUTRAGES AND THERE ARE OUTRAGES, AND SOME
are more outrageous than others.

Mankind is resilient: the atrocities that horrified us a week
ago become acceptable tomorrow.

The death of Socrates had no effect upon the history of
Athens. If anything, the reputation of the city has been improved by it.

The death of no person is as important to the future as the
literature about it.

You will learn nothing from history that can be applied,
so don't kid yourself into thinking you can.

"History is bunk," said Henry Ford.

But Socrates was dead.

Plato does not report that he wept that day.

He would have been only twelve at the time of his *Symposium* and therefore was not present to hear those affecting
encomiums of Alcibiades to Socrates which he so eloquently
represents.

Death by hemlock is not as peaceful and painless as he

portrays: there is retching, slurring of speech, convulsions, and uncontrollable vomiting.

The Rembrandt painting of Aristotle contemplating the bust of Homer may not be by Rembrandt but by a pupil so divinely gifted in learning the lessons of his master that he never was able to accomplish anything more and whose name, as a consequence, has been lost in obscurity. The bust of Homer that Aristotle is shown contemplating is not of Homer. The man is not Aristotle.

THE END

About the Author

Joseph Heller is author of CATCH-22, SOMETHING HAP-
PENED, GOOD AS GOLD, GOD KNOWS, and, with
Speed Vogel, NO LAUGHING MATTER. He lives with his
wife in East Hampton, New York.